DAILY PRAYER
SPAIN

To my parents, who had no idea that holidays in Spain might lead me along such paths.

DAILY PRAYER IN CHRISTIAN SPAIN

Graham Woolfenden

Alcuin Club Collections 76

SPCK

First published in Great Britain in 2000
Society for Promoting Christian Knowledge
Holy Trinity Church
Marylebone Road
London NW1 4DU

Copyright © The Alcuin Club 2000
Alcuin Club Collections

All rights reserved. No part of this book may be reproduced or transmitted in any form or by any means, electronic or mechanical, including photocopying, recording, or by any information storage and retrieval system, without permission in writing from the publisher.

British Library Cataloguing-in-Publication Data

A catalogue record for this book is available from
the British Library

ISBN 0 281 05328 6

Typeset by David Gregson Associates
Printed in Great Britain by
The Athenaeum Press, Gateshead

CONTENTS

Abbreviations and Notes Concerning Sources	vi
Introduction: The old Spanish Office and its Place in the Development of Daily Prayer	vii
The Schemes of Vespers	xx
The Schemes of Matins	xxi
The Hours of Terce, Sext and None	xxii
Part One: The Order and Components of Vespers	1
1 Early Testimonies to the Structure of Vespers in Spain	3
2 The *Oblatio Luminis* and *Lucernarium*	5
3 The Psalmody of Vespers	14
4 The Use of Hymns in the Divine Office	29
5 The Prayers	38
6 The *Psallendum*	48
7 Vespers – Some Concluding Remarks	54
Part Two: The Order and Components of Matins	59
8 Early Testimonies to the Structure of Matins in Spain	61
9 Matins – the Introductory Material	63
10 The Antiphons of Matins and the Question of the Psalter in Course	73
11 The Canticles at Matins	96
12 The Morning Psalm or Matutinarium, and the Sono	112
13 The Laudate Psalms	121
14 Readings in the old Spanish Office	125
15 The Morning Hymn	133
16 The Concluding Prayer of Matins – the Completuria	138
17 Matins – Some Concluding Remarks	140
Part Three: Conclusion	143
Bibliography	165
Index	169

ABBREVIATIONS AND NOTES CONCERNING SOURCES

Translations in the text are by the author except where otherwise indicated. Translations from the psalms are from the *Grail* version, except where the author's translation is used as closer to the sense of the passage in question. The Psalm numbering is that of the Septuagint.

AL *Antiphoner of Leon* (MS Leon. Arch. Capit. 8) – tenth century, for both Mass and Office, edited by Brou and Vives (see Bibliography).

Antiphon Unit typical of the Old Spanish rite, comprising antiphon (see below) and verse(s) of psalm or psalms. (Similar to a Responsory which involves repeat of a whole antiphon and also seems to be derived from a full psalm.)

antiphon A psalm (or other scriptural text) originally used as a form of response to a psalm. These were progressively elaborated everywhere, so becoming the preserve of skilled cantors.

Br. *Breviarium Gothicum* – the printed version as found in Migne's *Patrologia Latina* 86 – reference is to *column* numbers.

LOP *Liber Orationum Psalmographus*, psalms collects edited by J. Pinell (see Bibl.).

LXX The Septuagint Greek translation of the Bible, which as basis for both older Latin versions and for the Vulgate is basic to these offices.

MM *Missale Mixtum*, printed missal available as *PL* 85.

MP *Mozarabic Psalter* (MS.Brit.Mus.add.30.851) edited by Gilson (see Bibl.).

MS (MSS) Manuscript(s).

OV *Orationale Veronense* (MS Bibl.Capit.cod.LXXXIX(84)), eighth-century collection of collects edited by Vives (see Bibl.).

Pr. or ***P*** *Pressa*, the second, repeated, half of an antiphon.

T1 MS Madrid Bibl.Nac.cod.10.001 (Toledo 35.1), canticles and hymns edited for Lorenzana edition of *Br*.

T2 MS Madrid Bibl.Nac.cod.10.110 (Toledo 35.2), weekday offices for Lent edited by Janini (see Bibl.).

T3 MS Toledo Bibl.Capit. 33.3 – monastic hours (edited Pinell, see Bibl.).

T4 MS Toledo Bibl.Capit. 35.4 (ninth/tenth cent.) – *Liber Misticus*.

T5 MS Toledo Bibl.Capit. 35.5 – Lent Masses and Offices (edited Janini, see Bibl.).

Note

The Septuagint numbering of the Psalms is the same as the Masoretic text numbering up to 9–10, which are treated as one, then one less until 114–15, treated as one but 116 divided into two after verse 8; one less again until 147, divided after verse 12. The Jerusalem Bible shows the alternative numbering.

Introduction

THE OLD SPANISH OFFICE AND ITS PLACE IN THE DEVELOPMENT OF DAILY PRAYER

Early Christian worship appears to have been characterized by quite considerable variety. Christian communities organized their worship to suit their own situation, as long as the forms that emerged remained true to the message of Jesus Christ handed on to them. While there do appear to be many common structures and other features, we cannot now believe that there was ever a single fundamental Christian liturgy from which all others have developed. Rather the course of liturgical history has been characterized by more or less successful attempts at reducing the considerable variety of the earliest years. This does not, however, preclude the possibility that a fundamentally similar shape and theological thrust may be found across many different traditions.[1]

This variety was especially true of the daily, non-eucharistic services of morning and evening prayer. The variety may probably be explained by the dearth of identifiable Jewish structures that could be taken over wholesale and adapted to Christian practice.[2] Only a few practices that found their way into Christian daily worship might be said to be definitely Jewish in origin. The common structure of Christian prayer, especially at the evening and in the morning, originated in Christian belief, even though much of the material used was from the Old Testament, and especially from the Psalter.

Paul Bradshaw has conveniently summarized the early history, and also outlined the way in which times of prayer developed, not only in the morning and evening, but also at midday and at night. Much of this appears to have been in the form of private devotions.[3] But from at least the fourth century there grew up broadly similar forms of daily worship, usually comprising an important and often lengthy vigil/morning service and another major service in the evening, which we shall refer to as Matins and Vespers respectively. To these were added services at the third, sixth and ninth hours (circa 9 a.m., 12 noon and 3 p.m.), and other monastic additions such as Prime (between Matins and the third hour) and Compline (before bed) and in some places, such as Spain and the Byzantine East, in between these day hour services, and during the night.[4]

SPAIN AND THE WESTERN ROMAN EMPIRE

In the Latin-speaking Western empire of late antiquity there were a number of major groupings of similar liturgical practices: Rome and Central Italy, Milan and the north of Italy, North Africa, Gaul and Iberia (modern Spain and Portugal). Gallican and Hispanic uses appear to have been similar in many ways but it is the latter alone with which we are here concerned.

A Spanish Church dates from the earliest days of Christianity; the see of Toledo claims very early foundation, councils were held in Spain and then, in the second half of the fifth century, the country was invaded by the Arian Visigoths. After some persecution of the orthodox, Arianism was officially abolished in 589. The Church and its liturgy flourished in the now Catholic Visigothic state and, at greatest extent, its liturgical influence was spread across Spain, Portugal and Narbonnese Gaul.[5]

Between 711 and 756 Spain was largely overrun by Muslim Arabs, who were, however, usually tolerant, and Christians continued worshipping in the way to which they were accustomed while becoming Arabized in daily life, thus giving rise to the name *Mozarabic* or 'mixed arab'. Meanwhile in the areas not conquered and then in those reconquered, the traditional liturgy was increasingly under pressure from a powerful Romanizing party, the most formidable opponent of the old Spanish tradition being Hildebrand, Pope Gregory VII (1073–85). After his time the old traditions were fighting a losing battle.[6]

After the capture of Toledo from the Moors in 1085 it was deemed politic to allow six parishes in that city to continue with what was now called the Mozarabic rite. As the years passed their manuscripts became more illegible and celebration of the rites became infrequent, or the parishes simply assimilated to the local version of the Roman rite. One parish in particular, Sts Justa and Rufina, remained strongly attached to the old tradition.[7]

In about 1495 Archbishop Pedro Gonzalez de Mendoza appointed

Alfonso Ortiz, a canon of Toledo, to head a commission comprising Ortiz and the three parish priests of the surviving Mozarabic parishes, charged with producing a new printed edition of the liturgical books. Mendoza's successor, Francisco Ximenez de Cisneros, became Archbishop of Toledo in 1495 and allowed the work to continue. Ortiz had already carried out some revision of the books of the local use of the Roman rite and was not always careful in his work, also tending to adopt a self-consciously archaizing style.[8]

Ortiz' sources included, among others, a number of manuscripts of the *Liber Misticus* type, so called because they 'mixed' both offices and Masses together. These books normally contained the Vespers, Matins and Mass for each day, and also Terce, Sext and None for the weekdays of Lent and some fasts at other times in the year. Other books were needed for the purely monastic minor hours which were especially numerous in the old Spanish rite. The monks had three or four services at night, then Matins; after which came Aurora, Prime, second hour, Terce, fourth and fifth hours, Sext, seventh and eighth hours, None, tenth, eleventh and twelfth hours; then Vespers and, finally, Compline.[9] By contrast, the normal type of medieval Roman breviary had services of Matins and Lauds (always joined together), Prime, Terce, Sext, None, Vespers and Compline. This too was burdensome for most clerics and the offices were commonly celebrated as a morning group and an evening group. Attempts at reform, such as that of Cardinal Quinonez of 1535, often made no attempt to change the number of services, though more radical reformers such as Cranmer combined many of the existing services into just two,[10] and thus recovered something of which Ortiz can only have been dimly aware, that in the Spain of late antiquity, the only services normally expected of the parish clergy and the laity were Vespers and Matins; the rest being purely monastic except in Lent.[11]

In the context of his period Ortiz could not produce a breviary with only Vespers and Matins in it, so his printed Breviary of 1502 is something of a compromise. It also came out very quickly (preceded by the Missal in 1500). If these books were originally intended just for the three parishes, their usefulness was increased by the endowment of a college in the new Corpus Christi chapel of Toledo Cathedral in 1504 specifically to celebrate the Mozarabic services.[12]

The Ortiz edition of the Breviary is now very rare. It was printed on vellum, in red and black, with two sizes of typeface to highlight separate units;[13] after a Calendar and brief directions there follows the Temporal cycle from Advent to Pentecost. Except on certain weekdays, mostly in Lent, the offices of each day comprise Vespers and Matins. There is often no Second Vespers of Sundays and Feasts but there is always a First Vespers and the book is, as it were, biased towards starting the liturgical day on the previous night. Whereas in the older manuscripts, offices of Saints were mixed up with those of the season, Ortiz separated them and also removed all the Mass texts to the printed Missal. After the Temporal Ortiz printed a Psalter, which was interrupted after Psalm 117[14] by the insertion of the Minor Hours of Aurora (dawn), Prime, Terce, Sext and None; also *Ante Completorium* and Compline itself. The relevant parts of Psalm 118 were included in the offices for which they were appointed, which entailed the omission of about half of that psalm because of the 'inter-hours' that Ortiz did not include. The seasonal material for these hours, which are very different from those given in the Temporal, is included after each of them. The Psalter starts again with Psalm 119 (Psalms 119–123 are also used in the minor hours). After the Psalter came the common and proper offices of Saints (which included newly composed offices for later medieval feasts such as Corpus Christi) and finally four pages of indices.

EARLY RESEARCH

Over the next few centuries almost all writing on the subject of the Mozarabic Office was based on this printed edition of 1502. The manuscripts were not widely known. In 1741 Bianchini published an edition of the *Orational* of Verona (OV),[15] the oldest surviving MS of the rite containing prayers for the festal and Lenten offices. In 1770 two former chaplains of the Mozarabic chapel, Francisco Antonio Lorenzana and Francisco Fabian y Fuero, then both bishops in Mexico, published an explanation of the Mass and Office of the Mozarabic rite, with directions for saying them.[16] Lorenzana later became Archbishop of Toledo and in 1776 produced a revised version of the Breviary.[17] He made a number of alterations; a new Psalter with canticles and hymns[18] was included between the Temporal and minor hours, all modern feasts were placed in an appendix, and a new introduction was provided by Lorenzana himself. This is the edition which we shall use in this work, referred to for convenience as *Br*.

When the first modern histories of the Divine Office appeared, such as Batiffol's in 1893,[19] few authors seem to have had any inkling of the special character of the Spanish services, but publication of other sources began to change this. Also in 1893 Dom G. Morin published the *Liber Commicus* of Silos, an eleventh-century Mass lectionary.[20] In 1897, in his series *Analecta Hymnica* 27, Clemens Blume SJ published all the known Mozarabic hymns from both *Br.* and from the MSS.[21]

The year 1904 saw the publication of Dom M. Férotin's edition of the *Liber Ordinum*, basically the documents relating to the administration of the sacraments other than that of the Eucharist; but he also published in the book a long prologue that pointed out the difference between the office as celebrated in the secular churches and that of the monks in this tradition.[22] This was followed in 1905 by J. P. Gilson's edition of a fragmentary Spanish Psalter with collects for each psalm, some of the minor hours and a few orders of Vespers and Matins, a book obviously relevant to the office[23] (hereafter *MP*). In 1912 Férotin's *Liber Mozarabicus Sacramentorum*, a critical edition of many texts for Mass, appended a summary of all the known manuscripts giving the first words of many of the structural units of the offices.[24]

Various studies in scholarly journals raised awareness of some of the interesting features of the old Spanish office, notably the way it used canticles, hymns and the Psalter. A major step in the interpretation of the Spanish material came with W. C. Bishop's studies, edited and published in 1924.[25] Bishop emphasized the monastic nature of continuous psalmody and saw that the Mozarabic and Milanese books contained relics of a genuinely secular church service, perhaps not originally of daily occurrence. He noted parallels between old Spanish and Milanese practice but did not live to draw his final conclusions. In 1928 an edition of the important Antiphoner of Leon was brought out by the monastery of Silos – this important manuscript will be referred to henceforward as *AL*.

Parallel studies of the chant agreed that the ancient notation (in neums, i.e., signs that indicate the shape of the melody but give no indication of pitch or tempo) was difficult to decipher.[26] As a result the offices in the Toledo chapel were mostly chanted on one note, but on certain feast-days at Vespers they used music from sixteenth-century Cantorals. In the 1930s the English scholar A. W. S. Porter provided a series of helpful studies. These included a four-part article on early Spanish monastic practice, the last two parts containing descriptions and schemes of the offices.[27] In the course of this outline Porter drew attention to the difference between the *ordo cathedralis* of the secular churches and the ordo of the monks. Vespers and Matins were the rites of secular churches that the monks had to perform as well as their own. In 1935 Porter seems to have been the first to suggest that *Br.* contained the relics of an older tradition.[28]

The rite nearly became extinct with the murder of the Mozarabic chaplains during the Spanish Civil War. Postwar restoration was on a smaller scale and, at first, far from edifying in its manner of performance.[29]

POSTWAR RESEARCH AND DEVELOPMENT

Research continued with various scholary articles.[30] In 1946 J. Vives and J. Claveras published a re-edition of the *Oracional Visigotico* (*OV*) and other sources.[31] An important contribution was made by Dom Brou's emphasis on the unsuitability of the term 'Mozarabic', since the rite was in existence before the Moorish invasions and changed little in essentials in that period. 'Visigothic' was inadequate since so much pre-dated the short-lived Visigothic-Catholic state, and 'Toledan' ignored the very wide spread of this liturgical family. He spoke of the 'old Spanish' rite and the printed books as 'neo-Hispanic'. In this study we will continue to use the term 'old Spanish'.[32]

In the meantime Hanssens' work on the history of the morning office (noting the Spanish and Milanese evidence)[33] saw it as one celebrated between dawn and daybreak, originally as a single service, only later perceived as two; i.e., Matins and Lauds.

In 1953 came Fabrega's edition of the *Passionary* (saints' lives read at Matins),[34] and in 1954, in *Archivos Leoneses*, appeared the first of the many articles of Dom J. Pinell on the old Spanish rites,[35] examining the sets of three Antiphons and a Responsory at Matins in *AL*. In 1955 he examined the different books used in the old Spanish office and concluded that the *Liber Misticus*, first mentioned around 900 CE, contained the material necessary for the Cathedral Office and the Mass, while a separate Book of Hours contained the purely monastic offices.[36]

In further studies Pinell tried to identify a primitive form of Matins that consisted basically of a psalm chosen for that time of day and a psalm prayer to go with it, and showed how the old Spanish books, including *Br.*, preserved relics of this system.[37] Regarding evening worship, Pinell showed that the *Lucernarium* or bringing in of lamps at sunset was the starting point for Vespers in the West as in the

East.[38] In his overall view of the office,[39] Pinell noted that although there were a few MSS that related to the material found in *Br.*, most of those used by Ortiz must have been lost. Against Brou he emphasized the use of selected psalms in the cathedral office but that there was no single established course of psalmody in this particular cathedral rite.

It was by now clear to many scholars that the recitation of the Psalter in course was a monastic feature imported into cathedral offices in Spain as elsewhere. This did not, however, preclude the use of *selected* psalms in full. In 1958 Anton Baumstark's *Comparative Liturgy* was published in English.[40] This important book highlighted the concept of a cathedral office that used selected psalms and was of a ceremonial and clerical type, as contrasted with the monastic use of the Psalter spread over some period of time, usually a week, a more meditative office and less in need of officiating clergy.

In 1959, a new critical edition of *AL* was published, a vitally important addition to the growing knowledge of the old Spanish MSS.[41] This was followed by Josef Jungmann's papers collected under the English title *Pastoral Liturgy*, in which Jungmann pointed to the Spanish evidence of a 'pre-Monastic' service of Vespers and Matins only, and advised treating *Br.* with caution.[42] However, the reliability of *Br.* was dealt with by J. M. Martin Patino in an article in 1963,[43] where he pointed out archaic features such as the use of the *Vetus Latina* Bible rather than the Vulgate for the canticles, and other structural archaisms, also showing that in spite of using variant material, *Br.* still had the same basic shape of office as that of other manuscripts and witnessed to a separate but legitimate tradition, perhaps one that was both parochial and deliberately archaizing. From about this time Pinell began to refer to the main manuscript tradition as Tradition A, and that of *Br.* and its few related manuscripts as Tradition B.[44]

In 1966 Pinell brought out a reconstruction of the night offices of the monastic rite.[45] Noting that A. Mundo had dated two of the Tradition B manuscripts to the thirteenth or fourteenth centuries, this appears to have been where Pinell first suggested that Tradition B may have been brought to Toledo by Christians fleeing one of the spasmodic persecutions by the Muslims in Seville.[46]

ATTEMPTS AT REFORM OF THE DAILY OFFICES AND THE CONTRIBUTION OF RESEARCH

The 1963 decree of the second Vatican Council, *Sacrosanctum Con-*

cilium,[47] eventually issued in a new Breviary, entitled *The Liturgy of the Hours*. Intended as a set of services that sanctify the day, many have found it, if anything, more complex than that which preceded it. Those responsible for this reform were not listening to the scholars. Juan Mateos SJ had, for instance, in 1968, attempted to outline the real nature of a cathedral office.[48] He proposed that early morning and evening offices used selected psalms, hymns and prayers that reflected the time of day so as to celebrate morning as a time of rebirth and renewal and the evening as a time of thanksgiving and of asking forgiveness and protection. W. Jardine Grisbrooke, in a study in *Studia Liturgica*, noted that there were ancient cycles of reciting the psalms at the cathedral office, which he saw as a sort of prologue to those services.[49] He also emphasized the ceremonial, 'dramatic' side of genuine cathedral worship and the fact that even today in Orthodox parish churches, it is the specifically monastic features, such as recitation of the Psalter in course, that are cut down or omitted. Criticisms of the still basically monastic concept operative in the Roman office have been further extended by Stanislaus Campbell's detailed study of how the reform was carried out.[50]

A growing realization in some circles that the old Spanish office might be a privileged source for understanding the ancient Western cathedral office was boosted by the publication of Pinell's reconstruction of the *Liber Orationum Psalmographus* (*LOP*).[51] In a lengthy introduction Pinell explained his thesis that a Psalter with collects for each psalm was basic to the ordinary evening and morning cathedral offices in Spain. The prayers provided a way of drawing out a particular interpretation of each psalm. In 1974 Pinell published an article examining the possibility of partially re-establishing the content of the *Liber Canticorum* of Tradition B probably seen and used by Ortiz.[52] Like Martin Patino he stressed the continuity of use between Tradition B and other parts of the ancient tradition outside of Spain. In general the Tradition B was archaic and less eclectic and developing than Tradition A. In the same year Gabriele Winkler published an article on cathedral Vespers in which she drew upon Pinell's work, and also emphasized the theology of Vespers as worship of God the Saviour, and of the morning office as worship of God the giver of covenant love. She noted the parallels between Spain and Milan and underlined the relics of an older tradition to be found in the old Roman rite.[53]

The increasing number of studies included V. Martin Pintado's of the Lenten readings, again identifying Tradition B as the older.[54]

Against the increasing acceptance of Ortiz' reliability was an article on psalm collects in the *Liber Ordinum* by J. Janini, who was very critical of Ortiz' work and some of Pinell's readings. He felt that *LOP* was too artificial and that Pinell was over-inclined to prefer pastoral and literary criteria.[55] The following year, in an introduction to an examination of the liturgical MSS of Toledo Cathedral, Janini and R. Gonzalvez saw Tradition B as an abbreviation of Tradition A, and emphasized Ortiz' deliberately archaizing tendencies and slipshod workmanship.[56]

It was partly because of such scholarly findings that articles, particularly in *Worship*, were stressing the real nature of the 'Liturgy of the Hours' in a cathedral tradition, as against the monastic style still perceived in modern revisions.[57] In 1978 Pinell published an article on the canticle collects found only in Tradition B, in the course of which he pointed out the interrelationships between the various traditions of the Western cathedral office, the function of these canticles as reminders of the Paschal Virgil and thus, of the resurrection theme permeating Matins.[58] Once again, as in so many other aspects of the old Spanish rite, he discerned the preservation of elements that have outlived their meaning. The elements that make up the structure of such rites as the old Spanish can allow the forming of an hypothesis as to the original shape and purpose of these rites of the daily service.

In 1979, Jose Janini published his edition of manuscript *T2* (a Tradition B Toledan document), dating it to about the fourteenth century. He was sceptical of Pinell's theory of a Sevillan origin, but suggested that Tradition B was simply a parochial use. These too are hypotheses, and Janini admits that there may have been other manuscripts available to Ortiz that no longer survive. Janini does stress the continued importance of *Br.* as a source for our understanding of the old Spanish liturgy, especially in the form in which it has survived in the Corpus Christi Chapel.[59] In the following year emerged Janini's edition of the Toledo manuscript 35.5,[60] also of Tradition B.

In 1980 the Church of England's Alternative Service Book was published and the daily Morning and Evening Prayer was basically a revision of Cranmer's revision of the sixteenth century, the Psalter still being arranged to be said in some sort of course, and scripture readings, no part of the primitive office, continuing to be important. As in the revised Roman services, variation of psalms, readings and other elements tended to reflect seasons and feasts rather than time of day.

Paul Bradshaw's 1981 study of the primitive office challenged much received wisdom. He noted that Jewish temple practice was to have three services, not two, and he emphasized the early appearance of 'minor hours' (at least of Terce, Sext and None). He wondered whether the evidence for the universal use of Psalm 140 in the evenings was as conclusive as some would hold, and the same applied to Psalm 62 in the mornings. He did, however, show that the monastic style of office with psalms and readings in course was today the prevailing model in most people's thoughts about the daily office.[61]

In 1986, Robert Taft brought out his very important overview of the whole tradition of public daily prayer. For the Spanish evidence he relies upon Pinell together with Isidore and the Conciliar legislation. As to original structures, he tends to follow Winkler and posits a single selected psalm, while allowing that in Spain, as elsewhere, Psalms 148–50 were integral parts of any morning celebration from a very early stage. Taft again, in contrast to the official provision being made everywhere of complicated and rather clerical liturgies of the hours, stressed its primitive character as being simple and popular.[62]

That the official provision was still drawing criticisms from those who felt it unsuitable to their pastoral needs was shown by a small book by David Cutts and Harold Miller, which showed how, for most Christians, such services remained largely a *terra incognita*, and a monastic one at that.[63] Their title, the question *Whose Office?* is the question that still needs to be convincingly answered. Is all that is necessary some sort of structure of daily devotion and edification to keep the clergy up to the mark, or is there to be a real possibility of providing for genuine, not imaginary, parish celebrations?

The continuing discussion is well illustrated by George Guiver's *Company of Voices* of 1988. Guiver noted how modern Western Christianity, especially in its most clerical guise, has had a tendency to see 'real' spirituality as very inward, in contrast to 'unimportant' outer forms. He prefers the title 'people's office' to cathedral office, quite rightly perceiving that English people see cathedral worship as characterized by highly sophisticated choral worship. He noted the Ambrosian and old Spanish parallels and suggested that they may well represent what was once normal in the West.[64] As to the content of modern offices, he pleaded for selected psalms, noted that the Gospel canticles and readings were later additions, and suggested that praise and prayer should be the characterizing notes of such a people's office. Very importantly he noted the tendency in the Vatican 'Instruction on the Liturgy of the Hours' to impose one type of structure, a still monastic Western one, as the only true form of the daily service.[65]

In the pages that follow, the services of Vespers and Matins of the old Spanish rite will be examined and analysed. The basis for this analysis is largely the printed Breviary as revised by Lorenzana and reprinted as *Patrologia Latina* 86, because it is relatively easy to obtain. Due attention will be paid to the Tradition B material edited by Janini, but also to the Tradition A manuscripts. Following the order of *Br.*, the various units that make up Vespers will be examined first. Then after some conclusions about Vespers, a similar analysis of Matins will be made. The final conclusions will attempt to draw out what can be learnt from this tradition for those revising daily prayer services today.

In order to provide an overview of these services, an appendix to this introduction contains plans of their general arrangements. These are based on those provided by Porter in his March 1934 article in *Laudate* (pp. 31–52) and adapted to suit the services of *Br.* where they differ slightly from those of the Tradition A MSS. As they will be referred to occasionally, the schemes of the different forms of the minor hours are also provided and are adapted from the same source.

NOTES

1. Especially with reference to the daily offices, see e.g. the present author's paper, 'Daily Prayer: Its Origin in Its Function', *Studia Patristica* XXX (1997), pp. 364–88. Delivered at 1995 International Patristic Conference, Oxford.
2. See esp. James W. McKinnon, 'On the Question of Psalmody in the Ancient Synagogue', *Early Music History* 6 (1986), pp. 159–62.
3. *The Search for the Origins of Christian Worship* (London: SPCK, 1992), pp. 185–92. New edition in preparation.
4. See also Robert Taft, *The Liturgy of the Hours in East and West* (Collegeville: Liturgical Press, 1986).
5. The area around modern Narbonne in SE France. Archdale A. King, *The Liturgies of the Primatial Sees* (London: Longmans Green, 1957), pp. 462ff.
6. ibid., pp. 466 and 513–14.
7. ibid., pp. 516–17.
8. J. Janini and R. Gonzalvez, *Manuscritos Liturgicos de la Catedral de Toledo* (Toledo: Diputacion Provincial, 1977), pp. 39–42.
9. A. W. S. Porter, 'Early Spanish Monasticism', *Laudate* XII, 45 (1934), pp. 31–52.
10. See e.g. G. Cuming, *A History of Anglican Liturgy* (London: Macmillan, 1961), pp. 22, 47 and 71.
11. Porter, op. cit., *Laudate* XI, 44 (1933), pp. 199–200.
12. King, op. cit., p. 519.
13. *Breviarium Secundum Regulam Beati Isidori* (Toleti, i.e. Toledo, 1502).
14. ibid., fol 294v.
15. MS Verona, Biblioteca Capitolare cod LXXXIX (alt 84).
16. F. A. Lorenzana and F. Fabian y Fuero, *Missa Gotica seu Mozarabica et officium itidem, Gothicum, diligenter ac dilucide explanata* (Puebla de los Angeles, 1770).

INTRODUCTION

17 *Breviarium Gothicum*, republished in J. P. Migne (ed.), *Patrologia Latina* 86 (Paris, 1862), the edition to which all further reference will be made. (There was also a missal of 1804 which is *PL* 85.)
18 From MS Madrid Biblioteca Nacional 10.001, a ninth/tenth-cent. Psalter with Canticles and Hymns.
19 *Histoire du Breviaire Romain* (Paris, 1893).
20 *Liber Commicus seu Lectionarium Missae* (Maredsous, Belgium: *Anecdota Maredsolana* I, 1893).
21 *Hymnodia Gotica*, in series *Analecta Hymnica Medii Aevi* (Leipzig, 1897).
22 *Le Liber Ordinum en usage dans l'Église Wisigothique et Mozarabe de Espagne du V à X siècle* (Paris: *Monumenta Ecclesiastica Liturgica*, 1904).
23 *The Mozarabic Psalter* (London: Henry Bradshaw Society, 1905), edition of MS Brit. Mus. Add. 30.851.
24 Paris: *Monumenta Ecclesiastica Liturgica*, 1912, see pp. 633–906.
25 *The Mozarabic and Ambrosian Rites, Four Essays in Comparative Liturgiology* (London: Mowbrays for the Alcuin Club, 1924), esp. pp. 55–97.
26 See e.g., C. Rojo and G. Prado, *El Canto Mozarabe* (Barcelona, 1929).
27 'Early Spanish Monasticism', *Laudate* X (1932), pp. 2–15, 66–79, 156–57; XI (1933), pp. 199–207; and XII (1934), pp. 31–52.
28 'Cantica Mozarabici Officii', *Ephemerides Liturgicae* 49 (1935), pp. 126–45.
29 King, op. cit., pp. 520–2.
30 E.g. C. Callewaert, 'Le Carême Primitif dans la liturgie Mozarabe', *Sacris Erudiri* (Steenbrugge, 1940), pp. 507–516, and J. Vives, 'El Oracinal Mozarabe de Silos', *Analecta Sacra Tarraconensia* 18 (1945), pp. 1–25.
31 *Oracional Visigotico* (Barcelona: *Monumenta Hispaniae Sacra* I, 1946).
32 'Liturgie "Mozarabe" ou Liturgie "Hispanique"?', *EL* 63 (1949), pp. 46–70.
33 *Nature et Genèse de l'Office des Matines* (Rome: *Analecta Gregoriana* LVII, 1952), esp. pp. 42–3 and 58.
34 *Passionario Hispanico* (Madrid-Barcelona: *Monumenta Hispaniae Sacra* VI, 1953 and 1955).
35 'Las *Missae*, Grupos de Cantos y Oraciones en el Oficio de la Antigua Liturgia Hispana', *ArchL* 8 (1954), pp. 145–85.
36 'El Liber Horarum y el Misticus entre los libros de la Antigua Liturgia Hispana', *HS* 8 (1955), pp. 85–107.
37 'El Matutinarium en la Liturgia Hispana', *HS* 9 (1956), pp. 61–85.
38 'Vestigis del Lucernari a Occident', *Liturgica I – Scripta et Documenta* 7 (Monserrat, 1956), pp. 91–149.
39 'El Oficio Hispana-Visigotico', *HS* 10 (1957), pp. 385–427.
40 Ed. F. L. Cross (Oxford: Mowbray, 1958).
41 L. Brou and J. Vives (eds), *Antifonario Visigotico Mozarabe de la Catedral de Leon* (Madrid: *MHS series liturgica* V, 1959). Edition of MS Leon Biblioteca Catedral cod 8–10th cent.
42 London: Challoner, 1962, esp. pp. 127–57.
43 'El Breviarium Mozarabe de Ortiz, su valor documental para la Historia de Oficio Catedralicio Hispanico', *Miscellanea 40 Comillas* (1963), pp. 207–97 (an article marred by a large number of typographical errors).
44 'Una exhortacion Diaconal a la Plegaria en el Antiguo Rito Hispanico, La *Supplicatio*', *Analecta Sacra Tarraconensia* 36 (1963), pp. 3–23, and see pp. 5–6.
45 'Las Horas Vigiliares del Oficio Monacal Hispanico', *Liturgica 3 – Scripta et Documenta* (Monserrat, 1966), pp. 197–340.
46 ibid., pp. 209 and 222.
47 W. A. Abbott (ed.), *The Documents of Vatican II* (London: G. Chapman, 1967), pp. 163–7.
48 'The Morning and Evening Office', *Worship* 42 (1968), pp. 31–47.
49 'Cathedral Office and Monastic Office', *Studia Liturgica* 8 (1971–2), pp. 143–159.
50 *From Breviary to Liturgy of the Hours* (Collegeville: Liturgical Press, 1995).
51 Barcelona-Madrid: *MHS* IX, 1972.
52 'Los Canticos de Oficio en el Antiguo Rito Hispanico', *HS* 27 (1974), pp. 5–54.
53 'Über die Kathedralvesper in der Verschiedenen Riten des Ostens und Westens', *ALW* 16 (1974), pp. 33–102.
54 'Las Lecturas Cuaresmales en la Antigua Liturgia Hispanica. Estudio de Liturgia comparada', *Salmanticensis* XII (1975), pp. 217–69.
55 'Las Collectas Salmicas del *Liber Ordinum*', *HS* 28 (1975), pp. 103–24.
56 *Manuscritos Liturgicos de la Catedral de Toledo* (Toledo: Diputacion Provincial, 1977), esp. pp. 26–45.

57 E.g. William Storey, 'The Liturgy of the Hours: Cathedral versus Monastery', *Worship* 50 (1976), pp. 50–70; and also see Carl Dehne, 'Roman Catholic Popular Devotions', *Worship* 49 (1975), pp. 446–60.
58 'Las Oraciones "de Cantico" del Antiguo Rito Hispanico', *Didaskalia* VIII (1978), pp. 197–329.
59 *Liber Misticus de Cuaresma* (Toledo: Instituto de Estudios Visigotico-Mozarabes, 1979), see pp. xxix–xliii.
60 *Liber Misticus de Cuaresma y Pascua* (Toledo: Instituto de Estudios Visigotico-Mozarabes, 1980).
61 *Daily Prayer in the Early Church* (London: Alcuin/SPCK, 1981).
62 *The Liturgy of the Hours in East and West* (Collegeville: Liturgical Press, 1986), see esp. pp. 156–63 and 211–13.
63 *Whose Office?: Daily Prayer for the People of God* (Bramcote: Grove Liturgical Study 32, 1982).
64 *Company of Voices* (London: SPCK, 1988), p. 85.
65 ibid., p. 183.

THE SCHEMES OF VESPERS
(Brackets indicate units not always present.)

Sundays and Feasts	**Weekdays**
Opening Service of Light	
Opening formula	Opening formula
Vespertinum/Lucernarium	*Vespertinum/Laudes*
Prayer (on most Sundays & Feasts)	
Sono (usually omitted in Lent)	(*Sono* only in Eastertide)
Variable Psalmody	
Antiphon	Antiphon & Psalm (most days)
(More ants. on Feasts and some Suns.)	
(Prayer on great feasts)	
Laudes/Alleluiaticum	*Laudes/Alleluiaticum*
Hymn	Hymn
Prayer & Conclusion	
Supplicatio & Kyrie	*Supplicatio* & Kyrie
Completuria	*Completuria*
Lord's Prayer & Embolism	Lord's Prayer & Embolism
Benedictio	*Benedictio*
Appendices	
Variable *Psallenda* & prayer	Variable *Psallenda* & prayer
(several in Lent, sometimes *Preces*)	
Concluding formula	Concluding formula
Fixed *Psallendum* & prayer	Fixed *Psallendum* & prayer
Concluding formula	Concluding formula

THE SCHEMES OF MATINS

Sunday	Feasts	Weekdays
Opening at Night		
Aeterne rerum & prayer		
Antiphon & Ps. 3	Antiphon & Ps. 3	Antiphon & Ps. 3
Antiphon & Ps. 50		(or Pss. 50 or 56)
Antiphon & Ps. 56		
Prayer	Prayer	Prayer
Variable Psalmody		
Antiphon 1 – prayer	Antiphon 1 – prayer	Ant. – Psalm – prayer
Antiphon 2 – prayer	Antiphon 2 – prayer	Ant. – Psalm – prayer
Antiphon 3 – prayer	Antiphon 3 – prayer	Ant. – Psalm – prayer
Responsory (prayer)	Responsory – Prayer (Whole unit may be repeated)	Responsory (prayer)
Morning Praises		
	(Ant. – Ps. 50 – prayer)	Ant. – Ps. 50 – prayer
Ant. – OT canticle	Ant. – OT canticle	Ant. – OT canticle
Prayer (usually)	Prayer (on some feasts)	Prayer
Ant. – *Benedictiones*	Ant. – *Benedictiones*	
Prayer (ordinary Sundays)		
		Matutinarium
Sono (not Lent)	*Sono*	
Ant. – Pss. 148–50	Ant. – Pss. 148–50	Ant. – Ps. 150 (148–50)
Lesson	Lesson	Lesson
Hymn	Hymn	Hymn
Prayer & Conclusion		
Supplicatio & Kyrie	*Supplicatio* & Kyrie	*Supplicatio* & Kyrie
Completuria	*Completuria*	*Completuria*
Lord's Prayer & Embolism	Lord's Prayer & Embolism	Lord's Prayer & Embolism
Psallendum & prayer	(*Psallendum* – prayer)	(*Psallendum*)
Benedictio	*Benedictio*	*Benedictio*
	Concluding formula	
Appendices		
Psallendum – prayer	(*Psallendum* – prayer)	*Psallendum* – prayer
Concluding formula		Concluding formula

THE HOURS OF TERCE, SEXT AND NONE

Cathedral Ordo	**Monastic Ordo**
Opening	
	Deus in adjutorium
Readings	
Wisdom (only one on wkds)	
Old Testament (Only one at Sext)	
New Testament (Occasionally at Terce and None)	
Psalmody	
	Antiphon
Antiphon – psalm – prayer	Psalm (T 94, S 53, N 145)
Antiphon – psalm – prayer	Psalm (T 118, S 118, N 121)
Antiphon – psalm	Psalm (T 118, S 118, N 122)
(Complete psalms omitted in second half of Lent)	Psalm (T, 118, S 118, N 123)
	Antiphon
Responsory (not at None)	Responsory
Readings, etc.	
	Short OT lesson
	Short NT lesson
Laudes (weekdays)	*Laudes* (1 or 2)
Prayer & other material	
Preces	
(Hymn)	Hymn
	(Versicle at Easter Terce)
	Clamores
(*Supplicatio*)	*Supplicatio* & Kyrie
Completuria	*Completuria*
Lord's Prayer (& Embolism)	Lord's Prayer & Embolism
Conclusion	
(*Benedictio*)	*Benedictio*
Concluding formula	

Part One

The Order and the Components of Vespers

At a first glance the old Spanish Vespers presents a very puzzling appearance to somebody who is used to the forms of evening worship contained in the old or new Roman Breviaries, in the Book of Common Prayer and its successors, or even in the modern compilation *Celebrating Common Prayer*. All these books have a discernible family resemblance. There are psalms to be said in order (even though the modern Roman form and *Celebrating Common Prayer* do try to be less tied to the recitation of the Psalter in numerical course). Continuous or semi-continuous reading of Scripture is to be found in all of them even though historically the Roman system reserved most of this aspect to Matins/the Office of Readings. The modern forms frequently begin the service with a hymn, and in all of them the *Magnificat* is perceived to be the evening canticle par excellence. Even the beginning of the offices is very similar, usually some version of the 'Lord open our lips'/'O God make haste to help us' dialogue.

Very few of these familiar landmarks can be found to guide one into the mysteries of the old Spanish Vespers: psalm verses and antiphons only occasionally seem to require the whole of a psalm – and then usually just the one. There is no reading of Scripture, the *Magnificat* is entirely absent (as is any other New Testament canticle), and the hymn follows the 'psalmody' and immediately precedes the intercessory section which includes the Lord's Prayer. The offices begin with a presidential greeting. One feature that does appear to exist is a form of lamplighting chant at the beginning, a once common ancient ritual that *Celebrating Common Prayer* is attempting to re-introduce to Western Christians.

There is no doubt that neither the present printed books, nor the surviving manuscripts, seem to envisage what one might call a 'well-rounded' vesperal celebration. In order to understand the nature of the office that these texts originally represented, we will examine first the surviving early descriptions of the office of Vespers, and then, taking the components in turn, try to discern how each developed. After that we should be able to show how the office was originally celebrated in the seventh/eighth centuries and by attention to the material contained in the surviving forms, say what sort of a theology of Vespers they represent.

1
EARLY TESTIMONIES TO THE STRUCTURE OF VESPERS IN SPAIN

One of the earliest surviving Spanish references to a vesperal celebration is a canon of the First Council of Toledo (400 CE) forbidding the celebration of the *Lucernarium*, i.e. lamplighting, in a place other than church.[1] (This very insistence may well indicate that another practice had in fact been common.) Other early references include the Council of Agde in Gaul, in 506, requiring the 'capitella de psalmis'[2] to end both Vespers and Matins, Tarragona in 516 requiring a daily celebration of Vespers and Matins; then in c. 549 Barcelona ordered a blessing of the faithful at Matins as well as Vespers, Toledo IV (633) required the recitation of the Lord's Prayer at all offices, while finally, but very importantly, the Council of Merida in 666[3] declared that Vespers should begin as follows:

1 *Oblatio luminis* (offering of light).
2 *Vespertinum*.
3 *Sonum* on feasts.

(The latter two terms will be explained below.)

A summary description of the order of Vespers in a women's monastery in North-West Spain is found in the Ordo of Bobadilla, itself contained in MS 113 of the Royal Monastery of the Escorial. The ordo is believed to be older than the eleventh-century manuscript. It is also possible that St Isidore may have based some of his rule, the *Regula Monachorum*, upon this source. Pinell puts the schemes of Bobadilla and Isidore together with his own scheme for the developed cathedral ordo:

Bobadilla	**Isidore**	**Cathedral Ordo**
		Oblatio luminis
Psalmus	Lucernarium	Vespertinum (*Lucernarium*)

		[*Sono*]
Psalmus	Psalmus	Antiphona
Psalmus	Psalmus	Alleluiaticum (*Laudes*)
Responsorium	Responsorium	
Laudes	*Laudes*	
	Hymnus	Hymnus
		Versus (Trad. A only)
		Supplicatio
Completuria	Oratio	*Completuria*
		Lord's Prayer
		Petitio (i.e. embolism)
		Benedictio
		[*Psallendum*][4]

In view of the importance of the evidence from Isidore, here is A. W. S. Porter's translation of the relevant section of PL 83, col. 867: 'But at Vespers the *Lucernarium* is first to be said, then two psalms, one responsory, the *Laudes*, a hymn and a prayer.'[5] From the above material Taft suggests this tentative reconstruction of the primitive Spanish cathedral Vespers:[6]

Oblation of light
Vesperal psalm with antiphon, doxology and collect
Hymn
Supplication
Completuria
Our Father
Petition Blessing
[*Psallendum*, not every day]

NOTES

1 J. Pinell, 'El Oficio Hispano-Visigotico', *HS* 10 (1957), pp. 385–427, 386.
2 Probably a form of intercession using psalm verses, see below, p. 39.
3 ibid., pp. 386–8.
4 ibid., p. 401.
5 'Early Spanish Monasticism', *Laudate* XI, 44 (1933), pp. 199–207, here at 199.
6 R. Taft, *The Liturgy of the Hours in East and West* (Collegeville: Liturgical Press, 1986), pp. 157–61.

2

THE OBLATIO LUMINIS AND LUCERNARIUM

THE OBLATIO LUMINIS

According to the rules at the beginning of the printed Breviary, all offices are to begin: 'In nomine Domini nostri Jesu Christi lumen cum pace' (In the name of our Lord Jesus Christ, light with peace), with the response: 'Deo gratias' (Thanks be to God). After this, the priest greets those present with the salutation; 'Dominus sit semper vobiscum' (The Lord be always with you) and they reply 'Et cum spiritu tuo' (and with your spirit).[1] The formula was to be made with a sign of the cross.

As Porter observed, the 'in nomine' formula is not found in the manuscripts, but it is mentioned in an eleventh-century letter from Etherius and Beatus to Elipandus of Toledo.[2] Porter interpreted the formula as one that accompanied the offering of a light at the altar. Pinell also described the ceremony as the lifting up of a lighted lamp or candle in a gesture of offering[3] and suggested that parallels to this formula were the 'Lumen Christi – Deo gratias' formula of the Roman Easter Vigil, and 'The Light of Christ illumines all' in the Byzantine liturgy of the Presanctified Gifts.[4] The latter, involving blessing the people with a lit candle, is as Nicholas Uspensky has shown, a misplaced vestige of an actual bringing in of the light at evening.[5]

In Milan, which has preserved a light ritual at Vespers to the present day, the only formula is the salutation, followed by the chant of the *Lucernarium*, and the light is now a lamp brought into church at the beginning of the service, from which lights for the altar and for the acolytes are taken.[6] The old Spanish *Vespertinum* also shares the themes of light with the opening formula, so does the Milanese *Lucernarium*. We cannot then make too sharp a division between the opening formula and the chants that follow it.

The ceremonial acknowledgement of the need of light as the sun sets has a long history in the Judaeo-Christian tradition. The Jewish Sabbath commences with the mother's blessing:

> Blessed art thou, O Lord our God, King of the Universe, who hast sanctified us by the commandments, and commanded us to kindle the Sabbath light.

The day closes at sunset the next day with:

> Blessed art thou, O Lord our God, King of the Universe, who created the light of fire.[7]

Tertullian spoke of a similar custom, though after rather than before the evening meal. Gregory of Nyssa's life of his sister Macrina shows us that in fourth-century Cappadocia there was an evening lamplighting accompanied by thanksgiving for the light, and Basil the Great regarded the custom as already ancient. In Jerusalem Egeria attended what she knew as 'Lucernare' back home and it obviously differed little from what she was used to.[8]

Hippolytus gives a prayer of thanksgiving to be said at the bringing in of the lamps after a communal meal,[9] but from the fourth or fifth century the *Lucernarium* was a church service rather than a domestic observance, and as such it lasted, especially in Spain, to a very late date and, in Milan, down to the present day.

Winkler suggested that the Jewish tradition of starting the day at sunset was commemorative of the redemptive acts of God who led his people out of Egypt, while the morning commemorated the God of the Covenant.[10] She also pointed out that the urban monks of Cappadocia prefaced this popular cathedral service with their recitation of the Psalter in course.[11] This has influenced other Eastern rites; in the present-day Orthodox Vespers the service of light and the hymn 'O Gladsome Light' are preceded by both the fixed vesperal psalms and the recitation of the Psalms in course (*psalmodia currens*).[12] The earlier form of Byzantine Vespers had similar psalmody preceding a light ceremony, and in the present Liturgy of the Pre-Sanctified Gifts there are relics of both forms of Vespers that have been used in Constantinople, giving rise to a double light ceremony at this interesting Lenten service.[13]

Other Eastern rites exhibited similar features: a period of psalmody preceding the fixed vesperal psalms (always including psalm 140), which were themselves bound up with the light service, the *Lucernarium*. Relics of such a light ceremony can even be detected in Coptic and Ethiopian services;[14] East Syrian Vespers also contained a light ritual early in the service.[15]

The Christian East then, knew an evening service that celebrated Christ as the light of the nations. Over the centuries, the related incense ritual came to overshadow that of light in many places and, almost everywhere, continuous psalmody of monastic type was added. Often only verbal allusions in prayers survive to witness to the existence of the ancient light ritual. In the West too, as Pinell pointed out, it was not so much that the *Lucernarium* was a part of Vespers, as that Vespers developed out of the *Lucernarium*.[16] The Spanish evidence and the survival of the *Lucernarium* at Milan would argue that such a ceremony was once common in Western Europe.

Pinell entitled the opening formula 'Oblatio Luminis' but it seems purely declarative. Nothing indicates the offering of the light to God; it is easier to interpret it as *the offering of God's light to his people*, which would accord better with the earlier thanksgiving for light in such sources as Hippolytus (see above), or the Apostolic Constitutions.[17] It would also fit in better with the symbolism described by Egeria.[18]

In the East the desire to make a symbolic offering in thanksgiving for God's gifts may have resulted in the growing popularity of the incense rite, also seen as a propitiatory offering. Although many of the prayers found in the Spanish and Milanese sources are prayers of thanksgiving for light, many of the Spanish prayers speak of offering light as the evening sacrifice of praise to God. This will be seen in more detail as we pass to the second element of the opening of the old Spanish Vespers: the *Lucernarium* or *Vespertinum*, and the prayer that sometimes accompanies it.

THE LUCERNARIUM AND VESPERTINUM

This unit, called *Vespertinum*, abbreviated as VPR in some manuscripts, is similar to the Milanese *Lucernarium* in that it largely comprises a very few psalm verses, one usually serving as a response, which refer to light in the evening. Some documents use no particular title or refer to the unit as either *Laudes* or *Antiphona* (*Br.* most often entitles the unit *Lauda*, a misreading of *Laudes*[19]). This Antiphon, like its Milanese counterpart, appears to have originally been a complete psalm chosen because of its reference to light. Later it became reduced to a few verses and, on weekdays, to the antiphon alone, probably because of the increasing complexity of the chants to which it was sung. Later versions of the unit might use verses taken from other scriptural passages or from psalms more suited to a feast than to the time of day.[20] As we have seen, Isidore referred to the first psalm at Vespers as a *Lucernarium* and because this term more obviously identifies the unit with the light ritual, we shall use it henceforward for all those texts that occupy the first place in the structure of Vespers, after the opening formula and salutation.

Br. contains a total of 32 *Lucernaria*, not a large number when compared to some other variable units in the book. There are two for Advent, three for the Christmas-Epiphany period, four for the Sundays of Lent and Palm Sunday, three for Easter to Pentecost and seven for the Sundays that follow Epiphany and Pentecost. Most of these have the text of a collect attached, but five for weekdays and seven for the common of Saints do not have any collect at all. The theme of light is frequently found even in some of the seasonal pieces. The archetypal evening psalm, 140, is quoted in 'Elevatio manuum' (185), only appointed for First Vespers of the First Sunday after Epiphany octave, while the remaining ordinary Sundays make up a kind of cycle for First Vespers:

Die mandavit (Ps. 41.9) 2nd & 7th after Epiph. & Advent of John.
Illumina oculos (Ps. 12.4) 3rd & 8th after Epiph.
In noctibus (Ps. 133.2) 4th & 9th after Epiph. & 2nd after Pentecost.
Ad vesperum (Ps. 29.6) 5th after Epiph.
Apud te est Domine (Ps. 35.10) 6th after Epiph. & 1st & 3rd after Pentecost.

If we treat Second Vespers of Sunday as being actually the First Vespers of Monday, the weekday cycle would be as follows:

1 *Usque ad Vesperum*	(Ps. 103.23–4)	Sunday.
2 *Tu illuminans*	(Ps. 17.29)	Monday.
3 *Illuminatio mea*	(Ps. 26.1)	Tuesday.
4 *Vespere, mane et meridie*	(Ps. 54.18)	Wednesday.
5 *Dominus illuminatio mea*	(Ps. 26.1)	Thursday.
6 *Sol agnovit occasum*	(Ps. 103.19–20)	Friday.
7 *In noctibus*	(Ps. 133.2)	Saturday.

The weekday cycle is particularly clearly marked in Lent when Sunday nights always feature nos 1 and 7, and Saturday nights by a cycle of three texts proper to the season, again showing the priority of the

'First Vespers' over the second.[21] The more important celebration, with the greater variety of texts, is the Saturday night, the First Vespers of Sunday. The importance of the celebration on the Saturday night is further emphasized by the fact that the texts for the Sundays of Lent rarely lose the light theme, even when texts are selected for a particular day, such as Palm Sunday. By contrast *AL* often gives texts that are hardly recognizable as *Lucernaria*.[22]

As to the texts themselves, Pinell has shown that the Spanish *Vespertina* have close parallels in the Milanese *Lucernaria*. In the following scheme of Milanese Vespers, the capitalized pieces refer to the theme of light:

I LUCERNARIUM
   ANTIPHONA IN CHORO
   HYMN
   Responsorium in choro
II Psalmody in course
   PRAYER: *Respice Domine*
   Magnificat
   PRAYER: *Deus qui operatus*
III Psallenda
   Completorium I
   Completorium II
   Prayer
   Psallenda
   COMPLETORIUM I: *Quoniam tu inluminas*
   Completorium II
   PRAYER: *Exaudi nos*[23]

The three sections that refer to light are the *Lucernaria* and other introductory material, the prayers that accompany the current psalmody and one of the final processional chants (NB the *completorium* or *complenda* is a chant, not a prayer as in Spain). On some occasions the Responsory in choro also refers to light.[24]

Nine Milanese *Lucernaria* have Spanish parallels, in fact nine evening psalms are found in the same place in both traditions: Psalms 4, 17, 26, 35, 96, 111, 118 (vv. 105–112), 131 and 140.[25] To these *Br.* adds Psalms 29, 41, 54, 103, 129 and 133, which are also suited to the evening.[26] Pinell makes much of the presence of Psalm 140 in the two rites, which may be unjustified since its appearance in the Spanish rite is rare. Pinell may rely too much on later forms in which the light ritual is less important. Some prayers, however, seem to show that the psalm was once more frequently used in Spain, and it is of more frequent occurrence in *AL*.

It is equally likely that the emphasis on light may have influenced the selection of additional psalms with a more obvious light theme than 140. This may even have happened at a time when full psalms were still normally employed, and would accord with a Western concern to maintain the light theme which in the East often disappeared completely.[27]

In contrast to the East neither Spain nor Milan have a monastic type psalmody before the *Lucernarium*. In Milan the psalmody following the *Lucernarium* is, in fact, the Roman monastic *cursus* of five psalms. In the Milan pattern given above, the prayers after the psalms and the *Magnificat* appear to be placed there by the process of Romanization.[28]

The old Roman Office was monastic from an early stage but a surprising relic may have survived. In its developed form this Vespers comprised five variable psalms, short reading, hymn, versicle and response, *Magnificat* and prayer. Rome resisted readings until the late sixth or early seventh century, and hymns until the twelfth. If the *Magnificat* was not primitive either, then all that remains is five psalms, versicle and response and prayer. The versicle and response every day but Saturday was:

Dirigatur domine, oratio mea: Sicut incensum in conspectu tuo.
(Let my prayer arise, Lord: as incense in your sight.)

In other words, a verse of Psalm 140, quite possibly a relic of the use of this psalm in full, was a main feature of the primitive Roman Vespers. Winkler quotes Jerome's reference to the use of this psalm in the evening and, much later, Amalarius identified the incensation at Vespers precisely with this versicle and response and not with the *Magnificat* that followed it.[29] Once again Spain and Milan and even Rome as well, it would seem, show signs of a primitive *Lucernarium*/Vespers of very similar structure: light ritual, an evening psalm (Ps. 140) and prayer. Pinell saw it as a service of thanksgiving for light, material and spiritual, which had developed by the fifth century into a thanksgiving for creation and redemption as well.[30]

A good example of a Spanish *Lucernarium* from *Br*. is the unique text drawn from Psalm 140:

Elevatio manuum mearum sacrificium *P* vespertinum. *V*.
Dirigatur Domine oratio mea in conspectu tuo sicut incensum.

P Vespertinum. (The lifting of my hands like an evening sacrifice. *V* Let my prayer arise Lord, like incense in your sight.) (*Pressa* omitted.)[31]

Prayer:

Deus, cujus nomen a solis ortu usque ad occasum laudabile est: sicut incensum in conspectu tuo nostra dirigatur oratio; tibique elevatio manuum nostrarum, sacrificium vespertinum, impleat solemnitatem. (O God, whose name is praised from the rising of the sun to its setting; just as in your sight our prayer may come before you like incense; so to you may the raising of our hands, the evening sacrifice, be the fulfilment of our accustomed duty.)

The somewhat ungrammatical arrangement of verse 2 in the actual *Lucernarium* may well indicate that this is indeed a relic of a full psalm with a response. The use of incense here cannot be excluded but it would most likely be as symbolizing prayer rising to God, rather than a purificatory or propitiatory sacrifice.

The *Lucernarium* for the Sixth Sunday after the Epiphany octave, for *both* Vespers of the First Sunday after Pentecost and for the Third Sunday after Pentecost, is from Psalm 35 (as is that of Pentecost):

In you Lord, is the fount of life and in your light *P* do we see light. *V* The sons of men hope in the protection of your wings. They feast from the riches of your house: and the stream of your delight gives them drink. *P* do we see light.

Prayer:

Lord, in whom is the source of life, and in whose light we see the light, nourish in us the knowledge of your refulgence: and impart to us who thirst, the cup of life; and restore by supernal light, understanding to our darkened souls.

The parallel Milanese text, *Apud te, Domine*, is appointed for Epiphany. The version given above is also found in *AL* on the First Sunday of Lent. This *Lucernarium* appears to use light as a symbol of God imparting grace to his people and as such is suited to Epiphany and Pentecost, both ancient baptismal feasts.

The weekday *Lucernaria* comprise a single verse or part of a verse, e.g. for Mondays:

> Tu illuminans lucernam meam, Domine. (Psalm 17.29a) (col. 194) (Your lamp, Lord, is my light.)

(On the third Monday of Lent (col. 396) this text is preceded by an interesting rubric declaring the service to be Vespers of Tuesday.)

Another ferial *Lucernarium*, for the Fridays of Lent and other fasts, and probably the original ordinary Friday text:

> The sun knows its setting. When darkness is spread, it is made night. (Ps. 103.19b–20a)

If we conclude that the balance of probability argues in favour of more frequent use of Psalm 140 at a primitive stage of the old Spanish Vespers, then as the emphasis on light becomes of greater importance it is not wholly surprising to find Psalm 140 relegated to very occasional use, for, although obviously an evening text, it makes no reference to light. By contrast Psalms 4, 26, 103 and 133 on Sundays and weekdays are all undeniably evening psalms. Other psalms may have been chosen simply because certain verses made reference to light, and an example might be Psalm 17, a song of gratitude for victory which has a reference to light in verse 29.

In addition to Psalm 140 (perhaps on Sunday), Psalms 4, 26, 103 and 133 (to which it may also be reasonable to add Psalms 118, 105–12 and 129, both very suitable for evening usage) may well have been the basic repertoire of *Lucernaria*. At a very early stage verses which contained the light theme were extracted from other psalms, possibly in imitation of Milanese usage. This stage of development enables us to understand why Psalm 140 became relegated and other psalms became more prominent, and thus made the Sunday cycle one of psalms of which only certain verses are vesperal. While this development went on though, the weekday cycle and the ordinary Sundays of Lent (Sundays 2 to 5 inclusive) retained the older form, i.e., the use of clearly vesperal psalms for the *Lucernarium*.

AL provides a measure of support for the hypothesis of a basic repertoire of evening psalms used as *Lucernaria*. Unlike *Br.* the *Vespertina/Lucernaria* for ordinary Sundays are not arranged in any order of services, but are simply given as a collection of texts from which to draw a suitable one. Eight are given,[32] and the psalms used are 4, 133, 41, 135, 103, 112, 138 and 29, in that order. The first, *Sacrificate sacrificium* is in the same form as in *Br.* with a verse from Psalm 104. Two others, drawing from Psalms 133 and 41 are also, more or less, as found in *Br.*'s Sunday cycle. Several others, from Psalms 135,

103, 112 and 138, are given as antiphons only, without verses, which may mean that they were intended for weekday use. The final text in this set, *Ad vesperum demorabitur*, is given in full with a verse of Psalm 29, and is also found in the Sunday cycle of *Br*.

NOTES

1. *PL* 86, 44.
2. A. W. S. Porter, 'Early Spanish Monasticism', *Laudate* XII, 45 (1934), pp. 31–52 at p. 42, and XI, 44 (1933), pp. 199–207, at p. 207, fn 12.
3. J. Pinell, 'El Oficio Hispanico-Visigotico', *HS* 10 (1957), pp. 385–427, at p. 401.
4. J. Pinell, 'Vestigis del Lucernari a Occident', *Liturgica I – Scripta et Documenta* 7 (Monserrat, 1956), pp. 91–149, at p. 102, fn 27.
5. N. Uspensky, *Evening Worship of the Orthodox Church* (New York: St Vladimir's Seminary Press, 1985), p. 136.
6. W. C. Bishop, ed. C. L. Feltoe, *The Mozarabic and Ambrosian Rites* (London: Alcuin/Mowbrays, 1924), p. 111; and G. Guiver, *Company of Voices* (London: SPCK, 1988), p. 240 – witnessed by the present author, August 1987 and September 1992.
7. S. Singer (ed.), *Daily Prayer Book* (London: Eyre & Spottiswoode, 1962), pp. 141 and 293.
8. See P. Bradshaw, *Daily Prayer in the Early Church* (London: Alcuin/SPCK, 1981), pp. 51 and 57, 75–6 and 78–9.
9. G. J. Cuming (ed.), *Hippolytus: A Text for Students* (Bramcote: Grove Liturgical Study 8, 1984), p. 23.
10. G. Winkler, 'Über die Kathedralvesper in Verschiedenen Riten des Ostens und Westens', *ALW* 16 (1974), pp. 33–4.
11. ibid., p. 58.
12. See e.g. Raya and De Vinck (eds), *Byzantine Daily Worship* (Allendale, NJ: Alleluia Press, 1969), pp. 37–48.
13. Winkler, 'Über die Kathedralvesper', pp. 72, 75; and Uspensky, *Evening Worship, passim*.
14. See R. Taft, *The Liturgy of the Hours in East and West* (Collegeville: Liturgical Press, 1986), pp. 241–63.
15. S. Pudichery, *Ramsa* (Dharmaram College, 1972), esp. pp. 166ff.
16. J. Pinell, 'Vestigis', p. 91.
17. ibid., p. 97.
18. Bradshaw, *Daily Prayer*, pp. 78–80.
19. See L. Brou, 'Deux mauvaises lectures' in *Miscellanea Mgr H. Angles I* (Barcelona 1958–61).
20. Pinell, 'El Oficio', p. 401, and 'Vestigis', pp. 110, 117.
21. See J. M. Martin Patino, 'El Breviarium Mozarabe de Ortiz, su valor documental para la Historia del Oficio Catedralicio Hispanico', *Miscellanea 40 Comillas* (1963), pp. 207–97, at pp. 273–5.
22. The Sunday tests of *AL* are clearly connected with light, see Martin Patino, ibid., p. 275, and *AL* 281v.
23. Bishop, *Mozarabic and Ambrosian Rites*, pp. 109–12.
24. Pinell, 'Vestigis' pp. 107–8.
25. ibid., 116–7.
26. An example of the psalms in common would be Psalm 140, used in Spain as we have seen above, and in Milan on the Fridays of Lent, a day which is likely to preserve ancient practice.
27. Pinell, 'Vestigis', p. 136.
28. Winkler, 'Über die Kathedralvesper', p. 95.
29. Winkler, op.cit., pp. 98–101.
30. Pinell, 'Vestigis', p. 147.
31. *P* or *Pressa* indicates the repeated second part of the verse.
32. *AL* ff. 281 and 281v.

3

THE PSALMODY OF VESPERS

The modern Western reader may find the strangest feature of the old Spanish Vespers to be the seeming lack of a group of psalms to be recited. Between the *Lucernarium* and the hymn there are a number of pieces usually composed of psalm verses but having a variety of titles. On many weekdays a full psalm with an antiphon is appointed in *Br.*, and, as the Bobadilla ordo and Isidore also assume there to be psalms after the *Lucernarium*, the term 'psalmody' will refer to this section in general. As we shall see, these probably all originated as full psalms.

The first of these pieces, occurring on Sundays and feasts only, is the *Sono*; then follow one or more pieces entitled *Antiphona* and finally, that which in *Br.* is called *Lauda*, a misreading for *Laudes*, the term we will use. (This last unit is often referred to in the manuscripts as *Alleluiaticum*, e.g. in *AL*.) In the weekday pattern there is generally either one *Antiphona* and one *Laudes*, or there is a psalm with antiphon and the *Laudes*.

On great feasts, e.g., Christmas, Epiphany, Ascension and Pentecost, the *Antiphonae* are multiplied (and may even be accompanied by prayers). After the First Sunday of Lent, there is no *Sono* so the office has a more ferial aspect. Some offices, mostly in Eastertide, have more than one *Laudes*. Maundy Thursday, Holy Saturday and the Office of the Dead exhibit special features which cannot be treated in detail.[1]

THE SONO

This may be described as an alleluiatic responsory sung in an elaborate manner, and it is a piece that does not really fit in with the others discussed in this chapter. Those given for the First Sunday of

Advent and for the majority of Second Vespers after the Epiphany octave in *Br*. do not use the word 'alleluia'. However, it may be because the chant was alleluiatic that it was not used in Lent and it may also be that the Lent Sunday Vespers reflects the more ancient form to which the *Sono* was added on other days. It is first mentioned by the Council of Merida in 666,[2] which decreed that the morning *Sono* replace the *Matutinarium*, the morning psalm, but at Vespers it was to follow the *Lucernarium* which *is* the evening psalm, not replace it. Many festal *Soni* are used in the evening and in the morning without distinction, and make no reference to the hour of the day. It is possible that the *Sono* was at first a festal addition to Vespers, that at a later period came to be repeated at Matins, thus displacing the *Matutinarium*.

The Advent Vespers *Soni* are good exemples of festal texts and are appointed for First Vespers, Matins and Second Vespers. Psalms quoted include 94 ('Come ring out our joy to the Lord'), 95 ('... all the trees of the wood exult in the presence of our Lord for he comes') and 79 ('And show us your face'), all redolent of joy at the Lord's promised coming, celebrated in the season of Advent. On the third Sunday, the *Sono* is composed of verses from Isaiah 61 and 62. The great majority of *Soni* in the Sanctoral and common of Saints are interchangeable between the Vespers and Matins, some used at one time in the evening and at another in the morning. The popular Wisdom 3.1 text, 'The souls of the righteous', is used on Holy Innocents' day (*PL* 86, col. 131) and in one of the commons of several martyrs (*PL* 86, col. 998), and will serve as representative of the festal type:

> Justorum animae in manu Dei sunt, et non tanget illos tormentum mortis. Alleluia. *V* Visi sunt in oculis insipientium mori: et aestimata est malitia exitus illorum: illi autem sunt in pace. Alleluia. (The souls of the righteous are in the hand of God, no torment shall ever touch them. Alleluia. *V* In the eyes of the unwise, they did appear to die, their going looked like a disaster, their leaving us, like annihilation; but they are in peace. Alleluia.) (JB version)

Some *Soni* were specially composed for a particular feast, a good example being 'Dum succenderetur fornax' ('While the furnace was being heated') for the feast of Sts Fructuosus, Eulogius and Augurius (21 January, col. 1054) and also the feast of Sts Faustus, Januarius and Martialis (19 October, col. 1225). This is a fairly free rendering of the story of the three young men thrown into the 'blazing fiery furnace' of Daniel 3 and was chosen because the former saints were probably and the latter, possibly, martyred by burning. Free use of scriptural texts, changing them to suit the circumstances, might argue a late composition. Another late feature is the lack of vesperal themes. These pieces are largely festal and thus independent of the time of day, and it is possible that this was a characteristic of the *Sono* from its introduction into Vespers, but is it also true of the Sunday *Soni*?

After Epiphany the *Soni* for each First Vespers comprise a rough cycle of psalms 29, 64, 90, 99 and 138. On the remaining Sundays, 'Qui extendit coelos' from Psalm 103 is given for both First and Second Vespers of the First Sunday after Pentecost, and continues the Pentecost theme, e.g., 'Who made his angels spirits and his ministers a flaming fire'. First Vespers of the Second Sunday has the *Sono* of Second Vespers of the Second Sunday after Epiphany, 'Deus in te speravi' from Psalm 70. 'Cantet tibi' is used for most other Second Vespers (Psalm 29, verse from Psalm 118.56, col. 189). The latter lacks an Alleluia and is composed of two psalms; it may be from another source or even be a later composition designed to give greater solemnity to Second Vespers of Sunday which had probably once been more ferial in nature, as appropriate to First Vespers of Monday.

The psalms of the *Soni*, 70, 90 and 138, express trust in God the healer and protector, as do the selected verses of Psalms 29, 64 and 99. The theme is one natural to the end of the day, since for most ordinary people Vespers would have been the final public prayer of the day. As an example, a *Sono* employing a psalm that has the theme of trust, Psalm 90, a classic *bedtime* psalm that many would associate with Compline (Fourth Sunday after Epiphany, col. 224):

> Refugium meum, Deus meus sperabo in eum. Quoniam ipse *P* Liberavit me de muscipula venantium, et a verbo aspero. Alleluia. *V* Qui habitat in adjutorium Altissimi, in protectione Dei coeli commorabitur. Dicit Deo: Suspector meus es tu Deus meus. *P* Liberavit. (My refuge, my God in whom I trust, for it is he *P* Who will deliver me from the snare of the hunter, and from the noisome pestilence. Alleluia. *V* He who dwells under the defence of the Most High, and remains in the protection of the God of heaven, says to God: my stronghold are you, my God. *P* Who will deliver me.)

The *Sono* may appear to be a purely Spanish phenomenon but there is a possible parallel in Milanese Vespers, where, after the *Lucernarium*, on all Sundays and feasts (including Lent Sundays), there is a short piece called *Antiphona in Choro* immediately before the hymn. It normally comprises a single psalm verse, or the equivalent, and varies for seasons and feasts. A cycle of seven were used on Sundays, employing verses from psalms 66, 5, 150, 29, 54, 68 and 17 respectively;[3] in them we see the same emphasis on trust in God as in the Spanish texts. In Milan this piece comes before the hymn, which is probably a more ancient component of Vespers at Milan than anywhere else. The Milanese *Antiphona in Choro* and the Spanish *Sono* appear to be additional chants linked to the *Lucernarium*, originally to give it a festal flavour and later, extended to Sundays as well, becoming more general in theme.

THE ANTIPHONA

This next unit bears a resemblance to the Antiphons found also at Matins and the cathedral hours; being made up of an antiphon, a psalm verse and 'Gloria' (usually). Pinell believes that prior to the period that produced the surviving manuscripts the antiphon accompanied whole psalms or substantial parts of psalms.[4] This is the form in *Br.* for Sundays and Feasts, but on weekdays the antiphon is to be accompanied by a full psalm. This may be illustrated by *T2* which gives the antiphon and, in Roman numerals, the psalm to be used. In contrast to what we find at Matins and the Hours in that season the weekday Vespers of the second half of Lent always presumes a complete psalm, both in *T2* and in *Br.*

Weekday Antiphons and Psalms

Weekday Vespers are provided in *Br.* after the Epiphany octave for Monday, Tuesday and Wednesday (though Sunday night may be ferial in origin). It is likely that the source used by Ortiz was fragmentary, as the remaining days are covered by using the Office for the Sick on Thursday/Friday and one of Our Lady for Friday/Saturday.[5]

The weekday psalms at Vespers are 8, 13 and 14 (col. 194-203). These may be part of an attempted current psalter as will be seen later. The Lenten ferias are very different. In *AL* the Vespers psalm is one of the gradual psalms (i.e. Psalms 119–133) or a section of Psalm 118, while in *Br.* there appears to be no system at all.

In the last three weeks of Lent Psalms 34 and 139 are both used twice, with the antiphons: 'O Lord plead my cause against my foes; fight them who fight me' (Ps. 34); 'Rescue me Lord, from evil men, from the violent keep me safe' (Ps. 139); 'Arise, stir to my defence, to my cause, O God' (Ps. 34 in Holy Week) (cols 484, 557 and 579). These psalms are clearly selected for a season which commemorated the betrayal and abandonment of Christ. This theme is even more obvious on the eucharistic days: e.g., fourth Wednesday: 'O Lord my God, do not forsake me! Be not far from me' (Ps. 37); fifth Wednesday: 'Plead, O Lord, my cause against my enemies' (Ps. 34), and fifth Friday: 'Deliver me Lord, from the evil man, preserve me from the violent' (Ps. 139). An examination of the Epistles alone for these days reveals in 2 Peter 2.9—3.3, a warning against false teachers who revile the faithful, and in the fifth week, 1 John 2.7–13; and 4.5—5.13, which speaks of having faith because evil is overcome, and of the love of God that casts out fear. There is then a possible connection, especially when we recall that the Mass was celebrated at the ninth hour, i.e., late in the afternoon, for if Vespers followed close on, perhaps without a break, the ideas of the readings would still have been fresh in the mind.

In its present form the period *de Traditione* is older than the first three weeks of Lent.[6] Certainly it seems likely that specially selected texts reflecting the theme of the day would first emerge on the eucharistic days with their readings. Later, psalms selected for the same general theme may have spread to other days and, later again, the system is applied to the office of the first three weeks as well. The themes of those first three weeks are very general: prayer to God for rescue (e.g. 'Help with your right hand and hear', Psalm 59, first Tuesday, col. 287) and also thanks for God's goodness (e.g. 'How good is God to Israel, to those who are pure in heart', Psalm 72, third Wednesday, col. 411).

Outside Lent, full psalms are also appointed for other fast days, the most frequently cited being Psalm 27, under antiphon: 'Save your people O Lord, and bless your inheritance' (e.g. col. 161). The emphasis on these days is prayer for rescue, possibly from the plague or disaster which was often the original reason for such fasts.

Sunday and Festal Antiphons and their Psalms

Sundays and Feastdays do not cite full psalms. The *Antiphonae* at Vespers for Lent Sundays are mostly composed of an antiphon from a non-psalmic scriptural text and the verse of a psalm. The psalms used are:

Sunday	First Vespers	Second Vespers
1st	Ps. 94	Ps. 133*
2nd	Ps. 81	Ps. 84
3rd	Ps. 93	Ps. 127
4th	Ps. 80	Ps. 139*
5th	Ps. 80	Ps. 66
Palm Sunday	Ps. 33	Ps. 21

* composed of psalm verses only

The two in which the entire unit is psalmic are important, as the first, employing Psalm 133, serves as the *Antiphona* for what is, in effect, the First Vespers of Lent (as the fast commenced on Monday) and the second, Psalm 139 'Ne tradas me Domine' – 'Grant not the wicked their desire'), is then the First Vespers of the period *de Traditione* (cols 263 and 447). The other psalms at these Second Vespers celebrations also appear to have been chosen to suit seasonal themes; for example, v. 23 of Psalm 21, 'My God, my God (...) why have you forsaken me?' (col. 568), at the beginning of Holy Week proper.

As to the *Antiphonae* for the First Vespers, that for the first Sunday (col. 258) uses the sixth verse of Psalm 94, the Latin version of which reads 'ploremus coram Domino' – 'Let us *weep* before the Lord' (presumably for our sins), rather than the more familiar English '... *kneel* before the Lord'. With the verse 'If we say we have no sin ...' from 1 John 1.8 as antiphon, we have a suitable introduction to Lent perceived as a penitential exercise, the acceptable time proclaimed in the Epistle of the Mass from 2 Corinthians 5.20—6.11 (*PL* 85, cols 298–9). The second Sunday combines Psalm 81's declaration of God's judgement on the unjust oppressor with Deuteronomy 10.17–19, that speaks of God's love for the widow and orphan (col. 322). The epistle for the day, James 2.14–23, insists on the necessity of faith issuing in good works (*PL* 85, col. 319). It is possible to discern a similar pattern for the rest of Lent, in Easter week and in Eastertide, and on Advent Sunday and, to some extent, Advent weekdays as well: a verse drawn from a psalm and an antiphon from another scriptural text, all reflecting in some way a theme or themes drawn from the scriptural readings for that day.

As an example we may look at the *Antiphona* for First Vespers of the Fourth Sunday of Lent, in which the antiphon is from Isaiah

1.3b–4a and the verse from Psalm 80.12 (col. 438). (The Gospel of the day tells of the Jews' rejection of Jesus, John 7.2–15, *PL* 85, col. 356.)

> Israel me non cognovit: populus meus me non intellexit. *P* Vae genti peccatrici, filiis sceleratis: dereliquerunt Dominum, blasphemaverunt sanctum Israel. *V* Et non audivit populus meus vocem meam: et Israel non intendit mihi. *P* Vae genti. (Israel does not know, my people does not understand. *P* Ah, sinful nation, sons who deal corruptly. They have forsaken the Lord, they have despised the holy one of Israel. *V* And my people did not hear my voice and Israel would not obey me. *P* Ah, sinful nation.)

(NB The 'Gloria' is not said in the second half of Lent.)

Festal Vespers have very similar *Antiphonae*. The First Vespers of Christmas (col. 113–14) has as its first *Antiphona* Isaiah 7.14: 'Hearken, house of David', and the psalm is 48.1: 'Hear this all peoples', this being followed by a prayer based on the antiphon; the second *Antiphona*, using Psalm 46.1, also has an antiphon collect. The First Vespers of Epiphany (col. 175) has a verse from Psalm 47 (v. 5): 'For behold the Kings assembled together as one', and an antiphon referring to the coming of the Magi with a corresponding prayer.

The *Antiphonae* for First Vespers of Sunday also exhibit the same structure. The psalms used may be tabulated as follows:

(Sundays after Epiphany octave)

1st	103
2nd	146
3rd	146
4th	94
5th	144
6th	112
7th	79
8th	103
9th	112

Some of these psalms are appropriate for the evening, e.g. 103 and 144, thanking God for creation, Psalm 79 praying that God's face may shine upon his people, and 112 with the line: 'From the rising of the sun to its setting' (v. 3). Psalms 94 and 146 may also be said to proclaim God's wonders. The antiphons have even more obvious references to the power of God in creation and to the vigil nature of the celebration: e.g. 'God wise of heart and strong in power, who shakes the earth out of its place ...' (Job 9.4 and 6, Second Sunday, col. 215), and 'Behold the watchman calls, morning comes and also the night ...' (Isaiah 21.12, Fourth Sunday, col 224). On the Sundays after Pentecost we find similarities except that on two Saturday nights there are more than one Antiphon; the psalms used include 44, 48, 49, 80, 84 and 144.

Two examples, one from after Epiphany and one from after Pentecost, will illustrate the differences in style between the two types:

1 Fourth Sunday after Epiphany octave (col. 224): Isaiah 21.12 and Psalm 94.1:
Behold the watchman calls: morning comes and also the night. *P* If you inquire, inquire; come back again. *V* Come let us sing unto the Lord: let us praise the God of our salvation. *P* If you.

2 Third Antiphon of Second Sunday after Pentecost (col. 699): Proverbs 8.14 and 15 and Psalm 49.7:
I have counsel and sound wisdom, I have insight, I have strength. *P* By me princes rule and rulers decree what is just. *V* Hearken my people and I will speak: Israel, I will witness against you. *P* By me.

AL has a large number of similar texts for ordinary Sundays that are not appointed to any particular day.[7] They are linked with corresponding *Laudes* and, for the most part, do exhibit the same structure as those of *Br.* A few are found in both sources. It is possible that faced with a similar collection, perhaps containing more *Antiphonae* than *Soni*, Ortiz put together several in one Vespers after Pentecost, when they may originally have been alternatives.

There are only two *Antiphonae* for Second Vespers of Sunday in *Br.* That for the second Sunday after Epiphany is given as an example, not least because it illustrates use of the classical evening psalm, 140 (col. 189):

Elevatio manuum mearum sacrificium vespertinum. *V* Dirigatur oratio mea, sicut incensum in conspectu tuo. *P* Elevatio. *V* Gloria et honor. *P* Elevatio. (The lifting up of my hands like an evening sacrifice. *V* Let my prayer come before you like incense in your sight. *P* The lifting up ... *V* Glory and honour ... *P* The lifting up ...)

AL has several *Antiphonae* of this kind, composed entirely of psalm verses,[8] but it is unique for a Sunday or feast in *Br.* and is very similar to the *Lucernarium* for the First Vespers of the same day (col. 185).

We may conclude, then, that the *Antiphona* at Vespers was a psalm chosen to harmonize with the season or feast, and may have replaced an evening psalm, following the *Lucernarium*, that had the theme of God as the refuge and protector of his people (as on the weekdays of the first three weeks of Lent); thus came the development of using psalms that stressed God's power and rule over creation. The fact that prayers are usually not provided shows there to be a different development from that of the Matins Antiphons, as does the rapid abandonment of psalmic responses in favour of other pieces of Scripture perceived to be even more expressive of God's creative power and rule.

THE LAUDES

In *de Officiis* Isidore described the *Laudes* as an alleluiatic chant.[9] In the monastic hours it follows a reading; at Mass it follows the Gospel. The pieces used in the cathedral office with this title have a distinctive function and are sometimes entitled *Allelluiaticum*, as for instance in *AL*.[10] In *T2*, the terms *Antiphona* and *Laudes* are used interchangeably for this unit and the number of the psalm is often cited; usually it is Psalm 118.[11] In the manuscripts the title *Laudes* was often written in a contracted form which led to Ortiz' mistaken reading of the unit as *Lauda*, as found in *Br*.

This unit is again made up of psalm verses and, only rarely, other scriptural sources. The most striking feature of the unit in *Br*. is the consistent use of Psalm 118. This longest psalm was associated with the daytime in the West, particularly with the old Roman and Benedictine day hours, while in other traditions it was used at night, especially at the midnight office as with Basil,[12] and even today in the Byzantine tradition on weekdays. Basil in fact quoted verse 62, 'At midnight I will rise and thank you', and Isidore quoted the same verse as scriptural justification for Vigils.[13] Why the psalm was so popular is not known; its dominant focus is on the word of God and the law of God.

In *Br*. the most consistent pattern for the use of this psalm is found in the first three weeks of Lent. On each night, Monday to Friday inclusive, the *Laudes* are drawn from eight of the first thirteen eight-verse sections of the psalm. There would of course be room to use fifteen of those sections had continuous recitation been desired; in fact several are repeated more than once. Once again there seems to be some influence of the eucharistic days on the choice of verses: e.g., Friday of the first week (col. 314) when the Gospel has Jesus describe himself as the bread of life (John 6.27–38, *PL* 85, col. 313):

> How sweet are thy words to my taste, sweeter than honey in my mouth. *V* I have kept my feet from evil ways; that I may keep your word. *V* Glory and honour to the Father. (Psalm 118, 103 and 101 – Pressa omitted from translation.)

In the second half of Lent also, Psalm 118 is commonly used for the *Laudes*. Most of the exceptions are Wednesdays and Fridays, eucharistic days, and then the passion theme predominates: e.g., 'See how many are my foes' (Ps. 24.19, col. 534) and 'All who see me wag their heads' (Ps. 108.25b, col. 557). It is clear that since the idea of *de Traditione* had become associated with Jesus handed over to suffering, the older idea of the three weeks of 'handing over' the faith to catechumens has been superseded. Psalms found in place of Psalm 118 appear to be chosen because of the changed theme, and thus we may surmise that the choice of Psalm 118 and its emphasis on instruction is the more primitive use.

On Lent Sundays all but the First Sunday and the First Vespers of Palm Sunday use Psalm 118 for the *Laudes*:

v. 169	'Lord let my cry come before you, teach me by your word.'	2nd Sun., col. 323
v. 57	'My part, I have resolved O Lord, is to obey your word.'	2nd Sun., col. 328
v. 71	'It is good for me to be afflicted, to learn your statutes.'	3rd Sun., col. 379
v. 18	'Open my eyes that I may consider the wonders of your law.'	3rd Sun., col. 385
v. 69	'Though proud men smear me with lies yet I keep your precepts.'	4th Sun., col. 438
v. 134	'Redeem me from man's oppression and I will keep your precepts.'	4th Sun., col. 447
v. 53	'I am seized with disgust at those who forsake your law.'	5th Sun., col. 501

v. 95	'Though the wicked lie in wait to destroy me yet I ponder your will.'	5th Sun., col. 505
v. 130	'The unfolding of your word gives light and teaches the simple.'	Palm Sunday, verse only, col. 568

While the system allows for more specialized material on the Sunday *de Carnes Tollendas* (the Sunday before Lent) and on Palm Sunday, Psalm 118 does not lose its pre-eminence and seems to have been the psalm most closely associated with the Lenten Sunday *Laudes*. In *AL*, *Laudes* are also mostly from Psalm 118.[14] Psalm 118 was then most commonly found in Lenten Vespers of the old Spanish rite, and probably was originally intended to accompany or reinforce an ancient catechetical instruction.

We also find in *Br.* that the First Vespers of the ordinary Sundays after Epiphany, and those of the Second and Third Sundays after Pentecost, mostly use Psalm 118 for the *Laudes*. For the period after Epiphany octave, the Pressa (without the appended Alleluias) will adequately illustrate the cycle:

1st (col. 186)	'As I meditate upon the justice of your decrees.' (v. 7)
2nd & 3rd (col. 215)	'Give me understanding that I may keep your law.' (v. 34)
4th (col. 224)	'Revive me by your word.' (v. 25)
5th (col. 228)	'For I believe your commands.' (v. 66)
6th (col. 232)	'For your law is my meditation.' (v. 77)
7th (col. 236)	'Your word endures forever in Heaven, O Lord.' (v. 89)
8th (col. 240)	'And keep your commandment.' (v. 100)

For the 2nd and 3rd after Pentecost:

2nd (col. 699)	'Your will is my inheritance for ever, your decrees are right.' (v.111)
3rd (col. 703)	'Lord you are just, and true is your judgement.' (v. 137)

There is a consistent emphasis on praying for God's teaching and the willingness to abide by his decreees, but the most common Second Vespers text actually uses Psalm 112 (col. 189).

The fragmentary weekday cycle uses psalms 1, 4 and 10; the following are the antiphons:

> Monday: 'He meditates upon the law of the Lord, by day and night.' (col. 194)
> Tuesday: 'Stand in awe and do not sin, say in your own hearts, have compunction in your hearts.' (col. 199)
> Wednesday: 'The Lord is righteous and loves righteousness.' (col. 203)

The theme is the same, even while the psalms are different.

Here is an example of the Sunday *Laudes*, that for the First Vespers of the Fifth Sunday after the Epiphany octave (col. 228), from Psalm 118 vv. 66 and 65:

> Alleluia. Teach me understanding and knowledge, O God; Alleluia. P For I believe in your commands, Alleluia, Alleluia, Alleluia. V You have dealt graciously with your servant, Lord, according to your word. P For I. V Glory. P For I.

A weekday version is that for Monday after the Epiphany octave (col. 194) from Psalm 1, vv. 2 and 3:

> Upon the law of the Lord, Alleluia, shall he meditate by day and by night, Alleluia. P And he gives him his fruit in due season. Alleluia, Alleluia. V And he will be like a tree, planted beside the waters and whose fruit will be given in due season. P And he gives.

The Sunday *Alleluiatica* in *AL* do not use Psalm 118 and have a protection theme, in line with the preceding *Antiphona*.[15]

The *Laudes* for seasons such as Advent and Eastertide are purely festal, and select appropriate themes and texts, e.g.:

> (Ps. 19.2) 'Send us help from your Holy Place.' — 1st Vespers of Advent 1, col. 48.
> (Ps. 49.3) 'God will come and will not keep silence.' — 2nd Vespers of Advent 1, col. 58.
> (Ps. 79.4) 'May your face shine upon us and we shall be saved.' — Easter Sunday, col. 620.

| (Ps. 117.22) | 'The stone which the Easter Monday, col. 623. builders rejected has become the head of the corner.' |

The last two are combined with antiphons from Revelation 5 and 1 respectively. The use of other scriptural texts with the psalm verses as antiphons makes the *Laudes* progressively more indistinguishable from the preceding *Antiphona* except for the large number of Alleluias. On some feasts of saints, non-scriptural compositions appear as well:

> The bodies of the Saints rest in this place, pray for us to the Lord. *P* That he give peace upon earth, and respite to our times. Alleluia, Alleluia. *V* Praise the name of the Lord, praise him, O servants of the Lord. *P* That he give. *V* Glory and honour. *P* That he give. (Verse from Ps. 112.1.)

This composition is appointed for the 'departing Vespers' (as Second Vespers are often entitled in *Br*.) of Sts Justa and Rufina in July (col. 1161).

It would appear to be in the ordinary offices of Sundays and weekdays that we find the original liturgical function of the old Spanish cathedral offices. The *Laudes* was a distinctive part of Vespers with a clear theological and liturgical purpose in that service; by contrast, the later festal and seasonal versions are but further elaborations of the festal or seasonal themes.

SOME CONCLUSIONS REGARDING THE USE OF THE PSALMS AT VESPERS

When Isidore wrote his monastic rule, he laid down the content of the monks' offices and this is what he said for the minor hours and Vespers:

> In tertia, sexta vel none tres psalmi dicendi sunt, responsorium unum, lectiones ex Veteri Novoque Testamenti duae, deinde laudes, hymnus atque oratio. In vespertinis autem officiis primo lucernarium, deinde psalmi duo, responsorius unus, et laudes, hymnus atque oratio dicenda est.[16]

There is no difficulty in identifying Isidore's description with the sort of minor hours found in *Br*. For example, the order of Terce at col.

946: three psalms, a responsory, two short lessons from the Old and New Testaments and a short *Laudes*, a hymn and a prayer. It is not so clear however with Vespers, which (according to the normal interpretation of Isidore) would require a *Lucernarium*, two psalms, then a responsory and the *Laudes* hymn and prayer. Has something disappeared or could Isidore have intended *responsorius* and *laudes* in this context to refer to the manner of performing the two psalms that followed the *Lucernarium*?

In *de Officiis* Isidore described the *Laudes* as an alleluiatic chant, and a responsory as a chant sung by one or more persons to which the choir responded – there is no reason to suppose that he was speaking of anything other than full psalms executed in different ways.[17] It may then be possible to interpret this passage from the *Regula Monachorum* as saying that Vespers comprised a *Lucernarium*, a psalm executed responsorially and one with the response 'alleluia', followed by hymn and prayer. With the exception of the *Sono* which must be later, such a shape is the most likely ancestor of what we find on Sundays and weekdays in *Br.*: *Lucernarium* (with *Sono* on Sundays and feasts a little later), *Antiphona* (Responsorial Psalm), *Laudes* (Alleluiaticum), hymn and prayer.

Since so much effort was expended to keep the monastic and cathedral orders distinct, even though the monks had to celebrate the latter as well, it seems unlikely that Isidore would have invented this three-psalm Vespers in imitation of tripartite monastic structures. Also, if the criteria for the selection of psalms were as described above, then they were criteria that would be foreign to monastic use of psalmody.

If, as some scholars have suggested, primitive Spanish Vespers consisted only of *Lucernarium* and prayer, then it rapidly developed into: *Lucernarium* (a lamplighting psalm), a psalm expressing confidence in God's protection, and a psalm (usually Psalm 118) asking God to teach his people and keep them faithful to that teaching. This simple rite has a progression, a shape; it may be seen as a miniature paschal vigil – light ritual, song of rescue, song concerning God's will. Thus God would be praised every night as the God who frees and saves his people, who shines his light upon them, brings them powerful aid, and leads them into the right way.

It is also possible to identify a parallel form in the office described in the *Manuale Ambrosianum* for the Sundays of Lent and for Sunday to Saturday inclusive of Easter week:

Lucernarium
Antiphon in Choro
Hymn
Responsory in *Choro*
A single selected psalm with Prayer – and so on as normal.[18]

The selected psalm on Easter Sunday was Psalm 113, 'When Israel came out of Egypt'. If the *Lucernarium* and *Responsory in Choro* were once full psalms, than we may assume there to have once been a three-psalm Vespers at Milan and, as in Spain, one of the psalms might treat of the season or day but, at other times, more generally of God's greatness and mercy. We seem to have a broadly similar shape of an office understood in much the same way.

NOTES

1. The Office of the Dead in *PL* 86, cols 976–8 comprises sets of verses drawn from different psalms that share the same opening word. Its history and provenance are uncertain.
2. J. Pinell, 'El Oficio Hispanico-Visigotico', *HS* 10 (1957), pp. 385–427, at p. 402.
3. M. Magistretti (ed.), *Manuale Ambrosianum* (Milan, 1905), pp. 411 and 413ff.
4. Pinell, 'El Oficio', p. 419.
5. The texts for the latter are taken from the 18 December feast of the Annunciation.
6. A. W. S. Porter, 'Studies in Mozarabic Office', *JTS* 35 (1934), pp. 266–86. The second three weeks of Lent were the original preparatory period for baptism and *de Traditione* referred to handing on the faith. With decline of the catechumenate came the alternative interpretation of *traditio* as surrender or betrayal, hence passion.
7. *AL* ff. 284–7.
8. *AL* f. 186v.
9. *PL* 83, col. 749, 'de laudibus'.
10. Pinell, 'El Oficio', p. 405 and J. M. Martin Patino, 'El Breviarium Mozarabe de Ortiz, su Valor Documental para la Historia del Oficio Catedralicio Hispanico' in *Miscellanea 40 Comillas* (1963), pp. 207–97, at p. 276.
11. J. Janini (ed.), *Liber Misticus de Cuaresma* (Toledo: Istituto de Estudios Visigotico-Mozarabes, 1979), p. 54.
12. See R. Taft, *The Liturgy of the Hours in East and West* (Collegeville: Liturgical Press, 1986), p. 54.
13. ibid., p. 157.
14. *Passim. Laudes* entitled *Alleluiaticum* even when lacking 'Alleluia' in Lent.
15. *AL*, ff. 284–7, e.g., 'The Lord is with me to uphold me ...'
16. *PL* 83, col. 876.
17. ibid., cols 749 and 744 respectively. NB: *Laudes* in the Eucharist and at the Hours are shorter and always follow readings which never existed at Vespers.
18. *Manuale Ambrosianum* pp. 122–6.

4

THE USE OF HYMNS IN THE DIVINE OFFICE

Eastern and Western hymnody developed very differently. In the Eastern offices hymnic material was characteristically interspersed among psalm verses and other biblical elements, sometimes completely displacing them. In the West the hymn became an independent unit of a rather different and distinctive kind. Ambrose (339–397) has been described as the father of modern hymnody and four hymns in iambic metre are attributed to him by Augustine. Other hymns with similar simple metres are attributed to Ambrose and his circle. From the fifth century onwards many hymns were composed for the daily offices. Benedict's Rule required a hymn, which he called 'Ambrosian', to be inserted at each hour of the Divine Office, but the Roman Church did not admit hymns into its offices until the twelfth century.

On the whole, the Western type of hymn was largely confined to the Divine Office and the specialized type for the eucharistic rite, the Sequence, only developed from the ninth century onwards. It seems likely that the spread of Benedictine usages encouraged the growing popularity of hymns. In Benedictine use the hymns normally came at the start of the offices except at Lauds and Vespers where they were inserted after the psalmody and the short readings, a positioning which may have been intended to keep them in line with the older cathedral morning and evening offices. When Rome finally accepted office hymns they were inserted in the same places as in the Benedictine rite.

At Milan, where so many hymns had their origin, the hymn at Vespers was placed after the *Lucernarium* and before the psalmody, whereas at Lauds it came at the end of the office.[1] The Benedictine custom of having the hymn *after* the evening psalmody may have been due to monks not having any form of *Lucernarium*.

There was a certain unwillingness to allow ecclesiastical compositions like hymns into public worship. It was often felt wrong to permit anything unscriptural; heretics sang hymns and so the orthodox shunned them. In 563 the Council of Braga forbade the use of poetical compositions in church, perhaps due to the Arianism of the Visigothic state. Braga was also pro-Roman and suspicion of hymns lingered in some places with a basically Roman rite down to the French Revolution, e.g. Lyons and Vienne, long after Rome itself had admitted them.[2]

THE USE OF HYMNS IN THE OLD SPANISH OFFICE

In this tradition the hymns are always included in the same place, after the psalmody and any readings, and before the concluding prayers. This is as true of the monastic style of day hours in *Br.* (cols 939–60) as it is of the cathedral hours. Compline is more complex, but the night services known from other sources also have hymns placed after rather than before the psalms.[3] The very consistency of this placing tends to support the late inclusion of hymns in these offices.

The Fourth Council of Toledo (633) required hymns and the Eighth (653) expected the clergy to have learnt them by heart. This sudden volte-face, together perhaps with Benedictine influence, probably explains why so many of the hymns in the old Spanish books were imported from elsewhere than Spain. Most of the hymns in *Br.* are late compositions for feasts, and especially the feasts of saints. Ortiz inserted the hymns in their respective offices in the Temporal or Sanctoral, but originally they were collected together into a *Liber Hymnorum*, arranged so as to facilitate access to the hymns as the office of the day might require. Such a collection is *Tl*, the document edited by Lorenzana and included with his revision of *Br.* (cols 739–940). (*MP* has a similar, more fragmentary collection.[4])

The following hymns are appointed for Advent to Epiphany (the asterisk indicates hymns that originated outside Spain[5]):

Advent

Christi caterva clamitet	(col. 48) Vespers of Sundays
Aeterne rerum conditor	(col. 50) Sunday Matins throughout year
Cunctorum rex omnipotens	(col. 57) Matins of Sunday
Cunctarum rerum omnipotens	(col. 61) Matins of Weekdays

THE USE OF HYMNS IN THE DIVINE OFFICE

*Verbum supernum prodiens	(col. 62) Vespers & Matins Weekdays
* Vox clara ecce intonat	(col. 65) Vespers & Matins Weekdays
Ecce salvator omnium	(col. 73) Matins of Weekdays
A Patre unigenite	(col. 74) Vespers of Weekdays
Mane nobiscum Domine	(col. 76) Vespers & Matins of Weekdays

From Christmas to Epiphany eve, most hymns are proper to the feasts and with few exceptions (e.g. *Veni redemptor gentium* at Christmas) have a Spanish origin.

Epiphany and Sundays after Epiphany, and Pentecost

*Inluminans Altissimum	(col. 176) Vespers
*Hostis Herodes impie	(col. 184) Matins
Inventor rutilis lux bone luminis	(col. 186) 1st Vespers
*Splendor paternae	(col. 149) Matins
Altissimi verbum Patris	(col. 190) 2nd Vespers
*Christi lux mundi, salus et potestas	(col. 215) 1st Vespers
*O lux beata Trinitas	(col. 220) 1st & 2nd Vespers

Weekdays

*Fulgentis auctor aetheris	(col. 192) Matins of Monday
*Christe salvator omnium	(col. 195) Vespers of Monday
*Deus aeterni luminis	(col. 197) Matins of Tuesday
Christe lumen perpetuum	(col. 199) Vespers of Tuesday
*Deus Pater ingenite	(col. 201) Matins of Wednesday
Adesto nostris precibus	(col. 203) Vespers of Wednesday
*In matutinis surgimus	(col. 205) Matins of Thursday

For Lent and the Period de Traditione:

1st Sunday
Alleluia piis edite laudibus	(col. 259) Vespers & Matins

2nd Sunday
Auctor luminis, Filius Virginis	(col. 323) 1st Vespers & Matins

Deus qui certis legibus   (col. 328) 2nd Vespers

3rd Sunday
Christe immense, Dominator   (col. 379) 1st Vespers &
sancte   Matins
Quarto die jam foetidus   (col. 385) 2nd Vespers

De Traditione
Verbum Patris, quod prodit   (col. 438) Vespers
factum caro
Noctis tempus jam praeterit   (col. 446) Matins

1st 3 weeks (Monday to Thursday inclusive, Matins as above after Epiphany):
Christe qui regis omnia   (col. 306) Thurs. Vespers
Aeternae lucis Conditor   (col. 310) Fri. Matins
Christe precamur annue   (col. 314) Fri. Vespers
Deus creator omnium   (col. 318) Sat. Matins

Minor Hours
O Nazarene, lux Bethlehem   (col. 269) All Lent
(Fourteen alternatives are provided in *Br.* at cols 270–274.)

Palm Sunday
Vocaris ad vitam, Sacrum   (col. 564) Vespers & Matins
Dei Genus

Holy Week
(Matins as rest of *de Trad.*, Vespers; *Vocaris ad vitam* above)
except *Jam legis umbra*   (col. 595) Wed. Vespers
clauditor

Good Friday
Pange lingua gloriosi   (col. 609) At Veneration of
                                                Cross

Easter to Pentecost
Eastertide
Hic est dies verus Dei   (col. 618) Matins & Vespers/
                                                Matins of Sundays
Te centies mille legionum Angeli (col. 637) 1st Vespers
                                                Sundays
Psallat altitudo caeli   (col. 641) 2nd Vespers
                                                Sundays

Ascension
Aeterne rex altissime (col. 653) Vespers and Matins

Sunday after
Sacrata Christi tempora (col. 658) Vespers and Matins

Pentecost
Sacrate veni Spiritus (col. 690) 1st Vespers of Feast
Beata nobis gaudia (col. 693) Matins & 2nd Vespers

When compared with the manuscript hymnals we see that *Mozarabic Psalter* has a number of lacunae and only a small number of hymns are given compared to *Br*. In *T1*, however, about half of those found in *Br*. are also to be found. It may then be asked if the remainder of the hymns came from some manuscript now lost but available to Ortiz, or whether he drew upon the repertoire of the Roman and Benedictine offices. Blume edited all the known Spanish hymns and his tables show that all but 15 of the hymns of the Temporal in *Br*. can be found in these two main MS sources.[6] These fifteen, really thirteen, include only three from outside Spain. Eleven are found only in *Br*. and are not ascribed to any non-Spanish source by Blume.[7] Unless these other hymns were written especially for *Br*., which seems unlikely, the only alternative is that Ortiz did indeed have another source which is lost to us.

The Sanctoral has no fewer than 84 hymns, only six having a non-Spanish origin. Eighteen of the 84 are found only in *Br*. and Blume again gives no other sources for these hymns, so they may be presumed to be later Spanish compositions. Eight hymns are for the feasts of Apostles and may have replaced hymns from the common. The hymns for the feasts relegated to an appendix of *Br*. by Lorenzana are all from outside Spain, and of the hymns for the common offices of Saints (cols 990 to 1032), seven out of ten are non-Spanish. The hymns for the Office of the Dead are found in other Spanish sources (cols 978 and 989). Roman and Benedictine offices possessed no hymns for the Office of the Dead until after Vatican II.

The sources indicate a rich vein of hymn-writing, particularly concerned with composing hymns for the feasts of martyrs. Among the hymns that have no other source but *Br*. are two for St Justa; with

St Rufina, patron of the parish in Toledo that remained most faithful to the ancient rite (see cols 1153 and 1157). Common offices acquire hymns at a later date, as do the feasts of non-local saints, even those of the Apostles. Not surprisingly, many of these offices took well-known hymns from elsewhere. The Benedictine monks may also have popularized both the cults of non-Spanish saints and the use of non-Spanish hymns in their honour. In their writing of hymns for Spanish saints the Spanish authors showed their greatest productivity, following their greatest exemplar Prudentius (348–413), in quantity if not in quality.

Perez de Urbel showed that many of the hymns are of relatively late composition; this lateness is illustrated by poor grammar, uneven metre and, in some cases, references to contemporary events such as persecution of Christians by the Muslims. An example is that for St James the Less (col. 136), to which he gives a ninth-century dating, and which refers to people compelled to live under the heavy yoke of an alien power.[8] Toledo IV's requirement of hymns meant that they were hurriedly composed or taken from elsewhere. It is possible that local use of hymns of martyrs may have been common in spite of Braga, which would explain the early dating of some of them. The seventh century appears to have been a period of great productivity, but also a time of frequent importation of hymns from outside Spain.[9]

Isidore died in 636 and mentioned hymns in *de Origine Officiorum*. In this work he used Scripture to justify the use of non-scriptural texts,[10] and in his rule required hymns in some of the offices.[11] Even allowing that the word 'hymn' could mean several things at this period, Isidore does seem to mean non-scriptural parts of the office, and this may well have paved the way for the change of Toledo IV.

It is still true to say that hymns are a late addition to the old Spanish office in the form in which it has come down to us. The remaining question of interest is why they were inserted where they were. If it had been desired to imitate the Benedictines, then the hymns of the minor hours should have come at the beginning; if Milan had been influential, then the Vespers hymn might have been near the beginning of Vespers too. It is possible that the attempt was made to keep the hymns, at least at Vespers and Matins, close to the primitive centres of the offices.

THE VESPERS HYMN IN THE OLD SPANISH OFFICE

In the list of hymns of the Temporal cycle of *Br.* given above a total of 21 are listed for the evening, while 19 may be used at both Vespers and

THE USE OF HYMNS IN THE DIVINE OFFICE

Matins. The latter are largely seasonal or festal and so it does not matter at what time of day they are sung. Those listed for exclusive evening use are not all explicitly vesperal – some are seasonal and some purely festal in theme.

Only 14 of the 21 hymns for Vespers are really *evening* hymns and of these, four are also seasonal: *Christi caterva clamitet* and *A Patre Unigenite* are both Advent evening hymns. *Agni genitor alme* for the Sunday before Epiphany (i.e. the new year celebration) had vigilial phrases such as 'Christus dominus vigilet' – translated in Bishop as 'May Christ our master vigil keep'[12] – and finally, *Jam legis umbra clauditur* ('Now is closed the shadow of the law') for the Vespers of the Wednesday of Holy Week is really a First Vespers hymn for Maundy Thursday, combining evening themes with those of that day. The 11 purely evening hymns are largely found after Epiphany or Pentecost, three of them being used only in Lent.

On Sundays, *Inventor rutilis lux bone luminis* and *Altissimi verbum Patris* are of Spanish origin, while *Christe lux mundi, salus et potestas* and *O Lux beata Trinitas* are from elsewhere. To these we may add *Deus qui certis legibus* in Lent (though not very Lenten in spirit). *Inventor rutilis* was probably in regular use from the seventh century if not earlier. *Altissimi verbum Patris* is a good example of the later type.

1. Most High Word of the Father
Jesus, born to a Virgin mother.
Your birth to us twice joyful,
You that made flesh and are so.

2. Now that the day declines away,
Let there be a heavenly light
Favour us with a happy evening
Look kindly on our thanksgiving.

3. To you at the setting of the sun
O Christ we (offer) incense,
To us your heavenly light
Grant to banish darkness.

4. From minds now wearied unto sleep
Hold back the clouding night,
From dark surrender unto sleep
enlighten our souls with purity.

5. Our bodies know not quiet rest
from creeping, wanton artifice,
But you, O God, bring to minds asleep
Quiet rest for inner selves.

6. With hearts and voices raised as one
through Christ, by Spirit, to the Father
The hymn resounds in chorus strong
And sing we with zeal eternally.[13]

Very much an evening hymn, there is a reference to a possible use of incense in the third verse, and the fourth and fifth verses suppose this to be prayer last thing at night. Similarly the fourth verse of *Inventor rutilis* as used in *Br.* (col. 186) speaks of the offering of light at the onset of night. The general thrust is to treat Vespers as the last prayer of the day, which as we have already said, it would have been for those who were not monks.

The hymns of the fragmentary weekday cycle and those of the first three weeks of Lent are all typically vesperal.[14] We may note in passing the popularity of hymns addressed to the second person of the Trinity.

The order of the hymns for the Sundays of Lent in *Br.* is the same as in *T5* of the ninth/tenth century. While other sources sometimes arrange the hymns differently, many others use them on the same days. On the other hand *AL* gives no hymns for ordinary Sundays between cols 281 and 287. Possibly it was still expected that users of that Antiphoner would normally draw hymns for ordinary Sundays from a *Liber Hymnorum*. *T1* listed six hymns for Sunday Vespers (col. 924), three of which are used by *Br.*, and another, *Intende nostris precibus*, is used by *Br.* on Wednesday. Although some hymns, especially on Sundays, reflect the older vesperal themes of light and incense, they are only reliable as evidence for the form of Vespers in Spain from the seventh century. The mention of light, incense and prayer for protection in these hymns possibly echoes something older that survived in the liturgical books long after the original points of reference had disappeared.

NOTES

1 See W. C. Bishop, ed. C. L. Feltoe, *The Mozarabic and Ambrosian Rites* (London: Alcuin/Mowbrays, 1924), pp. 100–14.

2 G. Guiver, *Company of Voices* (London: SPCK, 1988), pp. 158–9; and J. Perez de Urbel, 'Origen de los Himnos Mozarabes', *Bulletin Hispanique* 28 (Bordeaux, 1926), pp. 5–21, 113–39, 209–45 and 305–20.
3 J. Pinell (ed.), 'Las Horas Vigiliares del Officio Monacal Hispanico' (Monserrat: *Liturgica* 3 – *Scripta et Documenta* 17 (1966), pp. 197–340, at pp. 275ff.
4 J. P. Gilson (ed.), *The Mozarabic Psalter* (London: Henry Bradshaw Society, 1905), pp. 184–291, and in night service, pp. 292–328.
5 Perez de Urbel, op. cit., pp. 18–19.
6 C. Blume, *Hymnodia Gotica* (Leipzig: *Analecta Hymnica*, 1897), pp. 290–6.
7 ibid.
8 'Plebi convulsae durum jugum pelle', Perez de Urbel, op. cit., p. 124.
9 ibid., pp. 13–15 and 305.
10 *PL* 83, col. 743, and Pinell, 'El Oficio', p. 385, fn 1.
11 *PL* 83, cols 875–7.
12 Bishop, op. cit., p. 72.
13 Latin text in Blume, op. cit., p. 72.
14 *Christe precamur annue* is so suited to night-time that two verses have been included in the revised version of *Te lucis anti terminum* in the Latin version of the new Roman Breviary – *Liturgia Horarum* (Vatican: Polyglot Press, 1975), p. 539.

5
THE PRAYERS

The old Spanish Vespers and Matins present a complex structure of concluding prayers, following the hymn and immediately preceding the processional/devotional appendices found at both offices. This is the structure:

- the *Supplicatio*, a variable prefatory unit with the response 'Praesta aeterne Omnipotens Deus' and then 'Kyrie eleison, Christe eleison, Kyrie eleison';
- that which *Br.* calls *Capitula*, a misreading of *Completuria*, which is the concluding prayer of the service and leads directly into
- the Lord's Prayer followed by an embolism, the *Petitio*;
- after a monition and salutation the *Benedictio* with its concluding doxology;
- a further salutation precedes one of the additional Antiphons and prayers, which is then followed by the formula of dismissal and any further Antiphons and prayers.

THE SUPPLICATIO AND ITS RESPONSES

Pinell pointed out this formula as common to both cathedral and monastic offices in *Br.* and aimed to show that it was originally a diaconal call for the people to pray privately.[1] The formula occurs only rarely in the manuscripts but may well have oral tradition behind it. It is not found at all in Tradition A manuscripts, and in Tradition B documents, such as *T2*, may often be marked by just a two-word reference.[2] It may also have been written down in a book used exclusively by deacons; similar diaconal formulae are found in the *Liber Ordinum*.

The *Supplicatio* is followed by what may be the relics of responses to litanies now lost: 'Praesta aeterne, omnipotens Deus' ('Grant this, almighty everlasting God') and the Kyries.[3] Pinell grouped together the formulae of the *Supplicatio* and tried to identify an hypothetic original from which others developed:

> Let us pray the Redeemer of the world, Our Lord Jesus Christ, with all supplication, that by his grace he will favour us and count us worthy of justification. (col. 49)

It was this, Pinell thought, that expanded in Advent to:

> Let us pray the Redeemer ... that by the grace of **his advent** ... (col. 49)

and at Easter to:

> Let us pray the Redeemer ... that by the **glory of his resurrection** ... (col. 619)

These do appear to be introductions to a litany, but other examples request prayer for a particular intention, e.g. delivery from evil devils at night or healing of the sick. Thus in spite of some references to the 'Angel of Peace', a common theme in litanies at the office,[4] Pinell still concludes that the formula originally introduced a period of silent prayer, even though there is no other evidence that this was so.

Bishop thought the Kyries a Romanization introduced by the Council of Vaison in 529, and the response 'Praesta aeterne' the ancient version.[5] Evidence for the existence of litanies in Spain is uncertain. In Gaul, the Council of Agde decreed that a *capitella* from the psalms be used after the hymn. This was a form comprising intercessory psalm verses which appears to have originated as scriptural responses to litanic invitations to prayer of, probably, the sixth century.[6] The litanic petition disappeared in time and resulted in the forms such as the *preces feriales* of the former Roman Breviary, from which developed the similar intercessory versicles and responses familiar to users of the Book of Common Prayer: 'O Lord show thy mercy upon us ...' etc.

There are no signs of such a form in the old Spanish rite. The nearest parallel is the freely composed and non-scriptural penitential *Preces* of the cathedral hours. On the other hand the responses 'Praesta aeterne' and the Kyries argue for there having been a litany. Milan's threefold or twelvefold Kyries in certain parts of the office, e.g. after Psalm 148–50 at Lauds,[7] may also represent former litanies. Generally speaking the comparative evidence makes a litany at this point more likely than a period of silent prayer.

THE COMPLETURIA

The fourth-century Apostolic Constitutions had the bishop conclude Vespers with a collect for a peaceful and sinless night. There was a similar prayer in the morning. Egeria spoke of a concluding prayer by a bishop or presbyter. Agde in 506 mentioned a collect by the bishop at Vespers but not at Matins. Toledo IV in 633 called such collects *Completuriae*,[8] indicating their function as completing the office. These prayers summed up evening or morning office as appropriate. Evening prayers were often for protection and the prayers in the morning sought God's blessing on the day.

Ancient Rome knew such prayers, morning and evening prayers being provided by the seventh/eighth-century Old Gelasian Sacramentary, the Frankish Gelasian and the Hadrianum of the eighth century.[9] From the ninth century these prayers were taken out of the Sacramentaries and put elsewhere, and then, possibly because of the increasing number of saints' days, prayers marking the time of day disappeared from use. With the exception of the minor hours of Prime and Compline the concluding prayer at the offices of the Roman Breviary, down to the revised office after Vatican II, was a prayer of the day and not of the hour. An ordinary weekday took the collect of the preceding Sunday, a practice that also passed into the Book of Common Prayer and modern Anglican use.

By contrast Spain retained prayers that referred to the time of day. Even many *Completuriae* that are seasonal or festal have a vesperal or matutinal allusion (especially if the morning *Completuria* is a psalm collect to accompany the *Matutinarium* or morning psalm). Purely festal prayers can be used interchangeably at morning or evening. At Vespers with a *Lucernarium* collect, that prayer has the light theme. *Completuriae* are, in general, prayers for protection during the coming night.

Was the *Completuria* intended to introduce the Lord's Prayer? Several of the prayers stand alone but some are obviously introductory, e.g. the following for Second Vespers of the First Sunday after Pentecost (col. 698):

> Let us bow our hearts with tears to God, dearly beloved brothers; acknowledge our sins to the most merciful Creator, let it be our burden to cry out with prayer from the earth.

There is nothing in this prayer that is particularly vesperal; it is simply an introduction to the Lord's Prayer. Another longer example, more obviously suited to the evening as it quotes from Psalm 140, is given for First Vespers of the First Sunday after the octave of the Epiphany (col. 186):

> Lord, let our prayer come before you like incense in your sight: so that we suffer not the tears of mortal sorrow this evening; but be granted to enjoy the tranquility of the morning sacrifice, our prayer taken up by your Angel, just as Tobias and Sarah were found worthy of your hearing; cure us of our infirmities and strengthen us in our weaknesses; so that as we place before you our belief, in this our daily worship; as the drawing on of night darkens the day so we shall be restored to life by him who merited it, who teaches us to pray:

Vesper prayers in *Br.* are likely to stress the themes of forgiveness of sins and protection for the night and many could easily be concluded without going on to the Lord's Prayer. The following is from First Vespers of the Fourth Sunday after the Epiphany octave (col. 224) and is also used at the Vespers of the Monday and Tuesday of Holy Week (cols 579 and 589):

> God, author of light, creator of the brightness, who drive away all works of darkness, so that the fullness of your light may reign in us: look, we beseech you, upon this burning light and pour out the grace of blessing that all beg of you: so, as this flame at your altar is set up to vanquish darkness and drive it away: may your light prevail in our senses over all shadow of evil.

Of the eleven Lenten weekday prayers in *Br.*, two are also used on ordinary Sundays. Of the remaining eight, *Propinquam passionis* for the Wednesday of Holy Week (col. 596) is proper to that day and time. *Sit festum jejunium*, the most frequently used (col. 278), and *Servis tuis* (col. 307) make mention of fasting and are not particularly vesperal. *Nonarum horarum* (col. 314), used on most Fridays, is vesperal and also mentions fasting; *Deus qui in hac vespertini* (col. 421) is purely vesperal. The remaining three prayers are found only in the period *de Traditione* (cols 458, 467 and 557) and, unlike most prayers in this second half of Lent, have no obvious reference to passion or betrayal. They are, rather, prayers for protection or forgiveness, in other words typically vesperal, and none are obviously introductions to the Lord's Prayer.

The most obviously Lenten of these prayers is that for the first and third Mondays and all Wednesdays except in Holy Week:

> Let our festal fasting be laid before you Lord, who cleanse iniquity and forgive sin: see us groan in confession to you, and be pleased to hear all our prayers; so that serving you in truth, no adversity upsetting us, removing all evil from our hearts, adhering to your precepts, we can be rejoicing in your peace. (col. 278)

A more vesperal example is appointed for the third and fourth Thursday of Lent (i.e. both parts of Lent) (col. 421):

> O God, who at this approaching eventide grant the gift of repose to frail humanity: permit, we pray, that we may take these good things and use them well, these benefits of which we know you as the author.

The following is an example of one used only in the second half of Lent, on the fourth and fifth Mondays and the fifth Tuesday (col. 458):

> Glorious, powerful and merciful God, deliver us from the wiles of the enemy; and, let not our souls be snatched away to ruin by the quickly pouncing lion, may we not lose the protection of your right hand as our guard; let not him who is saved, perish violently, for if he is not guarded he is destroyed. But do you, Lion of the tribe of Judah, arise in your anger and in severity of judgement, and make an end of the hosts of the treacherous: that we may be granted to believe in and remain in the precepts that you have laid down.

Most Wednesdays and Fridays employ *Sit festum jejunium* and *Nonarum horarum* – typically vesperal prayers that are thus connected with the eucharistic days. This may well indicate their antiquity. We may note again that these prayers are not obviously introductions to the Lord's Prayer.

There is not the space in this study to undertake a more searching examination of these texts, as they are too numerous. Those cited have been chosen because of their allusions to evening. They, rather than the festal and seasonal prayers, contribute to our understanding of the theology of daily worship that pervaded the old Spanish office.[10] The approach of night was a symbol of life-threatening darkness, the darkness of sin that can only be overcome by God. Once again echoes of the Paschal Vigil are heard, the service is a service of light, the beginning of a nightly vigil, a watch against that which would threaten Christian life. The service acclaims God as creator of the darkness as well as the hoped-for day. This creator God is beseeched to forgive his people's sins and grant them protection so that, although they recognize their unworthiness, still they may know his power and protection.

THE LORD'S PRAYER AND PETITIO

Many of the *Completuriae* could easily be completed by a doxology; others, as we have seen, lead into the distinctive old Spanish version of the Lord's Prayer:

> Pater noster qui es in coelis. *R* Amen. Santificetur nomen tuum. *R* Amen. Adveniat regnum tuum. *R* Amen. Fiat voluntas tua, sicut in coelo et in terra. *R* Amen. Panem nostrum quotidianum da nobis hodie. *R* Quia Deus es.* *V* Et dimitte nobis debita nostra, sicut et nos dimittimus debitoribus nostris. *R* Amen. Et ne nos inducas in tentationem. *R*. Sed libera nos a malo. (col. 49)
>
> (*For you are God.)

This is also found in the Mass and is traditionally chanted by the priest alone, the choir/people responding. The singing of the Lord's Prayer by the celebrant alone was a distinctive feature of the Roman rite at the time of Gregory the Great and down to the 1950s.[11] As King noted, *AL* has a rubric: 'Pater noster ab omnibus fidelibus recitantur' ('Our Father is said by all the faithful'),[12] but the *Liber Ordinum* has the inserted Amens, so it may have been a common practice in Spain.

In 517, canon 10 of Gerona ordered the Lord's Prayer to be added to morning and evening prayers. This 'innovation' was still resisted a century later, for Toledo IV was critical of clergy who omitted it. Bradshaw suggests that it may have been brought in as an imitation of monastic practice. Benedictine influence could be important here for they had no priests in early communities, and the Lord's Prayer may have replaced the collect.[13] St Benedict mentioned only the Lord's Prayer and not the collect.[14] While modern Christians may be surprised by a service without the Lord's Prayer, in the early Church it was seen as a model of prayer rather than a formula. As a formula it may first have been used in private worship and thus became the prayer that those who were not clergy would use when they came together, since the collect was presbyteral and could not be pronounced by a lay person.[15] Even today in the Byzantine tradition, in the absence of clergy, a group, religious or laity, may celebrate the offices, but the repeated singing of 'Lord have mercy' replaces all litanies and presbyteral prayers. Many of the *Completuriae* that are obviously not introductions to the Lord's Prayer might date back to the sixth century at least, when they would have still concluded the service. Though the Lord's Prayer was resisted for a time, it eventually became common in Spain.[16]

An embolism called *Petitio* is added to the Lord's Prayer (col. 49). From the words 'deliver us from evil' it expands into a lengthy conclusion to the Lord's Prayer and includes brief intercession for sinners, captives, the sick and the dead; for peace and for the defeat of enemies. The same form is used in the Mass (*PL* 85 *passim*). The Gallican version was variable.[17] It is probably a medieval addition to the Spanish office; the mention of captives and defeat of enemies suggests the possibility that it reflects the period of Moorish domination. A shorter form is used for weekday offices and minor hours (col. 62 and see cols 939ff.):

> A malo nos libera, et in tuo timore opere bono nos confirma Trinitas, Deus noster, qui es benedictus, et vivis, et omnia regis in saecula saeculorum. Amen. (Deliver us from evil and in your fear, keep us in good works, O Trinity, our God, who are blessed and live and reign over all for ever and ever. Amen.)

A variant form was used at the rarely celebrated office of Aurora that preceded Prime (col. 940).[18]

THE BENEDICTIO

Some form of Blessing or prayer over the people seems to have been common from at least the fifth century. The Eucharist concluded with Communion (which was perhaps blessing enough) but the offices with the bishop's blessing, as we can see from Egeria's account of the bishop blessing and the people 'coming to his hand' for an individual blessing.[19] Agde in 506 laid down that '... after the concluding prayer the people should be dismissed at Vespers by the bishop with a blessing'.[20] In 549, canon 2 of the Council of Barcelona required a

THE PRAYERS

blessing at the end of Matins too,[21] but this seems not to have been observed in areas of Spain that followed Tradition B.[22] *Br.* often has no blessing at Matins, or Matins uses the one from the previous night. There is no mention of a Matins blessing in *T2*.

The arrangements in *Br.* vary, e.g., on the Sundays of Advent the rubrics require the use of the blessing of the previous evening at Matins (see cols 50 and 58); Second Vespers of Sunday has a different blessing and the rubrics make no mention of a blessing at Matins on weekdays. (The Sunday night blessing is used through the week and is probably a ferial text.) Vespers blessings are frequently re-used at Matins, but for many of the Sundays of Lent no rubric requires a blessing at Matins at all, while the Vespers texts are proper to each Sunday. Very briefly, the only pattern that can be discerned is that Matins usually uses the Vespers blessing, if it has one at all, and the variety of rubrics or lack of them in *Br.* may indicate that not only is the blessing a later insertion at Matins, but it may have been Ortiz who inserted it.

In form these blessings are similar to the Gallican ones and to those that were inserted *before* Communion in Spain as well: usually in the second person and, in *Br.*, preceded by a diaconal monition: *Humiliate vos ad Benedictionem* (col. 49) with the salutation. There are three parts and a fixed conclusion.

A first example is that for Second Vespers of the Fourth Sunday after the Epiphany octave (col. 228):

> May the prayers you pour out in petition ascend to the Lord. *R* Amen. May that which you have earnestly entreated be given by the most merciful Pastor. *R* Amen. May he guide your minds to an understanding of salvation, and let not your souls fall into temptation. *R* Amen.

This is appropriately vesperal with its reminiscence of Psalm 140 in the first petition. It is noteworthy that even the blessings for Lent are more general than seasonal; the following example is appointed for the third and fourth Thursday of Lent (col. 421):

> May the Almighty bless you from on high. *R* Amen. May he maintain a gracious countenance towards your labour and graciously hear your prayers. *R* Amen. May your work be seen as pleasing and your life guarded in holiness and peace. *R* Amen.

The blessing is always completed by the following doxology:

Per misericordiam ipsius Dei nostri, qui es benedictus, et vivit, et omnia regit in saecula saeculorum. R Amen. (col. 50) (Through the mercy of our God, who is blessed and lives and reigns over all things for ever and ever. R Amen.)

This changes accordingly when the blessing is in the second person, and the doxology is also very similar to that used in the eucharistic rite.

While in many places blessings were the prerogative of the bishop, in Spain a presbyter could bless in the bishop's absence.[23] The large number of blessings in the Spanish books might be the consequence of their being presbyteral, and hence of more frequent occurrence than in Gaul and elsewhere.

THE DISMISSAL

Manuscripts such as *T2* show Vespers as ending with a blessing (followed by *Laudes* in the second half of Lent) and Matins with just *Laudes*. In *Br.* at Vespers there is a salutation after the blessing, then usually *Laudes* with a prayer and this dismissal:

In nomine domini nostri Jesu Christi perficiamus cum pace. R Deo gratias. (col. 50) (In the name of our Lord Jesus Christ, let us finish in peace. R Thanks be to God.)

This is repeated after a further invariable *Laudes* and prayer, bringing the office to a close. The formula 'May the souls of the faithful departed ...', often found elsewhere, is placed after the fixed *Laudes*, and was probably imported by Ortiz. The manuscripts do not have the dismissal formula; it was probably part of oral tradition. There are often additional *Laudes* between the blessing and dismissal at Matins (e.g., col. 123). If, as we have suggested, the Matins blessing was a later interpolation, then that service may have closed with the dismissal alone, *after* the *Laudes*, a form that will be dealt with in the next section.

NOTES

1 J. Pinell, 'Una Exhortacion Diaconal a la Plegaria en el Antiguo Rito Hispanico, La *Supplicatio*', *Analecta Sacra Tarraconensia* 36 (1963), pp. 3–23, at p. 3.
2 See e.g., J. Janini (ed.) *Liber Misticus de Cuaresma* (Toledo: Istituto de Estudios Visigotico-Mozarabes, 1979), p. 15: 'Oremus. Redemptorem'.
3 Pinell, op. cit., pp. 12–13.
4 ibid., pp. 23–4.

5 W. C. Bishop, ed. C. L. Feltoe, *The Mozarabic and Ambrosian Rites* (London: Alcuin/Mowbrays, 1924), pp. 83–5.
6 Paul de Clerck, *La prière universelle dans les liturgies latines anciennes* (Munster: Aschendorff, 1977), pp. 269–73.
7 Bishop, op. cit., pp. 103, 107.
8 See, e.g., R. Taft, *The Liturgy of the Hours in East and West* (Collegeville: Liturgical Press, 1986), pp. 44–56, 147–60.
9 Listed in Cyrille Vogel, *Medieval Liturgy: An Introduction to the Sources* (Washington, DC: Pastoral Press, 1986), pp. 66–9, 76–8 and 80–86.
10 An example of a seasonal prayer is given in Bishop, op. cit., p. 73 (from *Br.* col. 147); light is mentioned in the last clause almost as an afterthought.
11 See e.g., A. Archdale King, *The Liturgy of the Roman Church* (London: Longmans, 1957), p. 347.
12 A. Archdale King, *Liturgies of the Primatial Sees* (London: Longmans, 1957), p. 619.
13 P. Bradshaw, *Daily Prayer in the Early Church* (London: Alcuin/SPCK, 1981), pp. 120, 136.
14 *Rule of St Benedict* 14.
15 See G. Guiver, *Company of Voices* (London: SPCK, 1988), p. 171.
16 Until recent changes, the Roman Lauds and Vespers only inserted the Lord's Prayer when the *preces feriales* were appointed to be used – largely in Lent.
17 King, *Liturgies of the Primatial Sees*, p. 619.
18 In 1935 (last year of the pre-Civil War establishment) this office was appointed for only nine penitential days in the year. See *Directorium Mozarabicum ad Divinum Officium* ... (Toledo, 1934).
19 Bradshaw, *Daily Prayer*, pp. 79–80.
20 ibid., p. 116.
21 J. Pinell, 'El Oficio Hispanico-Visigotico', *HS* 10 (1957), pp. 385–427, at p. 386.
22 J. Pinell (ed.), *Las Horas Vigiliares del Oficio Monacal Hispanico* (Monserrat: *Liturgica* 3 – *Scripta et Documenta* 17 (1966), pp. 197–340, at p. 211, fn 14.
23 King, *Liturgies*, p. 621 and also pp. 131–9 for the practice of Lyons.

6

THE PSALLENDUM

The old Spanish Mass possesses a unit with this title but in a position analogous to that of the Roman Gradual. In the office this unit comes near the end of Vespers and Matins and is rather different. It is a simple antiphon with one or more psalm verses followed by a prayer, and is found before or after the blessing. In *T2* and *Br.* the *Psallendum* is called *Laudes* or *Lauda* but in Tradition A manuscripts is called *Psallendum* or *Psallendo* (sometimes in abbreviated form). *Psallendum* will be used here so as to distinguish this unit from the *Laudes*.

Isidore did not mention it but there are parallel chants and prayers that accompanied processions at Milan.[1] Some texts in *Br.* are entitled *Lauda ad Fontes* or *Lauda de fonte* (see cols 201 and 198/205), implying a procession to the Baptistery. Most authors agree that the origin of these pieces may be in imitation of fifth-century practice in Jerusalem where processional stations that followed the offices were described by Egeria.[2]

In *Br.* and other old Spanish sources there is usually one *Psallendum* and, perhaps, a prayer. *T5* and *Br.* multiply these units at the Sunday Vespers of Lent. Akeley[3] and Porter[4] identified those given for the Second Vespers of the Sunday *de Carnes Tollendas* as accompanying a procession to seal the Baptistery for Lent.

Martin Patino noted that, on ordinary Sundays and in Lent, the *Psallenda* were usually taken from Psalm 118 but in no particular order.[5] The prayers are usually taken from those accompanying the first Antiphon at the next morning's Matins, so there is little connection between the chant and the prayer. As an example, here are the *Psallendum* and prayer for First Vespers of the Fourth Sunday after the Epiphany Octave (col. 225, Psalm 118.4 and 20):

THE PSALLENDUM

You have commanded your commandments. Alleluia. *P* To be kept with care. Alleluia, Alleluia. *V* My soul desires eagerly your decrees, at all times. *P* To be kept. *V* Glory and honour to the Father. *P* To be kept. O God our refuge and strength, be to us a helper in time of distress, so that in no way may our conscience be afraid before your earth-shaking judgement: may the waters of the river give joy to the city, the place where the most high dwells: in it indeed; for from you comes our help, who, with your Holy Spirit, allow your people to reap abundant grace.

The prayer is a psalm collect for Psalm 45; the theme of Matins and Mass on this day is to do with the new Covenant in which God inspires his people to goodness. The prayer may have been added to the *Psallendum* in order to stress the preparatory, vigilial nature of First Vespers. The Second Vespers of ordinary Sundays usually has an invariable *Psallendum*, 'Your statutes have become my songs ... This has made for me, because of the keeping of your precepts' (col. 190, Psalm 118.54 and 56).

On ordinary Sundays, the Matins *Psallendum* is always from Psalm 149.1: 'Sing a new song to the Lord, his praise in the assembly of the faithful', which is accompanied by a psalm collect on the First, Fourth and Sixth Sundays (cols 189, 227 and 236). Where no blessing is appointed the collect takes its place. It may well be that the Blessing was the later alternative to the prayer:

Lord, we sing to you in the assembly of the faithful: we proclaim your graciousness: grant to us to deserve your praises; in which we believe we obtain your everlasting reward.

In the first week of Lent *Br.* indicates no blessing at the end of Matins, only a *Psallendum* and prayer. The same *Psallendum* and prayer are repeated *after* the blessing at Vespers but no reference to Vesperal *Psallenda* is to be found in *T2*.[6] The *Psallenda* in the first week are not taken from Psalm 118. In the second and third weeks they mostly are. The Matins *Psallendum* is again from Psalm 149. In the second half of Lent *T2* refers to a *Psallendum* after the blessing at Vespers (though not on the fifth Tuesday and Friday).[7] In this period almost all weekday *Psallenda* are drawn from the multiple ones of the preceding Sunday, even in Holy Week. Particular preference is for the *Psallenda* of the Second Vespers of the Sunday. The numerous *Psallenda* of Lent Sunday Vespers and the relative fixity of the Matins *Psallendum* allows us to suggest that the original place for this unit was at the end of Sunday Vespers, and also that these psalmodic texts were independent of any seasonal or festal theme in Lent, whereas at other times they were further comments on the theme of the feast or season.[8] Taking collects from Matins to accompany the *Psallenda* may be a later attempt to bring them into line with the Sunday theme. In Lent however (excepting the First Sunday – see col. 264) the collects are all psalm collects for Psalm 118.

What then is the function of the *Psallendum*? It is most likely a stational chant. Parallels include an ancient Roman procession to the baptistery after Easter Vespers, and the East Syrian/Chaldean rite which possesses the relics of such a stational procession, accompanied by Psalm 118 recited over two weeks. Jacob Vellian observed that this chant may be a late addition but there is ancient evidence of a procession 'to the martyrs' (probably to a chapel of relics).[9]

It seems possible then that Psalm 118 was used to accompany a procession to the baptistery or to a reliquary chapel. In *Br.*'s fragmentary weekday cycle titles such as *Lauda de Fonte* (col. 205) accompany texts that stress water and another text, 'In sanctis tuis ...', appears to be connected with visiting the relics (the *Pressa* reads 'ubi sunt repositae sanctorum reliquiae ...' – 'Where are deposited the relics of the saints ...'). These examples are untypical, one coming before and the other after the blessing, and having no collects. The fact that this weekday cycle is fragmentary must make one wary of drawing too many conclusions from it. It can be said, however, that Psalm 118 with its stress on doing God's will and obeying his law as the joy of religious life would be a suitable reminder of baptismal commitment, and the martyrs would then be seen as examples of the costliness of following the Christian call.

As the Lenten *Psallenda* are the fullest versions in *Br.*, texts for First Vespers of the Fifth Sunday of Lent are given as examples (col. 501):

> Many they are that persecute me and trouble me, Lord: but I have not turned from your law, O my God. *V* See my humiliation and save me for I will not forget your law. (Psalm 118.157 and 153) Lord, may your numberless mercies cancel all our iniquities; and lead us, corrected, to your forgiveness. *R* Amen. (Quotes Psalm 118.156.)

> I call with all my heart, hear me Lord. *V* I cry unto you, save me that I may keep your testimony. (Psalm 118.145a and 146) Lord, we call to you; that you hear us, that you lift up our lowered eyes to you: so that, enlightened by your brightness, we may remain

always in the light. *R* Amen. (References to Ps. 118.145 and 147–8.)

These *Psallenda* are very general and have little specific reference to the season *de Traditione*. *AL* indicates *Psallenda* at the end of Vespers on a few Sundays in Lent; they are also from Psalm 118 but only one quotes a section of the psalm also used in *Br*.[10]

In *Br*., after the *Psallenda* Psalm 50 is said and then some *Preces* with a prayer, before the concluding formula; at least on Lent 1 (Second Vespers – col. 264), Lent 2 (both Vespers, cols 324 and 329–30), Lent 3 (First Vespers, col. 380), and Lent 4 (First Vespers, cols 439-40). The others, except Palm Sunday which has only the *Psallenda* and prayers, do not appoint the psalm. The First Vespers of Lent 1, having a somewhat different character, has only one *Psallendum*, Psalm 90 and the *Preces* (cols 259–60).

The *Preces* that follow the *Psallenda* above for the Fifth Sunday of Lent are as follows:

Lord of mercies, *P* Forget our sins. *V* Who rising from the dead, sit at the right hand of God the Father. *P* Forget. *V* Who promise the prize to the just; and punish the doings of iniquity. *P* Forget. *V* Who judge not the sinners; but call them to embrace penitence. *P* Forget. *V* Who call the just to endurance; and, after the challenge of temptation, to crowning. *P* Forget.

Prayer
Lord, hear our prayers; let our groaning come to your ears: we truly acknowledge our iniquities and lay open our faults before you: We have sinned before you O God: confessing before you we implore pardon. And, as we return to your laws, and to that little observance that you ask of us, look again, Lord, upon your servants, who are redeemed by your blood. Pardon us, we pray, and grant forgiveness of our sins: that we may be worthy to receive the bounty of your merciful kindness. *R* Amen.

This somewhat repetitive 'apologia' appears at the end of Vespers on each of the Sundays of Lent (there is a shorter alternative at most Second Vespers – see col. 330) but not on Palm Sunday. The *Preces* and the prayer seem to be much later additions. It may not be altogether fanciful to understand this addition to the *Psallenda* as a way of turning a now redundant procession to the baptistery into a penitential exercise for Lent. The theological emphasis of Lent has passed from baptism to penance.

The Palm Sunday *Psallenda* retain much more of the baptismal atmosphere. For example, First Vespers, the collect of the second is entirely baptismal: 'Aedifica Domine ...' 'Build Lord, upon the waters of refreshment, a people formed from the baptismal water ...' (col. 565). And at Second Vespers (col. 569) the second changes Psalm 118.33 to read: 'Teach *them* Lord, the demands of your statutes ...' and the third changes verse 34 to read: 'Grant *them* understanding, Lord ...'

In Easter Week (cols 616–37), by contrast, the texts are all to do with the resurrection and there is no obvious connection with the newly baptized as one might have expected. (*AL* provides a similar series[11] – on the whole this source only provides texts for a limited number of feasts and very few Sundays.) Most other *Psallenda* are simply extra festal additions to the office, and the only point to note is that those for Matins are always taken from the previous Vespers. Ordinary Sundays have only a limited repertoire of texts and the use of the *Psallendum* on those days may be a later development.

What we have seen of the texts in Lent and on Palm Sunday inclines to the conclusion that the original purpose of these texts was to do with Baptism. This would mean that they might date back to the time when there were still adult catechumens, and would also explain why some sources say nothing of them – they may have been contained in books such as the *Liber Ordinum*. When adult catechumens disappeared the procession to the baptistery became one of penance and an increasingly penitential/devotional atmosphere pervaded Lent and extended these texts to weekdays as well. The next stage was to provide similar texts for other occasions, and also to use them at Matins. Thus, except for the titles such as *Lauda de Fonte*, the original purpose of the *Psallendum* was lost to sight.

After the *Psallendum* the dismissal was said and an invariable 'commemoration' followed (col. 50), comprising Psalm 54.17: 'At evening, morn and midday, we will praise you Lord', a collect and the reiterated dismissal. Something similar came at the end of Matins (col. 58). These *Psallenda* were treated as of secondary importance, being recited not sung, even on feasts.[12] The final commemorations may have been added in order to ensure that some reference to the time of day did not disappear entirely. By the early sixteenth century, saints' days had almost completely obscured the liturgical year, and in 1935 they so dominated the Corpus Christi chapel that the first ferial day in that year was 1 April, Monday of the fourth week of Lent![13] Even today the office is, on most days, of a saint.[14] The commemorations alone kept alive the memory of the original purpose and function of the offices of Vespers and Matins.

NOTES

1 See W. C. Bishop, ed. C. L. Feltoe, *The Mozarabic and Ambrosian Rites* (London: Alcuin/Mowbrays, 1924), pp. 84 and 126–7.
2 G. Winkler, 'Über die Kathedralvesper in Verschiedenen Riten des Ostens and Westens', *ALW* 16 (1974), pp. 33–102, at p. 85, fn 19; R. Taft, *The Liturgy of The Hours in East and West* (Collegeville: Liturgical Press, 1986), p. 162; J. Pinell (ed.), 'Las Horas Vigiliares del Oficio Monacal Hispanico' (Monserrat: Liturgica 3 – Scripta et Documenta 17 (1966), pp. 197–340, at p. 219 – Egeria 24.7.
3 T. G. Akeley, *Christian Initiation in Spain* (London: Darton, Longman & Todd, 1965), pp. 143–4.
4 A. W. S. Porter, 'Studies in the Mozarabic Office', *JTS* 35 (1934), pp. 266–86, at pp. 277–9.
5 J. M. Martin Patino, 'El Breviarium Mozarabe de Ortiz, su Valor Documental para la Historia del Oficio Catedralicio Hispanico', *Miscellanea 40 Comillas* (1963), pp. 207–97, at pp. 277–9.
6 Cols 267–318, see J. Janini (ed.), *Liber Misticus de Cuaresma* (Toledo: Istituto de Estudios Visigotico-Mozarabes, 1979), pp. 6–46.
7 Janini, op. cit., p. 184, 205.
8 See also Martin Patino, op. cit., pp. 280, 283–4.
9 *East Syrian Evening Services* (Kottayam: Indian Institute for Eastern Churches, 1971), pp. 17–19.
10 *AL*, ff 169, 223 and 261.
11 *AL* 308 and 321.
12 F. A. Lorenzana and F. Fabian y Fuero, *Missa Gotica seu Mozarabica et Officium itidem. Gothicum, diligenter ac dilucide explanata* (Puebla de los Angeles, 1770), pp. 189ff.
13 *Directorium Mozarabicum* ... (Toledo, 1934), p. 19.
14 Personal communication from Fr George Guiver CR, July 1988.

7

VESPERS – SOME CONCLUDING REMARKS

On pages 3–4 were given schemes of Vespers as it would have appeared in the Ordo of Bobadilla, the works of Isidore, and in the developed cathedral office; together with Taft's suggested reconstruction of the most primitive form. It was noted earlier that Isidore (possibly following Bobadilla) appeared to speak of a *Lucernarium*, two psalms, a Responsory and *Laudes*. If the developed cathedral ordo has a *Lucernarium*, *Antiphona* (possibly the Responsory?) and an *Alleluiaticum*, one has to ask what happened to the two psalms. It was suggested that Isidore was in fact describing the method of performing the psalms, for otherwise he is speaking of a Vespers of *five* psalms of which no other trace remains. Though it is of course possible that Isidore and Bobadilla are speaking of a monastic addition of extra psalms, an addition soon stamped out by the legislation that required the monastics to follow the cathedral ordo for Vespers and Matins.

Confusion may be thought to be worse confounded by the fact that the *Antiphona* is often a complete psalm on weekdays and the unit is multiplied on some feast days. The former fact seems to argue in favour of our hypothesis; the latter may imply a period when there was far less fixity in the number of chants to be rendered. So then let us ask if comparative evidence is in favour of the hypothesis that there was a form of service based on three psalms, no more and no less, as the primitive norm.

Magistretti's edition of the *Manuale Ambrosianum* takes us back to the rite of Milan as it was in the eleventh century. The scheme of this Vespers is given on p. 9 above and divides into three parts of which the second comprised the psalms of the day, i.e., the Roman cursus of five consecutively numbered psalms; then follows a prayer, the Magnificat and another prayer. On certain days, notably the Sundays of Lent, the ferias of Holy Week and the ferias of Easter Week, this was reduced to a single proper psalm, followed by Psalms 133 and 116 combined under one antiphon, a prayer and the Magnificat.[1] An even simpler form lasted until modern times in Holy Week and comprised a single psalm and a prayer – most notably this lacked the Magnificat.[2] Winkler has shown that Psalms 133 and 116 occur in many places as the beginning of the midnight office and suggests that they originally led into a form of 'All-night Vigil', in which case the proper psalm mentioned above would be the last psalm of the actual office of Vespers on the eve of a great feast.[3] So it is perfectly possible that the original form in Milan was that of the feriae *in Autentica*, i.e. the weekdays of Holy Week:

1 Greeting
2 *Lucernarium*
3 Hymn
4 *Responsory in Choro*
5 Psalm
6 Prayer
7 Kyrie (12 times)
8 Normal conclusion[4]

If the *Lucernarium* and, possibly, the *Responsory in Choro* were originally complete psalms, then we may have evidence of a three-psalm Vespers at Milan (the hymn being inserted between the *Lucernarium* and the *Responsory in Choro* at a very early stage). This service was completed by a Litany of which the 12 Kyries are a relic, except when a vigil followed immediately.

The use of early Celtic Christians is to be found in the Antiphonary of Bangor which also appointed three psalms for Vespers, Psalms 64, 103 and 112, all well suited to the vesperal themes of God's creation, and the praise of his wisdom and goodness. They were followed by the 'Gloria in excelsis' and prayer.[5]

Some most intriguing evidence is to be found in an Easter custom of the Roman clergy described by S. J. P. Van Dijk.[6] He described an Easter Sunday afternoon celebration of Vespers at the Lateran Basilica, at which three Alleluiatic antiphons were interspersed among the normal Sunday cursus of Psalms 109–113 and at which the Magnificat was sung no fewer than three times: after the first three psalms, then at the Baptistery after the fourth psalm, and finally at the church of St Andrew after the fifth psalm. The clergy were then given a well-deserved drink and went home to their parishes to celebrate Easter Vespers with their people. If the fourth antiphon is a later addition, as some think, the original form from which the antiphons evolved may be evidence of an older form of Vespers consisting of three antiphons. To this we may add a decree of Gregory III in 732 requiring the singing of three psalms in honour of the saint of the day *after* monastic style Vespers.[7] When the clergy got back to their parishes it was the three-psalm form that they celebrated, perhaps Psalms 129, 140 and 11, later integrated into the five-psalm monastic form as the people became less involved in the celebration. Van Dijk also emphasized that there would have been no reading and we are aware that hymns were only allowed at Rome at a very late date. Thus there seems to be evidence of a Roman urban Vespers of cathedral type that consisted of little more than three psalms and prayer. The earliest form of the monastic office of the Roman basilicas was possibly five psalms, the versicle and response from Psalm 140, and prayer. It is possible that the monks' five psalms in course were originally followed by the cathedral Vespers of the clergy and people, the three fixed psalms, including Psalm 140 of which the single verse alone survived. Such a pattern of variable monastic psalmody followed by the cathedral office would match what was to be seen in parts of the Christian East.

Thus the comparative evidence, especially that from Milan, together with the fact that the surviving texts (omitting the *Sono* as a later addition) usually number three, suggests that a three-psalm form of Vespers was the original form in Spain as well. The psalms were: a light-psalm to accompany the *Lucernarium* ceremony, an evening psalm and a psalm of praise. They were followed by prayer, notably by the *Completuria* and/or the Lord's Prayer and, from at least the late fourth century or early fifth, a final Blessing. The seventh century saw a metrical hymn added after the psalmody, in imitation of monastic practice, and before the prayer. Then later in the same century the *Sono* was added to the *Lucernarium* on Sundays and Feasts. Later again an occasional procession at the end of Vespers became a daily devotional addition.

Once again we can conclude that Old Spanish Vespers was a sort of miniature Easter Vigil. The light of Christ's presence was welcomed and the Creator God thanked and praised for his redeeming work among his faithful people, who prayed confidently for protection and new life. Even on days when the faithful were not watching in prayer all night, the light of Christ had been greeted as that light that conquers the darkness of sin and death. The function then of this evening service, as elsewhere in Europe at that time, was not so much to end the day as to begin the night.

NOTES

1 M. Magistretti (ed.), *Manuale Ambrosianum* (Milan, 1905), pp. 122–226.
2 ibid., pp. 175ff.
3 G. Winkler, 'Über die Kathedralvesper in Verschiedenen Riten des Ostens und Westens', *ALW* 16 (1974), pp. 33–102, at p. 96.
4 See, e.g., Monday of Holy Week, *Breviarium Ambrosianum, pars Hiemalis II* (Milan, 1944), p. 205.
5 M. Curran, *The Antiphonary of Bangor* (Dublin: Irish Academic Press, 1984), pp. 171–2.
6 S. J. P. van Dijk, 'The Medieval Easter Vespers of the Roman Clergy', *Sacris Erudiri* XIX (1969–70), pp. 261–363.
7 ibid., p. 330, and M. Andrieu, *Les Ordines Romani du Haut Moyen Age* (Louvain; 1931–61), p. 464, #18: 'Ad vesperum tres psal[mos] usque in sabbato et per singulos psalmus *Alleluia*' ('At Vespers three psalms until Saturday, and at each psalm, *Alleluia*').

Part Two

The Order and Components of Matins

When we turn to the old Spanish Matins in *Br*. we find what seem to be rather more familiar landmarks than we found at Vespers. The order for the First Sunday of Advent starts with a hymn and prayer. The psalms are then indicated (with short antiphons), and a further prayer. Three *Antiphonae* and a Responsory, all with prayers, take us back to unfamiliar territory, though the fragmentary weekday cycle expects whole psalms to be part of these *Antiphonae*. Under the heading in *Laudibus* (at Lauds), we find an Old Testament canticle at full length, followed by an abbreviated version of the canticles from Daniel 3. The traditional Lauds psalms, 148–50, are followed by a reading and hymn, and then prayers and concluding material similar to that already seen at Vespers (see *PL* 86, cols 50–8).

The division into Matins and Lauds is deceptively familiar, but we may notice that there is still no New Testament canticle; although the reading is in much the same place as the 'Little Chapter' used to be in Roman Lauds, it is rather longer, and the few psalms that are used at full length on a Sunday appear to be used every Sunday without fail, so there is still little sign of the whole Book of Psalms being recited in any particular order. Even the division into Matins and Lauds is deceptive; no ancient works indicate such a division, which was probably entirely of Ortiz' making, and intended to make the service look more like that of the Roman Breviary. We shall be treating the whole service as one.

8
EARLY TESTIMONIES TO THE STRUCTURE OF MATINS IN SPAIN

Isidore hinted at the use of Psalm 118 (verse 148) and Psalm 62 at morning prayer.[1] The Council of Agde in 506 spoke of the proper hymn and at the end, the *Capitella de Psalmis*.[2] The Council of Tarragonna in 516 required a daily celebration of Matins with the presence of a priest and a deacon. At Gerona, the following year, the Lord's Prayer was appointed to be said daily at Matins. Barcelona (c. 540) required Psalm 50 'before the Canticle', a blessing to be given at the end, and collects (probably with each psalm) to be said by the priests, even when the bishop was present. Toledo IV in 633 required that the Daniel 3 canticle be not omitted, as it was in use throughout the whole world.[3]

Three monastic rules, of Isidore, of Fructuosus of Braga, and the ordo of Bobadilla,[4] refer to 'three psalms' to begin the morning celebration following hard upon the monastic nocturnal vigils. Those vigils opened with the 'canonical psalms' (Pss. 3, 50 and 56) which on Sunday were replaced by Psalms 46, 99 and 116. The cathedral Matins, as it developed, acquired the three canonical psalms, so the monastic arrangement might well have been avoided to obviate duplication. The documents speak of groups of three psalms known as *missae*, Isidore and the ordo of Bobadilla also speak of a *missa* of three canticles. There then follows the morning part of the service, three psalms (according to Fructuosus and Bobadilla) or a fifth *missa* (Isidore). Bobadilla also stipulates a hymn and the Lord's Prayer.

Schematically, the three patterns look like this:

Isidore	Fructuosus	Bobadilla
	VIGILIAE	
Psalmi Canonici		*Psalmi Canonici*
Missae Psalmorum	*Responsoria sub ternorum psalmorum divisione*	*Missae de Psalterio*
Missa Canticorum		*Missa de Canticis*
	MATUTINIS	
Quinta missa matutinarium officiorum	*Tres Psalmi*	*Psalmi matutinari tres*
		Responsum
		Laudes
	cum laude et benedictione sua	*Hymnus*
		Dominica Oratione

This shape is very similar to what we find in *Br.*, especially if the three morning psalms spoken of are psalms 148–50, as seems most likely. Probably the later pattern, canonized by Barcelona, changed this by adding Psalm 50 before the Canticle. This pattern is shown schematically in Taft (morning section only):

Psalm 50 with antiphon and collect
Canticle with antiphon and collect
Psalm (Dan. 3 canticle on Sundays and Feasts), antiphon and collect
Psalms 148–50
Hymn
Supplication – *Completuria*
Lord's Prayer – *Petitio* (embolism)
Blessing
Psallendum

NOTES

1 *PL* 83. cols 743–760 and also see R. Taft, *The Liturgy of the Hours in East and West* (Collegeville: Liturgical Press, 1986), pp. 156–63.
2 See above, p. 39.
3 J. Pinell, 'El Oficio Hispanico-Visigotico', *Liturgica I – Scripta et Documenta* 7 (1956), pp. 386–9; and Taft, op. cit., pp. 158–9.
4 Pinell, op. cit., p. 385.

9

MATINS – THE INTRODUCTORY MATERIAL

The following elements comprise the introductory material of Matins:

1. The invocation and salutation.
2. On Sundays outside of Eastertide the hymn *Aeterne rerum Conditor* with a collect.
3. The Canonical Psalms, 3, 50 and 56 with antiphons and a collect, on Sundays outside of Eastertide, **or**
4. Psalm 3 with an antiphon and collect in Eastertide and most weekdays, **or**
5. Psalm 50 with an antiphon and a collect (Psalm 56 on certain weekdays of Advent) on other weekdays, and on all the feasts of saints.

THE INVOCATION AND SALUTATION

The invocation and salutation found at Vespers are required by *Br.* (cols 50 and 203), which seems odd as they are distinctly vesperal. The formulae may simply be misplaced.

AETERNE RERUM CONDITOR

This hymn, reliably credited to St Ambrose, was probably not known to the editors of *OV*, who did not provide any collect to go with it. A ninth/tenth-century manuscript mentions the hymn and gives collects for it, and it is also referred to in other sources. The hymn was sung daily at Milan at the beginning of the morning office which also was not originally divided artificially into Nocturns and Lauds. Borella stressed that its inclusion indicated the vigil nature of this first part of the morning office.[1] St Benedict required hymns at the beginning of the night office and towards the end of the morning office.[2] By his time monks were saying the morning office earlier and had inserted the office of Prime between the Lauds and Terce.[3] This would mean that a service of nocturns permanently linked to the morning service would probably start much earlier and the morning hymn would probably occur about cockcrow – and that is where *this* hymn is inserted in the Benedictine and old Roman monastic offices. In both cases *Aeterne rerum Conditor* was the hymn for Lauds (i.e. the morning hymn) in winter.

If this hymn was carried into Spain by monastic influences from the eighth century onwards, then it is interesting that it did not take a similar place but was placed at the very beginning of Matins. Possibly there was an awareness that the morning office, Matins, was, like that of Milan, a single service starting at cockcrow, and so the hymn was placed at the beginning. There may also have been continued resistance to its inclusion, which might explain why it never became a daily item as at Milan and was totally omitted in Eastertide. The first verse reads:

> Everliving ruler of all,
> Maker of all things,
> You made the day and the night,
> Giving us this morning light
> So that we might herald the dawn
> With hope reborn.[4]

If the hymn entered the Spanish office between the early eighth and late ninth centuries, then the prayers composed to accompany it are rather late specimens of old Spanish prayer style. The nine prayers given are for all Sundays except those of Eastertide – though one is appointed for Pentecost. Several are also found in Tradition A sources.[5] They were for use at any time of the year, and nothing in them ties them to any particular season. No other prayers in the Breviary quote a hymn, which may itself be a sign of their relative lateness. They keep closely to the themes of the hymn: the dawn as the end of the night watch; the identity of darkness with sin, both banished by the new light; the new resurrection hope that gives God's people a renewed strength and knowledge of his forgiveness.

The following is one of the prayers (also found in *MP*):

> Now that the paean of cockcrow has driven forth the silence of the night, before you O Lord the elder night gives birth to day, heralded by the cockerel's flourish. As they give voice to a

jubilant morning hymn, so, Lord, to you in heaven be given praise; you who command the dissolution of darkness by the incoming rays of the sun. Almighty Father, these wonders are yours alone; we can bring only the pledge of ourselves, offering to your holy name this morning sacrifice; that we may be acquitted of and escape our sins, made worthy to be freed from the danger that threatens. Amen. (col. 240)

In the old Spanish rites, all prayers have 'Amen' without a doxology and then, another doxology and a second 'Amen':

Per misericordiam tuam Deus noster, qui es benedictus, et vivis, et omnia regis in saecula saeculorum. Amen. (Through your mercy, O our God, who live and reign and who are blessed for ever and ever. Amen.)

THE CANONICAL PSALMS WITH THEIR ANTIPHONS AND COLLECTS

Psalms 3, 50 and 56 are 'canonical' in the sense that they are, according to rule, always the same and the antiphons and the psalms were all sung to the same melody, as is made clear by *AL*. Psalm 3 is used alone in Eastertide. Bishop concluded that the group was not original, not being found in *OV*, and Psalm 3 alone being required for special occasions.[6] *AL* gives a large set of undifferentiated antiphons for these psalms, arranged in sets of three, and comprising texts from each of the psalms in turn.[7] In this source 'Psalm 3' in the rubrics often indicates the use of all three. One document gives 52 antiphons for these psalms and 12 prayers to follow them, and *MP* gives three antiphons and a choice of two prayers for a Sunday in ordinary time.[8] Usually the prayers quote all three psalms so they are not real psalm collects but prayers that synchronize themes from these psalms.

Pinell concluded that the prayers were the work of a single seventh-century author, implying that the group of psalms was in use before then, at least informally and, as a result of this practice, the saying of Psalm 50 before the Canticle was dropped in order to avoid duplication. Psalm 50 had been the original introductory feature of the Cathedral Matins.[9]

In the monastic office, the three psalms were used daily at Nocturns, but on Sunday Psalms 46, 99 and 116 were substituted.[10] It seems, then, that a monastic beginning to the office was adopted by the cathedral and parish churches and the alternative use was established in order to avoid duplication. Isidore's reference to the canonical psalms probably intended the monastic use.[11] It was possibly for monastic use too, that the prayers were composed in the seventh century. The whole unit was perhaps adopted by the cathedral ordo in the next or even in the ninth century.

The antiphons with each psalm are also found in *AL*. Several are short and could have originated as easily memorized responses, e.g. 'Domini est salus, et super populum tuum benedictio tua' (Salvation is from the Lord, and your blessing is upon your people), an ordinary Sunday antiphon in both *Br*. (col. 80) and *AL*.[12] In the Grail Psalter Psalm 3 is subtitled 'Confidence under persecution; a morning prayer', and the antiphons maintain this same theme of confidence in the face of adversity.

The prayers too are general, not seasonal. Only three out of thirteen in *Br*. have festal themes. As an example, this prayer is from the Sixth Sunday after the Epiphany octave (col. 233) and the Fifth Sunday of Lent:

> Lord our upholder, our glory and the lifter up of our heads, who enrich us in your mercy: cleanse our innermost hearts from guilt and purify us of polluting sins; send from heaven and save us from those who oppress us; so that hastening back to this your altar; we may offer to you a morning sacrifice in the temple. Amen.

The prayer quotes from Psalm 3.3 and Psalm 56.3 with general echoes of Psalm 50, and is listed in *T4*.

PSALM 3 WITH ANTIPHON AND COLLECT (Sundays of Eastertide and most weekdays)

As we have already indicated above the invitatory use of Psalm 3 alone may be older than the use of all three canonical psalms. On the other hand, on the weekdays of the fragmentary cycle in *Br*. and on a great many feasts, Psalm 50 takes its place. Psalm 3 is always used in Tradition A. In Pinell's reconstruction of *LOP*, he dated the psalm collects from the sixth century and divided them into four chronological series.[13] The first and second series have only one collect used in *Br*. for Psalm 3, but the third series has no fewer than seven, of which six are found in *Br*. Pinell surmises that this group may have been originally provided for each day of the week. If his further hypothesis is correct and Leander of Seville was the author, then the collects were written before his death in 596. This would mean that Psalm 3 was in use as an invitatory from at least the early sixth century, Leander adding the collects to draw out the themes of the psalm.

In the Roman and Benedictine offices Psalm 94 (*Venite*) was the normal invitatory of Matins. Psalm 3 was popular in monastic circles to begin prayer in the night because of the theme of waking from sleep: 'I laid down to rest and sleep. I awoke, for the Lord sustains me.' This use of Psalm 3 was also common in the East. It would then appear that we have a version of a monastic type of vigil *preceding* the cathedral morning prayer proper, and the first element of this vigil was a psalm closely connected with such vigils in their normal monastic form.

Twelve prayers are associated with this psalm in *Br*. One of the two not in Pinell's *LOP* is found in both Traditions A and B for Easter Sunday and throughout Eastertide; 'Domine Jesu Christe, qui pro nobis soporem mortis ideo suscepisti ...' (col. 615) – 'Lord Jesus Christ, who for us undertook the sleep of death ...'. Though not a psalm collect it takes the theme of waking that is found in the psalm, and applies it to the resurrection. The ten genuine psalm collects are largely found on the weekdays of Advent and Lent and on the other fast days outside Lent. The following is a good example because frequently used:

> Although, Lord, the great horde of evildoers deny it, our salvation is in you, Lord our God; to us however, from this strength comes an increase of hope, for you deign to be our shield: so then, stop the mouth that speaks iniquity, and lovingly surround with your mercy those who hope in you. Amen. (col. 150)

The prayer quotes verse 3 of the psalm – it is appointed 18 times in Lent and for fast days. Pinell notes the theme of persecution here, perhaps by Arian heretics.[14] It remains, like the psalm, an expression of hope in the certainty of God's eventual vindication of those who remain faithful.

There are only fifteen antiphons for Psalm 3 on its own and of these, only two are in any sense seasonal. For the most part, then, we can say that the prayers take up the theme established by the antiphons and all of these themes are simply ways of expressing the same ideas: that we may have confidence and trust in the Lord who is our refuge, and who banishes the darkness of night that represents sin and evil. The prayers for the canonical psalms, as we have seen, elaborate on these themes but the general thrust is the same, an invitatory that calls on God's people to arise and take up their stand against evil in the power of God's protection.

PSALM 50 WITH ANTIPHON AND COLLECT (see p. 63, no. 5)

On the Wednesday of the first three weeks of Advent, on the Tuesdays and Fridays of the fourth and fifth[15] weeks of Advent and on Christmas Eve, Psalm 50 is used instead of Psalm 3 as the Matins invitatory. The same collect is used each time and this same collect is also used on the first three Fridays of Advent, the fourth and fifth Wednesdays and on the only Saturday for which an office is supplied, the fifth, but on those days Psalm 56 is the invitatory psalm. The collect, 'Deus Dei Filius ...' is not listed by Pinell in *LOP*.

The incomplete weekday cycle also uses Psalm 50 as the invitatory of Matins, as do the Friday and Saturday of that week when the Offices for the Sick and of the Blessed Virgin Mary supply the missing days. Then, most interestingly, although in Tradition A MSS such as *AL* Psalm 3 is used on the feasts of saints, in *Br.* all feasts of saints use Psalm 50 instead. The office of the departed also follows this custom.

An examination of the antiphons and collects connected with Psalm 50 both at the beginning of the office and before the Canticle, shows the following interesting features:

- All the prayers appointed for the weekday cycle are also used before the Canticle on other days and often the same antiphon is used in both places.[16]
- There is, again, little connection with any feast or season.
- It is the whole unit, antiphon, psalm and collect, that appears to be movable, and it may be found in either place at Matins.
- The unit is only found *before* the Canticle on days when Psalm 3 is used alone at the beginning, and these are all days that may be regarded as penitential: the fasts in January, before Pentecost, September and November, and in Lent.

On some days Psalm 3 is used by *Br.* as the invitatory at services which have no trace of Psalm 50 at all: in Eastertide, on Christmas Day, the Circumcision, the Epiphany, the Invention of the Holy Cross (which always falls during Eastertide), and the more recently composed office of Corpus Christi. In addition, Christmas, Circumcision and Epiphany have an extra Antiphon and prayer before the Canticle that do not reflect the themes that one would normally associate with Psalm 50.

Bradshaw noted the universality of the use of Psalm 50 at Matins and thought that the psalm may well have originated in the cathedral tradition. He quoted Gregory of Tours' description of an office comprising Psalm 50, the Canticle from David 3, Psalms 148–50 and the *capitellum*.[17] Caesarius of Arles regarded the psalm as a daily component of Matins and seemed to envisage a system where at the end of Vigils, the morning service commenced with Psalm 50.[18] Aurelian, in Arles after Caesarius (546–553), spoke of Psalm 50 beginning Nocturns, not Matins.[19] The Roman Lauds commenced with Psalm 50 on weekdays, a practice carried over into the Rule of the Master and later Roman and Benedictine use. The latter further prefixed Psalm 66 as an 'assembling psalm'. At Milan, there were no Canticles on weekdays and Psalm 50 immediately preceded Psalms 148–50. Similar patterns are found in the East, Psalm 50 normally commencing the morning office as we can see from Taft's reconstructed Cappadocian Matins.[20] In the Armenian office the psalm follows the vigil and precedes Psalms 148–50. In modern Byzantine Orthodox use, Psalm 50 comes after the lengthy monastic *psalmodia currens* and before the Canticles, the Canon of Matins.

It is then reasonable to conclude that Psalm 50 was once almost universally used as the opening element of the service of morning prayer. And if that is so, how does this square with the fact that in the old Spanish sources, the psalm is found before the vigil psalmody at Matins but after it at other times? Before attempting to answer that question, we will examine some of the texts.

As an example of the prayers listed to accompany Psalm 50 as an invitatory in the fragmentary weekday cycle:

> According to the multitude of your mercies, Lord, blot out our offences, and because they weigh upon us, lift them from us: a humbled contrite heart in us do not spurn: but by the Holy Spirit may the power of the ineffable Trinity dwell in us; renewing a right spirit, sustaining a spirit of fervour; and may goodness be its only proof, so that renewed by the Father and sustained by the Son, we may be kept always in joy by the Holy Spirit. Amen. (col. 195)

Whether at the beginning of the office or before the Canticle, this prayer is always associated with the same antiphon: 'Secundum magnum misericordiam tuam dele Domine iniquitates meas' ('According to the multitude of your mercies, do away my offences') from verse 1, and quoted in the first lines of the prayer.

The antiphons and prayers that occur only when Psalm 50 appears before the Canticle are not usually tied to any season; e.g. the prayers, 'Miserator Domine' (col. 349) of the second Wednesday of Lent and 'Quinquagesimum psalmum' (col. 547) of the fifth Friday of Lent. They are all rather general texts and usually have no essential connection with the Lenten or fast days for which they are appointed. The prayers tend to be penitential in tone, because they are part of a penitential beginning to the office.

On feast-days, as we have seen, *Br.* uses Psalm 50, while Tradition A documents use Psalm 3. There are, however, very few variants in both the antiphon and the prayer: four antiphons for saints' days or the common offices, and of the two most frequently used, 'Labia mea, Domine, aperies' ('O Lord, open my lips') from verse 15 is cited 35 times in *Br.* (e.g. col. 125), and 'Da nobis laetitiam' ('give us joy'), from verse 12, 32 times (e.g. col. 133), the latter usually for the celebrations of more than one saint. Five prayers accompany Psalm 50 on these festal occasions, of which three are listed in *LOP* as psalm collects.

As an example of an antiphon:

> Give to us the joy of your help: with a spirit of fervour sustain us, Lord.

And a prayer:

> Give us again the joy of your help, Lord; that we be loosed from the iniquity we bear and our neglects passed over; so that you may call us to the joy restored to us; and with sins driven forth, righteousness may enter in, unfaithfulness be repulsed, and eternal joy made present. We beseech you, grant that with this joyfulness we may be worthy to attain eternal salvation. Amen.

This antiphon and prayer are used at the beginning of Matins on the feasts of the Holy Innocents (col. 133–4), Sts Peter and Paul on 29 June (col. 1141) and also on such typically Spanish feasts as St Torquatus and his companions (1 May, col. 1113) and Sts Adrian and Natalia (17 June, col.1126). Although these are feast days, there is nothing especially festal about the antiphon or the collect – rather, they are very appropriate for use with Psalm 50 at the beginning of the office on any day.

If, as elsewhere in the world, the ancient morning office in Spain started with Psalm 50, then we may describe this psalm as the original invitatory. How then did Psalm 3 become the actual first element of this office on some days and Psalm 50 find its place halfway through the office; while on Sundays, both of these psalms, together with Psalm 56, made up the complex invitatory group of the canonical Psalms?

A clue may lie in the constant Eastertide use of Psalm 3 and the total exclusion of Psalm 50 from the Matins of that season. We have already shown that although Psalm 3 was a common invitatory to monastic *night* offices, it was not universal. Possibly the Spanish cathedral office, in the natural process of 'festivalization', adopted Psalm 3 because of its resurrectional overtones as an alternative to Psalm 50 which might seem too penitential for Eastertide: 'I lie down to rest and I sleep. I wake for the Lord upholds me' is certainly appropriate for Easter.

The collect is common to both Spanish traditions:

> Lord Jesus Christ, who for us undertook the sleep of death, that we should no longer slumber in death; grant that in dying to you, we may be reborn, living also for you as we rise from the bed of sin; and let us not be overburdened by the punishment our sins deserve, you who redeem us by your holy and precious blood that we may rejoice with you. Amen. (col. 615)

This prayer, addressed as it is to the second person of the Trinity, would be unacceptable to Arians, so there may have been an apologetic interest in using it thus in Eastertide. Monastic traditions would also influence the use of Psalm 3 at the beginning of the office on other days and especially on Sundays, the weekly commemoration of the resurrection.

The hypothetical stages of the development may now be set out as follows:

Stage 1 Psalm 50 is the first element at Matins each day.

Stage 2 Psalm 50 is the invitatory on ordinary days but Psalm 3 replaces it in Eastertide.

Stage 3 The increasing use of a cathedral vigil of psalms with prayers and later, Antiphons with prayers (as we shall see in the next chapter) on Sundays and saints' days, pushes Psalm 50 back to before these vigil elements.

Stage 4 Barcelona insists on Psalm 50 being recited before the Canticle, so Psalm 3 becomes the only invitatory on the next two strata of days to which a vigil is appended; the period *de*

Traditione and then, the fast days and the other Lenten weekdays.

Stage 5 Possibly because of older customs and possibly because of distance from Barcelona, in some places other days, such as saints' days, continue to commence Matins with Psalm 50.

Stage 6 Meanwhile the monastic custom of the canonical psalms results in the use of Psalms 3 and 50 together on Sundays, with Psalm 56 added in order to form a symmetrical group of three psalms.

Stage 7 In the later regulations of the Advent cycle, Psalm 56 is used as an invitatory on certain weekdays but, being a later addition to the weekday offices, has to make do with a borrowed collect normally associated with Psalm 50 in that season.

NOTES

1 P. Borella, 'Il Breviario Ambrosiano' in: M. Righetti (ed.) *Manuale di Storia Liturgica II* (Milano: Ancora, 1946), pp. 603–41.
2 *Rule of St Benedict* 9 and 12.
3 For full discussion, see R. Taft, *The Liturgy of the Hours in East and West* (Collegeville: Liturgical Press, 1986), pp. 191ff.
4 Trans. T. J. G. S. Cooper.
5 E.g., J. P. Gilson (ed.), *The Mozarabic Psalter (MP)* (London: Henry Bradshaw Society, 1905), p. 352.
6 W. C. Bishop, ed. C. L. Feltoe, *The Mozarabic and Ambrosian Rites* (London: Alcuin/Mowbrays 1924), p. 84.
7 *Antifonario Visigotico Mozarabe de la Catedral de Leon (AL)*, ed. L. Brou and J. Vives (Madrid: Monumenta Hispaniae Sacra, ser lit. 5 (1959), ff. 287–8v.
8 *MP*, p. 363.
9 J. Pinell (ed.), *Liber Orationum Psalmographus (LOP)* (Barcelona-Madrid: Monumenta Hispaniae Sacra IX, 1972), Introduction, p. [291].
10 See, e.g., *MP*, pp. 307 and 312.
11 *PL* 83, col. 867.
12 *AL*, f. 288v.
13 *LOP*, pp. [175]ff.
14 *LOP*, pp. [283]ff.
15 Advent is six weeks long, as is that in Milan.
16 See, e.g., *PL* 86, cols 191 and 459; 204 and 449.
17 See P. F. Bradshaw, *Daily Prayer in the Early Church* (London: Alcuin/SPCK, 1981), pp. 82, 118; Taft, op. cit., p. 146.
18 Bradshaw, ibid.; Taft, pp. 154–5.
19 Bradshaw, op. cit., pp. 127–8.
20 Taft, op. cit., p. 41.

10

THE ANTIPHONS OF MATINS AND THE QUESTION OF THE PSALTER IN COURSE

In *Br.*, with the exception of the canonical psalms and certain others of frequent occurrence, there is an almost total absence of complete psalms, as we have already seen at Vespers. On certain days there are indications of psalm numbers between an antiphon and a collect, on other days there is the 'Antiphon', a unit comprising what we normally call an antiphon, psalm (or other scriptural) verse and *Gloria*, with a collect that probably draws its theme from the antiphon. After three Antiphons or three antiphons with psalm numbers, there is a Responsory, the structure of which is very similar to the Antiphon and which may have a prayer attached to it. On feasts, the whole complex of three Antiphons with prayers and a Responsory (known as a *Missa*) may be repeated several times.

Bishop recognized that the cathedral office used selected psalms and not the whole Psalter in course, and he gave as an example the office for the Sunday before the Epiphany.[1] He concluded that the psalm verse of the Antiphon stood for a whole psalm or part of a psalm that had been reduced to a single verse, and in that case the *Missa Psalmorum* of *OV* originally comprised three psalms and a Responsory, or even four full psalms. Isidore described the *Missa* as a series of psalms sung by a soloist to which the congregation or choir responded, and which developed into a form in which two or three sang verses.[2]

Both *AL* and *Br.* provide offices for the first half of Lent that expect there to be complete psalms in each Antiphon of Matins, Terce, Sext and None. The second half of Lent has Antiphons with a psalm verse only. *AL* provides an irregular reading of the whole Psalter, with a few omissions, spread over the three weeks. Porter's table of this scheme is the basis for the following, to which has been added, in square brackets, the numbers of the psalms appointed for the same days in *Br.* (corrected with reference to Janini's edition of *T2*).[3]

DAILY PRAYER IN CHRISTIAN SPAIN

		Week 1	Week 2	Week 3
Sunday	Vesp.		121, 118.41	124, 118.90
Mon.	Matins	1, 2, 104	34, 34, 110	78, 79, 115
		[1, 2, 4]	[1, 2, 9]	[18, 19, 21]
	Terce	4, 5, 6	35, 36, 36	80, 81, 82
		[9, 10, 11]	[9, 10, 11]	[21, 31, 32]
	Sext	7, 7, 8	36, 37, 37	83, 83, 84
		[13, 15, 17]	[122, 123, 124]	[32, 33, 35]
	None	9, 9, 9	38, 39, 39	85, 85, 86
		[21, 18, 19]	[21, 21, 27]	[32, 33, 33]
	Vespers	118.1 [27]	118.49 [74]	118.97 [65]
Tues.	Matins	10, 10, 104	40, 41, 111	87, 87, 116
		[28, 31, 32]	[32, 32, 33]	[44, 45, 43]
	Terce	11, 11, 12	43, 43, 44	88, 88, 88
		[32, 33, 35]	[44, 45, 53]	[48, 57, 59]
	Sext	13, 14, 15	44, 45, 46	89, 89, 90
		[43, 44, 45]	[57, 125, 123]	[44, 45, 53]
	None	16, 16, 16	47, 47, 48	91, 92, 93
		[48, 64, 65]	[59, 65, 69]	[64, 65, 95]
	Vespers	119, 118.9	122, 118.57	125, 118.105
		[59]	[128]	[13]
Wed.	Matins	17, 17, 105	49, 49, 112	94, 95, 117
		[15, 68, 69]	[136, 72, 73]	[88, 64, 71]
	Terce	17, 17, 17	51, 52, 53	96, 97, 97
		[59, 71, 72]	[124, 82, 82]	[48, 72, 73]
	Sext	18, 18, 18	54, 55, 57	98, 99, 100
		[122, 128, 129]	[60, 129, 130]	[74, 75, 76]
	None	19, 19, 20	58, 59, 59	101, 101, 102
		[–]	[–]	[–]
	Vespers	118.17 [66]	118.65 [115]	118.113 [72]
Thurs.	Matins	21, 21, 105	60, 61, 113	102, 102, 134
		[70, 74, 78]	[91, 93, 94]	[77, 77, 77]
	Terce	22, 23, 23	63, 64, 65	103, 103, 109
		[77, 77, 77]	[101, 101, 102]	[78, 80, 81]
	Sext	24, 24, 24	65, 67, 67	128, 130, 131
		[80, 82, 83]	[113, 125, 127]	[82, 82, 85]
	None	25, 25, 26	67, 68, 68	131, 132, 133
		[84, 85, 89]	[134, 136, 144]	[89, 91, 93]
	Vespers	120, 118.25	123, 118.73	126, 118.121
		[113]	[69]	[94]

Fri.	Matins	26, 26, 106	69, 70, 113	136, 137, 134
		[57, 93, 94]	[102, 104, 104]	[77, 77, 77]
	Terce	27, 27, 28	70, 71, 72	138, 138, 139
		[99, 95, 97]	[78, 105, 105]	[88, 104, 104]
	Sext	29, 29, 30	73, 74, 75	139, 140, 141
		[96, 127, 130]	[122, 125, 128]	[105, 105, 105]
	None	30, 30, 31	76, 77, 77	141, 142, 143
		[–]	[–]	[–]
	Vespers	118.33 [125]	118.81 [84]	118.129 [95]
Sat.	Matins	31, 32, 106	77, 77, 114	144, 144, 135
		[101, 102, 102]	[106, 106, 106]	[144, 134, 135]
	Terce	32, 33, 33	77, 77, 77	145, 146, 147
		[104, 105, 105]	[111, 134, 135]	[134, 136, 144]
	Sext	–	–	–
		[106, 114, 122]	[145, 146, 122]	[145, 146, 147]

While *AL* follows a more or less orderly plan, *Br.* and *T2* appear to have no discernible order. The scheme in *AL* omits psalms that are used elsewhere (e.g. 3, 50, 56 and 148–50), also Psalms 108 and 127. Brou, who denied that full psalms were used in the old Spanish cathedral office, examined the second half of Lent and concluded that this was the original material, drawing its psalm verses from an older version of the Latin Psalter, the variant readings being preserved because they may have been set to elaborate music.[4]

When Pinell turned his attention to the *Missa* of Matins in *AL*, he saw the unit as a group of three psalms and a Responsory, later reduced to three antiphons with psalm verses and a Responsory. He showed how a linking word or theme might run through the *Missa*, such as 'veniet' or 'ecce' in Advent and 'exurge' in Lent. Greater feasts multiplied the *Missae*, Epiphany having no fewer than eight in *AL*, all recalling different aspects of the feast.[5]

Pinell suggested that this thematic use may have developed from something once more spontaneous, and questioned whether there had ever been an ordered *Psalmodia currens*. As for the first three weeks of Lent, he showed that the texts in *AL* were not specifically Lenten and so this may be the relics of an ordinary weekday office at which the Psalter was indeed recited in course, especially as the collects were often very general in their themes. (This can only be correct if the cathedral minor hours became an ordinary daily event, instead of something largely confined to penitential seasons.)

Pinell concluded that there had been several arrangements in Spain, spread over particular stages:

1 whole psalms with antiphons and collects;
2 whole psalms recited only in the ferial office until the rite was suppressed in the eleventh century;
3 the gathering into Antiphoners like *AL* of the material for the Antiphons of Lent and for feasts;
4 no single arrangement for reciting the psalter was in use but
5 the most likely one spread the Psalter over three weeks.

As has been seen, the arrangement of the psalms in *Br.* and *T2* is very disordered by comparison with *AL*, which only omits nine psalms from its three-week psalter while *Br.* omits 71. In order to try to understand this contrast, we shall first examine the rationale for arranging the Psalter for worship in any form of consecutive recitation.

SYSTEMS FOR RECITING THE PSALTER

Most ancient cathedral offices used psalms that were selected for their suitability to the time of day. Egeria mentioned ascetics coming together in church *before* the cathedral offices to recite psalms and antiphons. This may differ from the use of selected psalms at any of the services she described. The early monks and these urban ascetics of Egeria aimed at the ideal of 'praying without ceasing' and drew their spiritual nourishment from the Psalter.[6] Many committed the psalms to memory and perhaps recited the whole Psalter every twenty-four hours. As with all reading at that time, recitation would be aloud even by those praying on their own. An alternative was for one to recite while the others listened in silence.

John Cassian described Egyptian monks c. 380–399 as occupying the night with psalmody according to the so-called 'Angelic rule' of a group of 12 psalms.[7] As Taft said, monastic psalmody was a twice-daily meditation (evening and morning) taken in common. The subject of the meditation was the psalms and the time of day was immaterial.

As already mentioned, there were urban monasteries elsewhere which combined meditative psalmody with the cathedral evening and morning offices, so these ascetics had their own prayer and also joined in the popular cathedral services. The continuous psalmody was often carried out at night, concluding at sunrise with the cathedral morning office. A constant feature almost everywhere was the grouping of the psalms in threes, widely known in Latin as a *Missa* as e.g. in Spain. St Benedict too spoke of psalms in multiples of three at the night offices.

The following important features of this development are relevant to understanding the old Spanish offices:

1 Monks carried out their office of psalmody in course before the morning and evening services of the people as a whole.
2 The psalms were normally grouped in threes.
3 As in the East, the greater number of psalms was recited in the night/morning.
4 Most Western cathedral offices were supplemented and eventually swamped by the monastic service.

As one example of how another system is used, the Byzantine Matins have two *Kathismata* each day in summer, Vespers have one (each *Kathisma* is divided into three *staseis*, and each *stasis* has three medium-length psalms or the equivalent). *Kathisma* 1 (Psalms 1–8) is recited on Saturday night, Sunday night has no Psalter in course and there is a swop over late on in the week so that Psalm 118 is said at Saturday Matins (an ancient custom). In this system Psalm 140, the central *fixed* psalm of Vespers, is also said on Friday morning! An alternative system exists to ensure the recitation of the Psalter twice a week in Lent.

Another example; the Milanese system of *Decuriae* is combined with the Roman system. *Decuriae* are spread over the Mondays to Fridays of a two-week period with, in the first week, the first half of Psalm 118 on Saturday, and the following week, the second half. Sunday Nocturns had canticles instead. The remaining psalms, except 117, 133 and 142, were assigned to Vespers in a one-week cycle – obviously the Roman system adopted somewhat uncritically.

The old Roman and Benedictine systems were similar to one another. There is a more sophisticated avoidance of duplication, but the greater part of the Psalter is still appointed for Matins or Vigils, with Psalms 109–147 (excepting Psalm 118, used at the minor hours) allotted to Vespers. It appears that Benedict simplified the Roman system, introducing more variety into the minor hours and thus was able to reduce the number of psalms at Vespers from five to four. The original ideal inspiring the recitation of so many psalms was to pray after each one, but the periods of silence following each psalm rapidly disappeared from all these arrangements. Dom Adalbert de Vogue believes there was still space for prayer after each psalm in St Benedict's concept of the night office.[8]

THE PSALTER IN COURSE IN SPAIN

By contrast with all these arrangements, Spain seems to have known only this three-week cycle of the first three weeks of Lent. This differs from other arrangements, not only in being spread over three weeks but also in having psalms in course spread over minor hours that normally have fixed psalms. The reason for this contrast may lie in the night services of the Spanish monks, which Pinell established were four in number, not three as Porter supposed: *ad Medium Noctis*, *Peculiaris Vigilia*, *Nocturnos* and *post Nocturnos*.[9] *Peculiaris Vigilia* and *ad Nocturnos* had *missae psalmorum* after introductory sections and *post Nocturnos* had twelve psalms after the introductory verse. *Nocturnos* had nine psalms on weekdays and twelve on Sundays and festivals. Isidore referred to pauses for prayer but not to collects which may have died out, or which simply never existed in the monastic office.

It is difficult disentangling the various testimonies but it is possible to state that the night was punctuated by services. These services largely consisted of psalms in groups of three:

- *ad Medium Noctis*, three introductory psalms (41, 132 and 133).
- *Peculiaris Vigilia*, three canticles and then nine psalms and three more canticles, with Responsories after each group of three.
- *ad Nocturnos*, three introductory psalms (3, 50 and 56 or 46, 99 and 116 on Sundays) then three *Missae* from the Psalter in order, with Responsories at the end of each.
- *post Nocturnos*, 12 psalms as they occur in order from where Nocturns left off.[10]

These offices developed in several books, later collated into a single *liber Horarum*. Fundamental to this process was the *Responsorial* with its basic 24 ferial responsories, four for each day of the week at Nocturns. This was, Pinell suggests, a system of simple recitation of three psalms followed by one sung responsorially.[11] On Sunday the Responsorial psalm would be Alleluiatic, which paved the way for increasing 'festivalization' of this unit when it became a Responsory of the cathedral office. The monastic form retained the simple structure of reciting these Responsorial psalms in psalter order. The more ancient Alleluiatic responsories remained part of both traditions.

In *Br.* the following psalms occur in Responsories in the fragmentary weekday cycle:

Monday	Matins, Psalm 24 and Terce, Psalm 50 (cols 191 and 194)
Tuesday	Matins, Psalm 26, also at Terce (cols 196 and 198)
Wednesday	Matins, Psalm 39 and Terce, Psalm 25 (cols 200 and 202)
Thursday	Matins, Psalm 123 and Terce, Psalm 108 (verse, Ps. 30), (cols 204 and 206)

This may indicate that a repertoire of Responsorial psalms was originally drawn upon to produce these Responsories.

Pinell divided the Alleluiatic Responsories into four categories; those with very brief responses, the more extended, those that followed the sense rather than the letter of the psalm and last, the very extended texts. These Responsories provided a repertoire from which texts were drawn as needed. Those with short responses, easier to memorize, are probably more ancient. This ancient Responsorial psalmody was combined with the perhaps more simply recited psalms of the monastic cursus said in order.

In the course of the night the monks must have recited around thirty psalms, finishing perhaps just before cathedral Matins. As Psalm 118 was used in the day hours and inter-hours, this would give ample opportunity for the monks to cover the entire Psalter in a week. Such a practice would be similar to that of Milan, the bulk of the psalmody being discharged at night. Similarly, the Spanish system may well have divided up the psalms without regard for duplicating those found elsewhere, as was also the case at Milan. It may be that the original Northern Italian monastic use was to recite three *decuriae* each night, a *pensum* of about thirty psalms, just as in Spain.

With so much Conciliar legislation directed at keeping the cathedral and monastic offices distinct, the peculiarly monastic night psalmody was probably not adopted by the Spanish cathedral office. The three-week arrangement of the first three weeks of Lent in *AL* would then be a later cathedral modification of the monastic Psalter in course. While the monks multiplied psalms, the cathedral office in Spain retained the ancient custom of praying after each psalm with a psalm collect.

Pinell also suggested that there developed a cathedral vigil that eventually was added before Matins on all occasions, and was a shortened version of the sort of vigil found in monastic practice; three variable psalms and a psalm formed into a Responsory, preceded by an introductory psalm, i.e. an introduction and a single *Missa*.[12] We have already seen that by the sixth century monasteries may not have been using psalm collects. The introduction of a vigil into cathedral worship could have been the incentive to authors like Justus of Urgel, Leander of Seville and Conancius of Palencia to compose or collect together suitable prayers, so that congregations of ordinary Christians could draw some greater spiritual value from the psalms used.

Pinell detects four strata in the psalm collects that survive; the first are usually of a short and pithy nature, perhaps based on already known examples; the second reflect a more ascetic and world-renouncing spirituality; the third are concerned with the struggles against Arians and others; and the fourth reflect a situation of opposition and perhaps persecution, but also a more mature theological synthesis. This pattern fits very well that of the life of Leander of Seville. Pinell goes even further and identifies the rather different liturgy of the St Gall palimpsest with that of Justus of Urgel who was also known to be a composer of psalm collects, and the collects of the Sunday Antiphons in Tradition A are identified with Conancius.

Since a more ordered cycle of psalms is found in the fragmentary weekday cycle, this will be dealt with before considering the Lenten arrangements in detail.

The Psalms used in the Missae of the Fragmentary Weekday Cycle

This cycle is unusual because it provides Terce on non-penitential weekdays, but no other minor hours. The psalms or parts of psalms are distributed over the three offices of Matins, Terce and Vespers, as follows:

Monday	Matins, 1, 2, 4	Terce, 5, 6, 7	Vespers, 8
Tuesday	Matins, 9, 9, 9	Terce, 10, 11, 12	Vespers, 13
Wednesday	Matins, 15, 16, 16	Terce, 17, 17, 17	Vespers, 14
Thursday	Matins, 18, 19, 20	Terce, 21, 21, 21[13]	

It would be possible to extend this pattern in much the same way, dividing up the longer psalms and avoiding using the 'Canonical Psalms' and Psalms 148–50 and also keeping the occasional shorter psalm out of order to be used at Vespers (see Wednesday above), thus ending up with a four-week or five-week cycle.

If such a system were once common, then we should note the following features of it: first, the scheme omits Sundays (we will see that there are traces of a different cycle for Sunday use). Second, this cycle must originate in a period in which the *Matutinarium* psalms have been reduced to a single verse (e.g. Psalm 5 is included at Monday Terce and elsewhere in *Br.* it is usually only used in the *Matutinarium*; see below). Third, the otherwise inexplicable occurrence of Terce on an ordinary weekday may be simply to provide a vehicle for a *psalmodia currens* that could be completed in a reasonable length of time for, otherwise, one would need some eight weeks to carry out the same pattern and complete the Psalter.

With a few exceptions the collects accompanying these psalms are to be found elsewhere with the same psalms, so we may assume that psalms and prayers together were brought into this scheme at a date posterior to that of the composition of the actual collects.

The Psalms and Psalm Collects of the First Three Weeks of Lent

In the course of Matins, Terce, Sext, None and Vespers of the first three weeks of Lent, 78 psalms are cited in *Br.*, presumably to be recited complete or in parts.[14] No attempt seems to be made to carry out any kind of orderly recitation of the Psalter. Of the 78 psalms, 18 are used in all three weeks and another 43 are used in two weeks out of three. There are then only 17 psalms that occur only one week each in this 'cycle', and four of them occur twice in the same week, sometimes at different times of the day. While there would appear to be some sort of order at the very beginning, with psalms 1, 2 and 4 at Matins on Mondays of the first week of Lent, 9, 10 and 11 following at Terce, and 13, 15 and 17 at Sext, at None, the order is lost and we find 21, 18 and 19 in that order. From then on although there appears to be a tendency to adhere to psalter order within each *missa*, there are many jumps and reversals of position.

There is no real relation to the hour of the day; Psalm 4 is an obvious night psalm and occurs at Matins, several psalms that are also used as *Matutinaria* (18, 64, 66, 75, 77 and 89) occur in the Antiphons and of them, Psalm 18 appears both at None and at Matins, 35 in both Terce and Sext, 64 at None and Matins, 66 at Vespers, 75 at Sext, 77 at Terce and Matins and 89 at None. The only possible remaining way in which the scheme could have been arrived at, must have been by consideration of their themes or of the themes that the liturgist editors wished to draw from these psalms.

On the Wednesday of the first week of Lent we find Psalms 15, 68 and 69 at Matins (col. 288); in English the antiphons are:

Keep us, Lord, for in you we hope, you O Lord, are our heritage.

Seek the Lord and your soul will live.
Come to our aid, Lord, make haste to our rescue.

The themes of all three psalms are those of hope and confidence in God in spite of difficulties and dangers. Of the prayers, that for Psalm 15, *Conserve nos, Domine in timore*, is a prayer for forgiveness with phrases such as 'keep us from the contagion of sin'. The other two prayers, *Quaerentibus te* and *Intende in adjutorium*, both quote the antiphons and seek the Lord's protection for his people: 'Lord, impart life to the souls of those who seek you ...' and 'Come to our aid, Lord, and quickly increase your assistance to us ...'

In Terce on the same day are cited Psalms 59, 71 and 72 (col. 292) with the antiphons:

Help us with your right hand and reply, O God, you have spoken in your holy place.
Pity the poor and weak and save the lives of the poor, Lord.
How good is God to Israel, to those pure of heart.

The first of the prayers is for God's help in time of tribulation, the second that he spare those who call upon him and the third (the *Completuria*) asks that those who place their hope in God's reign may obtain their wish. At Sext, Psalms 122, 128 and 129 have the antiphons:

To you have we lifted up our eyes, you who dwell in the heavens, have mercy on us.
The blessing of the Lord be upon you, we have blessed you in the name of the Lord.
With the Lord there is mercy; and plenteous redemption. (col. 294)

God is prayed to have mercy and spare those who look to him fearful of their sins, to grant help against oppressors, while lifting from our backs the heavy burden of sin, and that our prayers from the very depths be accepted that we may rise to share the perpetual joy of heaven.

There is no None as, on Wednesdays and Fridays of Lent, the Eucharist was traditionally celebrated at the ninth hour instead. At Vespers, Psalm 66 with the antiphon: 'The Lord our God has blessed us. May God still give us his blessing till the ends of the earth revere him' (cols 294-5) brings the office of the day to an end.

From a prayer of confidence in God's mercy through the realization that he protects his people and gives hope of eternal redemption, we come at Vespers to a fitting song of confident joy in the knowledge that God is among his people and upholding them. This picture fits well with a day when the Gospel of the Eucharist is the account of Jesus' temptation in the wilderness, Matthew 4.1–12. Several eucharistic texts, notably the *inlatio* (Preface), stress fasting and prayer as the remedy for the attacks of evil (see *PL* 85, col. 309). Further examples can be found, though many themes are very general.

Compilers may have drawn appropriate psalms, antiphons and prayers from a large repertoire in order to express themes such as God's merciful protection and forgiveness, themes entirely suited to Lent. If *T2* was typical of a parish liturgy at the church of Sts Justa and Rufina in Toledo,[15] then this may be the pattern of old Spanish liturgy as it might have been performed outside the greater monastic churches. In such places, *psalmodia currens* may never have had much importance and anyway, monks and nuns recited the Psalter in course during their long night offices.

The Psalms in the Period de Traditione

Except for Vespers and for None of the fourth Tuesday, *Br*. does not give psalm numbers in the Antiphons for this second half of Lent. Also the prayers are of the festal kind and not psalm collects; in fact they are Antiphon prayers of the type that would be found in the *Orationale* rather than *LOP*. The *Completuriae* of these offices are, however, psalm collects arranged in psalm order. While there may be vestiges here of an older use of psalms, such vestiges are so fragmentary as to be unrecoverable. This period concentrated on the theme of the passion from an early stage and was therefore heavily 'festivalized'.

The Psalms of the Fasts outside Lent

In *Br*. these fasts are before the Epiphany, before Pentecost, and in September and November. Psalms are cited for Matins, Terce, Sext, None and Vespers for each day except the last, which normally does not have Sext, None or Vespers (the latter being replaced by First Vespers of the feast being prepared for). There appears to be no system other than choosing very general themes of the worship of, and hope in God. The November fast does emphasize prayer for protection and arranges its psalms accordingly (cols 724–40). Not only may there have been local traditions of psalm selection for these fasts, there seems to be confusion as to how many fasts there should be. Ortiz may have tried to combine differing traditions, or he simply arranged the material from different sets of undifferentiated antiphons and psalms. He also used the material of the first day of the November fast as the service for Ash Wednesday, newly created for the printed books (col. 246).

The Antiphons of the Ordinary Sundays

In *Br.* orders of Sunday Matins all have three Antiphons (there are no cathedral minor hours on Sundays), comprising an antiphon, psalm verse with *Gloria* and a psalm collect. In Tradition A the Sunday *Missa* for the most part uses Antiphon collects instead. Pinell thinks that the festal type of Antiphon was not developed for ordinary Sundays in Tradition B, which latter retained an older use that was more similar to that of weekdays, especially after Epiphany and Pentecost.[16]

The following table indicates the psalms used in the Antiphons after Epiphany (*Br.* does not give the psalm numbers):

1st Sunday	Pss. 2, 4, 6	(cols 187–8)
2nd Sunday	Pss. 9, 11, 12	(cols 217–18)
3rd Sunday	Pss. 18, 19, 20	(cols 221–2)
4th Sunday	Pss. 45, 84, 21	(cols 225–6)
5th Sunday	Pss. 29/122, 32, 33	(cols 229–30)
6th Sunday	Pss. 21, 84, 61	(cols 233–4)
7th Sunday	Pss. 27/85, 28, 30	(cols 237–8)
8th Sunday	Pss. 122/85, 79, 78	(cols 241-2)
Sunday before Ash Wednesday	Pss. 4, 102, 122	(col. 244)[17]

The first three weeks seem to attempt a *psalmodia currens* quite separate from that of the weekday cycle already discussed. On the other hand, this may have been Ortiz trying to impose order on a set of undifferentiated Antiphons for these Sundays. If, as seems likely, the musical development of these Antiphons advanced further and earlier than in the ferial offices, reducing the psalms to a single verse, then the history of these Antiphons is more similar to those of the festal offices, except that they have remained much more faithful to the Psalter. This is true in spite of the loss of full psalms at quite an early stage. The Sundays after Pentecost are similar but show fewer signs of order. The *Missae* for two of the Sundays after Epiphany will be given and the collects may stand as examples for the weekdays as well, as they are often also used then. (The *Pressa* is omitted for clarity's sake.)

First Sunday after Epiphany

Antiphon I
Serve the Lord with awe, and rejoice in him with trembling, lay hold of instruction – *P* lest he be angry and you perish from the right way. *V* Why this tumult among heathens, among peoples who meditate vain things? *P.* and *Gloria. P.*

Prayer
Before you Lord, we serve with awe, your warning instruction takes hold of us and trembling we rejoice and raise modest joy: you do not allow us to perish from the right way and be lost; but in you, may we confidently expect to find happiness.

Antiphon II
You have put off from us our affliction, O God. *P* Have mercy upon us and hear our prayer. *V* When I called upon thee, O God of justice, you heard me; you have put off from me my affliction. Have mercy on me and hear my prayer. *P. Gloria* and *P.*

Prayer
Lord, you always come to those who invoke you, and your delight is mercifully to work our rescue: grant that, hating always that which is futile and turning away from all that is false, *your Christ (in whom we recognize your greatness)* may be to us the highest and eternal prize in which we shall rejoice.

Antiphon III
Turn O Lord, rescue our souls: save us in your mercy. *P* For in death, no one remembers you. *V* Lord, do not rebuke me in your anger; chasten me not in your wrath. *P. Gloria* and *P.*

Prayer
Lord do not reprove us in your anger; punish us not in your rage: but from harsh words relieve us mercifully; so that instead of the pain of hell, we may grow wiser *by devoting ourselves to your instruction.*

Responsory
The abundance of our iniquities is greater than the expanse of the ocean and now your righteous anger presses down upon our

head: we have sinned, Lord, we have sinned. *V* We have sinned with our fathers, we are wrongdoers, we do evil. *P. Gloria. P.*

The italicized phrases show signs of a common theme of Christ instructing his people to recognize him. The theme at Mass for this day is the finding of Jesus in the Temple as a child (*PL* 85 col. 242 – Luke 2.42–52). The collects are also used on the Monday of the second week of Lent, the Monday after the Epiphany octave at Matins and at the third prayer of Terce on that day; in other words, they go with the psalms.

Seventh Sunday after Epiphany

Antiphon I
Bless Lord, your inheritance: *P* And govern them, raise them up for ever. *V* O Lord, you are good and gentle, full of mercy to all who call. *P. Gloria* and *P.*

Prayer
Lord, *we call upon you in prayer: that you will not withold consolation from us, nor leave us to the devices of our own hearts, neither drag us away with the wicked*; save your people, whom you have created, and bless your inheritance redeemed by your precious blood.

Antiphon II
Give strength to your people, Lord: *P* and bless your people with peace. *V* And govern them, raise them up for ever. *P. Gloria* and *P.*

Prayer
Give strength to your people Lord, against all evil enemies; that your people may be enriched by the blessing of your peace; so for abundant rest, may all in your temple cry 'Glory' to you, giving both praise and honour and, though stained by this evil life, may we always give glory to you.

Antiphon III
Be unto us, Lord, a God to defend us *P* and house of refuge to save us. *V* How great is the multitude of your goodness O Lord, which has been hidden for those that fear you, which you have done for them before the sons of men. *P. Gloria* and *P.*

Prayer
Be, Lord, a protecting God, nor let us be held hostage; may we rejoice in integrity of mind, for in this place may we deserve to find

your protection; for you overshadow us; nothing is so strong as to crush virtue: *nor can we be turned back by temptation, if you pour out upon us* in your generosity, the strength of your right arm and our place of sure refuge.

Responsory
God of power, in tranquillity you judge sinners and with reverence correct faults. You give to sinners a place of repentance: you give time and space, by which we may be cleansed from wickedness. *V* And, Lord God of power, good and forgiving, in patience and in mercy, dispose of us. *P. Gloria* and *P*.

The first Antiphon has an antiphon from Psalm 27 from which is drawn the theme of the collect, which also quotes verses 1 and 3 as well as alluding to 11, the verse of the antiphon. The versicle of the Antiphon is from Psalm 85.4. The other two Antiphons both possess prayers that appear to quote more of their respective psalms than just the verse(s) used for the antiphon. The Gospel of the day is the story of the Prodigal Son (*PL* 85, col. 274 – Luke 15.11–32) and there is a strong emphasis on forgiveness and on being ready to turn back to God's merciful love.

After Pentecost there is less possibility of linking the Matins Antiphons to the Mass reading themes, especially because, whereas *Br.* provides only three Sundays after Pentecost, the Missal provides eight. The rubric at col. 705 suggests that these offices after Pentecost are to be repeated when there are no feasts. Since there were so many feast days in the late Middle Ages, often obscuring the Sunday office, it is possible that three services were felt to suffice.

The Sunday Antiphon of Lent
On the first three Sundays of Lent there are Antiphons and collects in which the psalms are readily identifiable:

Lent 1	Pss. 48, 61 and 84	(cols 260–1)
Lent 2	Pss. 81, 104 and 102	(col. 325)
Lent 3	Pss. 84, 81 and 31	(cols 380–1)

On the First Sunday of Lent, the Gospel is that of the Samaritan woman from John 4.3–42 (*PL* 85, col. 299). The Matins Antiphons have general themes that could go well with the idea of Jesus addressing his mission to the Samaritans and declaring that true worship must be in spirit and in truth (John 4.23). On the Second Sunday, the Gospel is the account of the man born blind (John 9.1–38 – *PL* 85, col. 319). The Antiphons suit the discussion in the Gospel as to whose sins were responsible for the man's blindness (vv. 1–3) and his constancy to Jesus when judgement is laid against him and he is expelled from the synagogue (see vv. 24–34). The Third Sunday has the account of the raising of Lazarus (John 11.1–52 – *PL* 85, col. 337), and the Antiphons stress calling upon God that he might act: 'Revive us now, God our helper! Put an end to your grievance against us' (Ps 84).

It is impossible to suggest more than an hypothesis, that these Antiphons and psalm collects *were* chosen to reflect on, or prepare for, the proclamation of that particular day's Gospel. It is likely that the eucharistic lectionary would have been established early on in the history of the old Spanish liturgy,[18] and it may well be that appropriate psalms and prayers were selected to accompany those readings (then becoming Antiphons with prayers in order to reinforce the theme). This resulted in the Sunday morning service being preceded by a short Vigil that reflected the day's theme.

The *Missa* in the first part of Lent has, as can be seen from the foregoing, a very similar structure and content to the *Missa* as it would appear on ordinary Sundays. Because of this it would be superfluous to give an actual example of a Lenten Sunday *Missa*, as the Sunday examples already given should suffice. However, it is likely that these three Lenten Sundays achieved their present form earlier than those for the ordinary Sundays. The development of both is likely to have been very similar, the theme of the day's Gospel influencing the choice of more or less suitable Psalms/Antiphons and collects from a large repertoire, so as to form the Sunday cathedral vigil.

The Festal Antiphon

In this context, 'festal' must be taken to include both the Sundays and weekdays of the second half of Lent (the period *de Traditione*), and those of Advent and Eastertide as well as the feasts of the Christmas season and Epiphany and of the saints.

Br. does not appear to be as rich in festal Antiphons as the Tradition A manuscripts. Most of the days on which these antiphons and their collects are used have only one *Missa Antiphonarum* consisting of three Antiphons with their collects and a Responsory (usually with a collect). There are 15 days that have more than one *Missa*, and one of the feasts relegated to the Appendix by Lorenzana (All Saints) also has more than one.[19]

The texts of the Antiphons are often taken from the psalms, especially in the period *de Traditione*. Other texts of Scripture are used as well, but the verse is usually from a psalm. It may well be that the Antiphons and psalms originated as an Antiphon with a psalm; festival development was triggered by the collects being derived from the theme of the antiphon rather than from that of the psalm. In the following example (Matins for the Fifth Sunday of Lent, col. 502) we can see how this process was worked out in the context of Antiphons deriving their texts from the Psalter.

Antiphon 1 (Psalm 9)
I sing psalms to your name, O most High. When my enemy be turned back, they shall weaken and shall perish before your face. *V* For you have maintained the justice of my cause; you have sat enthroned, you that judge righteousness.
(*NB Gloria is not said in this season.*)

Prayer
Your church sings psalms to your name for ever, O Most High God; who by the triumph of your passion, turned back the enemies of our souls; we pray therefore, that he with all his accomplices be debilitated and lost, and that we may always have the sufficient protection of your glorious passion.

Antiphon 2 (Psalm 10)
The wicked have bent their bow; they have prepared arrows for the quiver, to shoot down the upright of heart in the dark. For what you have formed they have destroyed; what has the righteous done? *V* The Lord is in his holy temple, in heaven is his throne.

Prayer
Against you, Lord Christ, do malignant sinners draw their bow; nevertheless his own cunning is transfixed by the arrow; so then in the dark of wickedness, the darts from their mouths cannot pierce through; we pray that your passion may be the protection that extricates us from their teeth; so may you, who reckon impious the persecution of the righteous in heart, be to us in all things our protector.

Antiphon 3 (Psalm 11)
Let the Lord destroy all deceitful lips, and the tongue that boasts.

Who say, our tongue is our own, who is Lord over us? Our tongue is our strength, our lips are our own, who is our God? I will grant them the salvation they seek, acting faithfully in it. *V* Save me, O Lord, for there is no righteous one; truth has vanished from the sons of men.

Prayer
Destroy, Lord, all lying lips and the tongue speaking high-sounding words, so that those who refuse to place trust faithfully in your salvation, may be confused in the wickedness of their lips: so that those called by repentance to Christ our Lord, may be effectively made one with us in the tongue of faith; so that all lying lips may ever be destroyed in us.

Responsory
The unjust will say: let us oppress the just man wrongly, and bring down his life even to the grave: let us erase his memory from the earth; *P* And let us divide his goods amongst us: so do the murderers stir up evils for themselves. The foolish and malicious spurn wisdom, and perform the bad deeds they have thought of. *V* They will say, come, let us strike him on the mouth, and listen not to any of his words. *P* And let us.

Prayer
Christ, Son of God, whose life, evil and repressive men plotted against and made to be swallowed up and held in the inferno, attempting to banish your mercy from the world, you who created heaven and earth; we ask and pray that you will make worthy to receive a share in the spoils you sent those who remain firm in faith: bear kindly with the lapses of our frailty, keep us expiating all traces of our sins: and, while our accustomed evil prevents us from being completely restored to union with you, yet unite us with the host of the saints in the hope of praising you in the future.

Although in this *Missa* the psalms occur in a consecutively numbered series, this does not necessarily hold for the *Missae* of this period in general. The Gospel of the day is of the Good Shepherd who lays down his life for the flock (John 10.1–16 – *PL* 85, col. 373).

An example of a *Missa Antiphonarum* of a more developed type is that for the Sunday before the Epiphany (cols 147–8), which is more readily available in the English translation of Bishop.[20] As can be seen there, the verses of these Antiphons are from the psalms, but the antiphons, and the prayers based upon them, are taken from other scriptural sources (Proverbs 8.22a and 26 in Antiphon 1, Isaiah 9.2 in Antiphon 2). As to the psalms used, 44 is often associated with Christmas because of its bridal imagery and 46 deals with God's reign. This *Missa*, then, is a reflection on the themes of Christmas and Epiphany.

Having established the custom of using these psalms at Christmas/Epiphany, the next stage may have been to emphasize further the festal themes by associating other scriptural texts with the psalms, and drawing the themes of the collects from them. At an earlier stage of this development complete psalms may have survived in use with their non-psalmic antiphons (something that can be seen also in the festal offices of the Roman and other ancient Western Breviaries); eventually musical elaboration of one verse would allow the rest of the psalm to disappear.

The Mass of the day (*PL* 85, cols 223–4) gives the following readings: Isaiah 49.1–6, 'The Lord called me from the womb'; Hebrews 6.13—7.2, God's promise to Abraham, and John 1.1–17, 'The Word was made flesh'. There is, again, some degree of consonance between the day's reading and the Antiphons of Matins.

Similar forms can be seen on other feasts. The verse is usually taken from a psalm and the antiphon (upon which the prayer is usually based) from another suitable scriptural text. Epiphany is a good example. In Matins for the day psalms are the basis for the verses of the Antiphons and the Responsory, other texts forming the antiphons. The following examples are from the first *Missa* (col. 177):

Antiphon 1 (The verse is Ps.71.5.)
Jerusalem, in you the Lord appears, *P* And his glory will be seen over you. The Kings come into your light, and the peoples flock to your splendour. *V* He shall continue as long as the sun, and before the moon from generation to generation. *P* And his glory. *V* Glory. *P* And his glory.

Prayer
Make us rejoice, Lord, in the blessed vision of Jerusalem, and in its bosom, raise up perpetual joy in that eternal light that you promised would shine and whose honour you promised: therefore grant us that we may put aside the desires of the flesh and be clothed with abundant virtues, so that we who bathed in the appearing of your undiminished light, may always deserve the embrace of your paternal love.

Antiphon 3 (The verse is Ps 47.5.)
In the days of Herod the King, behold wise men from the east came to Jerusalem P Saying: Where is he who has been born King of Jews? For we have seen his star in the east, and have come to worship him. V For the Kings of the earth were assembled, they came together in one. P Saying. V Glory. P Saying.

Prayer
King of all ages, Christ, most High God, who in the days of King Herod were born of a virgin; and the wise men seeking you declared by a new sign from on high: let there appear in us your excellence, as a protection to drive away all the destructions of darkness, thus making your majesty to shine like a star in us, so that in seeking you, none of our errors may interpose as barriers to you, and that we may run eagerly in your sight, and come quickly to the enjoyment we seek.

The feasts of the saints show similar features, the antiphon often from elsewhere in the Scriptures than the Psalter. In some cases, the choice of text would be influenced by the legends of the saints' lives as related by the Passionary. Readings from this book may have been interspersed between the *Missae* or even between the Antiphons. The Passionary sometimes indicates the points at which a reading would have been interrupted.[21]

It may well be that the *Missa* or *Missae* were a 'mini-vigil' that first began to be used in non-monastic churches on feasts, particularly those of local saints, which included the reading of the passions of these saints as well as suitable psalms and prayers. This was probably very freely organized early on, becoming more fixed later. In the process of becoming more fixed the 'mini-vigil' was extended to other days, but continued to be based on the unit of three psalms with prayers and a Responsory, a unit that could be multiplied on more important feasts. It may well be that a 'mini-vigil' on some days and not on others reflects the difference between an office intended for ordinary Christians who could manage an extended vigil only now and again, and a daily vigil of the monks. The 'mini-vigil' was itself, Pinell believes, an imitation of the monastic vigil but adapted to the exigencies of the more parochial churches.[22]

CONCLUSIONS

Regarding the Recitation of the Psalter in Course

1 It appears to be clear that in Spain and, no doubt, elsewhere, there was originally no tradition of reciting the Psalter in course in the cathedral office.
2 The monasteries did use a current psalter and may have used psalm collects, perhaps as a result of North African influence.[23] Composition of these prayers may have begun in the second half of the fifth century.
3 By the seventh century the monasteries had lengthy vigils largely comprising psalms in course while, it would seem, the psalm collects became part of the cathedral office with its smaller number of psalms.
4 After the seventh century the influence of St Benedict's rule may have caused Spanish monks to re-think their somewhat burdensome office.
5 There was probably growing pressure on the secular clergy to recite the whole Psalter and so we may have the rise of attempts to distribute the psalms over some weeks in the cathedral offices, for example in the first three weeks of Lent as found in *AL* by the tenth century.
6 However, it seems likely that recitation of the Psalter in course had not been established securely before the suppression of the rite.

The Missa Psalmorum/Antiphonarum as a Unit of the Old Spanish Matins

1 From around the late fifth/early sixth centuries the cathedral Matins was lengthened on feasts by the addition of selected psalms and prayers.
2 During the sixth century, this vigil became more frequent and the collections of collects grew accordingly. As the process of 'festivalization' went on, non-psalm texts were often used as the inspiration for new collects.
3 By the seventh century, musical elaboration had reduced many psalms to a single verse on Sundays and feasts, and by the later part of the century Antiphon collects had replaced those of the Psalter at Matins in Tradition A.
4 Sunday and festal *Missae* continued to become more elaborate, as did those of other seasons; first, *de Traditione*, and later, Advent and Eastertide.

5 Other days, such as the first three weeks of Lent and the lesser fasts, adopted a less elaborate vigil and eventually this was extended to other weekdays.
6 As Sunday and festal vigil spread to other days, it became more general in its themes.
7 By the end of the development, the ordinary vigil with its complete psalms had less connection with any theme for the day and so was perhaps seen as an appropriate vehicle for some kind of current psalmody – but this may have been so late on as to never have become securely established.

In conclusion, since monks had their own night vigils, as well as being expected to perform the cathedral office, there would a strong influence preventing the latter from becoming too long and unwieldy.

NOTES

1 W. C. Bishop, ed. C. L. Feltoe, *The Mozarabic and Ambrosian Rites* (London: Alcuin/Mowbrays, 1924), pp. 56, 78–9.
2 See A. W. S. Porter, 'Early Spanish Monasticism', *Laudate* XI (1933), pp. 199–207, at p. 201.
3 A. W. S. Porter, 'Studies in the Mozarabic Office', *JTS* 35 (1934), pp. 266–86, at pp. 282–6.
4 L. Brou, 'Le Psautier Wisigothique ou les Éditions Critiques des Psautiers Latins', *HS* 8 (1954), pp. 337–60, at p. 338, fn 1.
5 J. Pinell, 'Las *Missae*, Grupos de Cantos y Oraciones en el Oficio de la Antigua Liturgia Hispana', *HS* 8 (1954), pp. 145–85, at pp. 146ff.
6 Paul F. Bradshaw, *Daily Prayer in the Early Church* (London: Alcuin/SPCK, 1981), pp. 93–4.
7 See R. Taft, *The Liturgy of the Hours in East and West* (Collegeville: Liturgical Press, 1986), pp. 58–60.
8 A. de Vogue, *The Rule of St Benedict: A Doctrinal and Spiritual Commentary* (Kalamazoo: Cistercian Publications, 1983), rules 19–20, and see also the present author's 'The Use of the Psalter by early Monastic Communities', *Studia Patristica* XXVI (1993), pp. 88–94.
9 J. Pinell (ed.), 'Las Horas Vigiliares del Oficio Monacal Hispanico' (Monserrat: *Liturgica III – Scripta et Documenta* 17 (1966), pp. 197–340.
10 Pinell, ibid., pp. 275–331.
11 Pinell, ibid., pp. 249–50.
12 J. Pinell (ed.), *Liber Orationum Psalmographus (LOP)* (Barcelona-Madrid: *Monumenta Hispaniae Sacra* IX, 1972), pp. [86]–[88].
13 Friday Terce is provided with Ps. 23 and two sections of 24, but that office was probably no part of this cycle originally.
14 In *T2* Roman numerals with the antiphon indicate the psalm appointed.
15 J. Janini (ed.), *Liber Misticus de Cuaresma* (Toledo: Istituto de Estudios Visigotico-Mozarabes, 1979), pp. xxiv–xxvi.
16 Pinell, *LOP*, pp. [206–11].
17 Where two psalm numbers are given, the first is that of the antiphon, the second the one that supplies the verse – in these cases, the collect draws from the antiphon psalm.
18 The first two Sundays mentioned are found in the ninth-century *Liber Commicus* (lectionary) edited by Urbel and Ruiz-Zorilla (Madrid, 1950), pp. 142–4 and 210–12.
19 E.g., two *Missae*: Purification (2 February); three: Sts Julian and Basilissa (9th January), and Christmas; four: Annunciation (18 December) and Epiphany; five: St Fructuosus and companions (21 January).
20 Bishop, op. cit., pp. 78–80.
21 A. Fabrega Grau, *Passionario Hispanico* (Madrid-Barcelona: *Monumenta Hispaniae Sacrae* 6, 1953 and 1955), see esp. pp. 12 and 46.

22 Pinell, *LOP*, pp. [87]–[88], and 'Las *Missae*', pp. 154 and 184–5.
23 See Porter, 'Early Spanish Monasticism', *Laudate* X (1932), pp. 2–15, at p. 6.
24 E.g., Christmas in Tradition A; see M. F. Férotin (ed.), *Liber Mozarabicus Sacramentorum* (*LMS*) (Paris: *Monumenta Ecclesiastica Sacra* IX, 1972), col. 760.

APPENDIX: PSALM 50 BEFORE THE CANTICLE

On certain days when Matins commenced with Psalm 3 (though *not* in Eastertide), Psalm 50 was to be recited before the Canticle of Matins. For *Br.* such days were the weekdays of Lent and the lesser fasts. Tradition A manuscripts, on the other hand, placed Psalm 50 before the Canticle on feasts, whereas *Br.* used it at the beginning of the service on many such days.[24] For Tradition A, then, one can state that Psalm 50 preceded the Canticle, as required by the Council of Barcelona in 549.

In *Br.* on many saints' days, we find Psalm 50 alone at the beginning of the service – on some days it does not appear at all. On four of these latter days, Annunciation (18 December), Christmas, Circumcision and Epiphany, an additional antiphon and collect follows the last *Missa*. These additional antiphons and collects all occur on days when the *Missae* are multiplied, and neither quote Psalm 50, nor in any other way relate to that Psalm. The collects are festal and inspired by the non-psalmic texts of the antiphons. This additional unit appears to be a form of summary following several *Missae* on some feasts. Perhaps it was confined only to the most important feasts.

Three of the four feasts mentioned are feasts of the Saviour, on which the invitatory is Psalm 3, as in Eastertide. Possibly these feasts were in some sense considered resurrectional. The additional antiphons and prayers do not appear to affect the conclusion to the previous chapter, that Psalm 50 was the original Matins invitatory of Tradition B.

11

THE CANTICLES AT MATINS

Unlike the Roman tradition, scriptural canticles in the old Spanish rite were confined to Matins and canticles from the New Testament were used very infrequently. Baumstark stressed the origin of the canticles as part of the Paschal Vigil, a point well illustrated by the Roman rite as it existed before the reform of 1951. There were then three Old Testament canticles in the Vigil, and all three were integral parts of the readings with which they were connected; e.g. the canticle of Exodus 15, *Cantemus*, followed directly upon the account of the Red Sea crossing. The Orthodox Easter Vigil (now normally celebrated on Holy Saturday morning) has only the two canticles, *Cantemus* and *Benedicite* (from Daniel 3), again both integral parts of the readings that precede them. Forms of the Isaiah 55 canticle, of *Attende* (Deuteronomy 32.1–43), *Benedicite* and *Cantemus* are found in the old Spanish Vigil as given in *MM*.[1] Baumstark concluded that these were the earliest non-psalmic canticles to be used in the Christian liturgy, both in the Paschal Vigil and apart from it. This view gains force from the fact that two of the canticles, *Cantemus* and *Benedicite*, are often found together, e.g. in the Coptic rite (separated only by Psalm 135) and in the Milanese Sunday Lauds. *Benedicite* appears in nearly all morning offices, at least on Sunday.[2] The use of New Testament canticles, particularly *Benedictus* and *Magnificat*, appears to be a later tradition which did not find favour in the East Syrian and Coptic rites, and was used only very sparingly in the old Spanish office. Other canticles replaced and supplemented the original ones in order to reflect changing liturgical seasons. Eventually, in most places, the basic repertoire was spread over the week, but in Spain the early stratum of canticles became identified with certain seasons or days.

Readings chosen for the Easter Vigil were appropriate to the paschal themes, and some of these included poetic sections originally added by the biblical redactors. The hymn attributed to the Israelites after their crossing of the Red Sea is one of the best known, as Christians have always seen something of their baptismal faith in this event. In Deuteronomy 31 Moses promises the people that they will inherit the land and sings of God's love and mercy in the canticle of chapter 32, *Attende*. The Daniel 3 canticle *Benedicite* is part of the account of the young men thrown into the furnace, traditionally seen as a type of the resurrection of Christ.

These poems became independent of the Paschal Vigil lesson context, but their paschal themes guaranteed them a continuing role as morning components of the Sunday morning prayer, in close association with the sunrise hymn of praise, Psalms 148–50. While the original paschal canticles maintained their pre-eminence, in Spain they were spread over several Sundays, and not normally used on weekdays.

To help see the diffusion of these traditions the following table is an abbreviated version of that given by Martin Patino.[3] The two Spanish systems of *Br.* and *Tl* are given in the central column. The numbers in the columns indicate the order in which the canticles are listed in the various collections. The order in *Br.* is the order they have in the Temporal and Sanctoral cycles, *Tl*'s order is numerical. The non-Spanish lists often do not list canticles that are used elsewhere in that tradition, but which may perhaps come from a different source or date, e.g. the Greek books *do* assign the prayer of Manasses at the Lenten office of Great Compline.

Canticle	Alex.[4]	Jer.[5]	Milan[6]	Spain Br./Tl	Coptic[7]	Greek Odes	Gall[8]	Roman[9]
Exod. 15	1	1	1	38/55	1	1	2	4
Deut. 32	2	2	2	1/62	2	2	3	6
1 Sam. 2	3	3	3	11/63	3	3	5	3
Isa. 26.9	4	5	5	12/–	10	5	7	–
Jonah 2	5	6	6	36/60	6	6	–	–
Hab. 3.2	6	4	4	8/–	7	4	–	5
Isa. 38.10	7	7	7	22/73	4	–	9	2
Pr. of Man.	8	8	8	–/22	5	–	12	–
Dan. 3.26	9	9	9	–/25	–	7a	–	–
Dan. 3.52	10	10	10	42*/–	11	7b	1	–
Dan. 3.57	–	11	11	–/–	(3.1–97)	8	–	7
Mag.	11	12	12	10/14	13	9a	6	9
Nunc.	12	14	14	2 Feb/16	15	–	–	–
Ben.	13	13	13	15/46	14	9b	–	8
GLORIA	14	15	15	–/77	16	–	–	–

DAILY PRAYER IN CHRISTIAN SPAIN

Canticle	Alex.[4]	Jer.[5]	Milan[6]	Spain Br./T1	Coptic[7]	Greek Odes	Gall[8]	Roman[9]
Isa. 25	–	–	–	–/71	8	–	–	–
Isa. 26	–	–	–	7/–	9	–	–	–
Judg. 5	–	–	–	39/41	–	–	–	–
Lam. 5	–	–	–	28/20	–	–	10	–
Isa. 5	–	–	–	30/56	–	–	–	–
Isa. 61.10	–	–	–	6/48	–	–	4	–
4 Esd. 8	–	–	–	23/61	–	–	11	–
Deut. 9.26	–	–	–	20/69	–	–	–	–
Deut. 32.36	–	–	–	21/–	–	–	–	–
2 Macc. 1.24	–	–	–	5/26	–	–	–	–
Tobit 13.10	–	–	–	14/52	–	–	–	–
Isa. 12.1	–	–	–	–/65	–	–	–	1

* = *Benedictiones*, a fixed canticle.

Cantemus and *Attende* are common to all the orders. The canticle of Hannah is found in all, but not in Verecundus' commentaries (which are not listed above), the only source that does not mention the New Testament canticles (the others have at least *Magnificat*).[10] Most lists have the same canticles as those most frequently used in *Br.* for Sundays. It was Martin Patino's opinion that there may have been a common usage of the canticles in North Africa, Spain, Southern Gaul and Northern Italy.

T1, the document included into the Lorenzana version, not having Habakkuk 3 and Isaiah 26 etc., is not the source that Ortiz used for *Br.* He must have used a different and perhaps more ancient collection.[11] Pinell, attempting an hypothetical reconstruction of Ortiz' source, listed all 43 canticles of *Br.* in biblical order, taking Deuteronomy 32.1–43 and 32.23–32 as two distinct canticles. The *Benedictiones* (Daniel 3) may be taken as number 44. Canticles from Sirach 35.2–9 and Matthew 22.23–32 for Corpus Christi and the Departed respectively may be omitted as inauthentic.

In the following list of the 43 canticles an asterisk denotes those also found in *T2*, edited by Janini. The canticles are given in biblical order, but are found all over *Br.*, so the column numbers in *PL* 86 are given as well. It is worth noting that several of the canticles were in *Vetus Latina* versions, not the Vulgate.[12]

The Canticles of Tradition B in Biblical order

Incipit	Biblical reference	Col. number in PL 86
1 Go from your country	Gen. 12.1–3; 13.14–15; 22.17–18; 15.7; 17.1–8	191*
2 He smelt the smell of his	Gen. 27.27–9; 28.3–4	196*

	garments		
3	O God of my Father Abraham	Gen. 32.9–12	200
4	Then Jacob called his sons	Gen. 49.1–27	120*
5	We will sing to the Lord	Exod. 15.1–19	616
6	From Aram Balak has brought me	Num. 23.7–10; 18–24	162*
7	Lord God, destroy not thy people	Deut. 9.26–9	204*
8	Give ear, O heavens	Deut. 32.1–43	52
9	He sees their power is gone	Deut. 32.36–9	209*
10	The Lord came from Sinai	Deut. 33.2–29	1005
11	Who offered themselves willingly	Judg. 5.2–31	1001
12	My heart exults in the Lord	1 Sam. 2.1–10	130
13	I took you from the pasture	2 Sam. 8.8–14; 16	64
14	Blessed art thou, O Lord	1 Chron. 29.10–18	373*
15	O Lord who inhabitest eternity	4/2 Esdras 8.20–36	245
16	(Give thanks worthily ...)	Tobit 13.(10) 11–18	171
17	O Lord, King who rulest over all things	Esth. 13.9–11, 15–17	289*
18	O my Lord, thou only art our King	Esth. 14.3–19	1282
19	Let the day perish	Job 3.1–26	349*
20	My words have been rash	Job 6.3–13	459*
21	But now he has made me weary	Job 16.8–20	485*
22	Behold, I cry out	Job 19.7–27	528*
23	Behold God is great	Job 36.26–32; 37.3–12	60
24	The gift of the Lord endures	Sir. 11.17; 26.1–3; 16.23–4	1127
25	I will give thanks	Sir. 51.1–38	1014
26	Let me sing for my beloved	Isa. 5.1–7	387*
27	We have a strong city	Isa. 26.1–8	78*
28	My soul yearns for thee in the night	Isa. 26.9–20	144
29	I said, in the noontide of my days I must depart	Isa. 38.10–19	234*
30	Arise, shine	Isa. 60.1–5	183
31	I will greatly rejoice	Isa. 61.10–11; 62.1–7	75
32	O Lord, thou knowest	Jer. 15.15–21	547*
33	Heal me, O Lord	Jer. 17.14–18	450*
34	O Lord, thou hast deceived me	Jer. 20.7–12	475*
35	Why should a living man complain?	Lam. 3.39–44	279*
36	Remember, O Lord	Lam. 5.1–22	367*

37 I called to the Lord	Jonah 2.3–10	535*
38 O Lord, I have heard the report	Hab. 3.2–19	81
39 Rejoice greatly	Zech. 9.9–16	67
40 O Lord, Lord God	2 Maccabees 1.24–9	73*
41 *Magnificat*	Luke 1.46–55	122
42 *Benedictus*	Luke 1.68–79	182
43 *Nunc Dimittis*	Luke 2.29–32	1091

THE SUNDAY CANTICLES

Ignoring the *Benedictiones* for the moment, nine canticles, all Old Testament, are used on Sundays. They are also the ones most widely used at Matins:[13]

1 *Attende coelum* ('Give ear, O heavens'), Deuteronomy 32.1–43:
1st, 2nd and 4th Sundays of Advent, 1st, 4th and 5th Sundays of Lent, Palm Sunday and the first three Sundays after the Epiphany octave.

2 *De nocte vigilat* ('My soul yearns for thee in the night'), Isaiah 26.9–20:
2nd and 3rd Sundays of Lent, 7th and 8th Sundays after the Epiphany octave, Pentecost Sunday and the three Sundays after Pentecost, and the Sunday before the Nativity of St John the Baptist.

3 *Cantemus* ('Let us sing to the Lord'), Exodus 15.1–19:
Easter Sunday, the Easter octave and Sundays of Eastertide.

4 *Confirmatum est cor meum* ('My heart exults in the Lord'), 1 Samuel 2.1–10:
4th and 5th Sundays after the Epiphany Octave.

5 *Domine audivi auditum tuum* ('O Lord, I have heard the report of thee'), Habakkuk 3.2–19:
3rd and 5th Sundays of Advent.

6 *Domine qui habitas in aeternum* ('O Lord who inhabitest eternity'), 4 (or 2) Esdras 8.20–36:
Sundays before Ash Wednesday and the November Fast.

7 *Ego dixi in dimidio dierum meorum* ('I said, in the noontide of my days I must depart'), Isaiah 38.10–20: 6th Sunday after the Epiphany.

8 *Gaudens gaudebo* ('I will greatly rejoice in the Lord') Isaiah 61.10—62.7:

6th Sunday of Advent.
9 *Vocavit Iacob filios suos* ('Then Jacob called his sons'), Genesis 49.2–27:
The Sunday before the Epiphany.

Only the last three of these canticles, used on but one Sunday each, are in Vulgate versions. All the others are *Vetus Latina*. It has already been noted that Milan uses *Cantemus* every Sunday, Numbers 1, 2, 3, 4 and 5 are odes 2, 5, 1, 3 and 4 of the Byzantine canon, and numbers 1, 3, 4, 5 and 7 are in both old Roman and Benedictine offices. In other words, the *Vetus Latina* canticles of *Br.* are part of the common, ancient tradition and in this respect, *Br.* is more traditional than the MSS of Tradition A.

A good example of the way these are used is the Deuteronomy canticle *Attende*, which occurs on ten Sundays of the year, in Advent, Lent and ordinary time. Outside Lent, the antiphons are simply verses taken from the canticle in order. The prayers with the canticle are provided for three ordinary Sundays and three in Lent (First, Fourth, and Fifth – no prayer is provided for Palm Sunday). The prayers often cite phrases from the canticles, e.g. (biblical phrases underlined):

> <u>Descendat, Domine, ut pluvia eloquium tuum; et sicut ros, verba tua super nos effundantur:</u> ut, ubertim tua miseratione rigati, <u>tibi magnitudinem demus,</u> cuius opera bona esse cognoscimus: <u>omnes viae tuae, judicia</u>; et iniquitas procul est a rectitudine tua ... (col. 188)
> <u>May your teaching Lord, drop as the rain and your speech distil as the dew</u> (v. 2); <u>to you we ascribe greatness</u> (v. 3); as you generously bestow your mercy so that we may learn that your works are good: <u>all your ways are justice</u> (v. 4) and wickedness is far from your rightness ...

The antiphon for the third Sunday after Epiphany, *Deus fidelis*, is quoted in the prayer for that day: 'Deus fidelis, in quo nulla est iniquitas: tu justus et sanctus ...' (from v. 4, col. 222: 'God of faithfulness and without iniquity; you are just and holy ...') Pinell thought this prayer ancient, and in fact, on both stylistic and doctrinal grounds, argues for the antiquity of the canticle prayers in general.[14]

Many of the prayers and texts do not seem particularly Vigilial or Matutinal; an example of a good vigil canticle is *De nocte vigilat* of

Isaiah 26, which is used on nine Sundays, the same collect being used on most of them (see e.g. col. 238):

> Our souls yearn for you in the night, O God, the beauty of your commands shines out and in the tempest of our expectancy, we watch for you, the light that comes at midday. Let nothing of the darkness obstruct our following of you, nor let even the traces of evildoing hold back your love from us, but give us strength to speak of your justice; for you are the source of the justice in which we earnestly seek to advance and thus we strive to endure in accomplishing this, whilst adhering to your all-embracing wisdom.

The third most frequently used is *Cantemus* of Exodus 15, on all Sundays of Eastertide and otherwise not at all in *Br.* (see col. 616). The other Sunday canticles are used much less often, and, among the Vulgate canticles, Isaiah 38.10–20 is used only once, on the Sixth Sunday after Epiphany, which is strange as it is popular in other traditions. Isaiah 61.10—62.7, *Gaudens gaudebo*, for the Sixth Sunday of Advent is of interest. In *T1* and elsewhere it is only appointed for the Common of a Virgin. The canticle may have come into the Advent office by extension of the concept of a virgin saint to the best known virgin, Mary. There was a Gallican feast of Mary in Advent and this would explain Marian themes on the Sunday before Christmas. Finally, Genesis 49.2–27, *Vocavit Jacob filios suos*, used on the Sunday before Epiphany (col. 148), is also the Old Testament canticle for Christmas.

It will be recalled that the variable canticle on Sundays is always followed by the *Benedictiones* from Daniel 3, except on Palm Sunday. Two prayers are given for this canticle; 'Domine Deus, patrum nostrorum' which quotes the canticle, and 'Domine Deus, qui super Cherubim sedes' which does not do so directly. The canticle is recited in this shortened form (col. 55):

> Blessed are you, Lord God of our Fathers, and praised and glorified for ever. And blessed be the glory of your name, which is holy and praised and glorified for ever. Blessed are you in the temple of your glory, in the firmament of heaven, and praised and glorified for ever. All you works of the Lord, heavens and Angels, bless the Lord, and all you who are above the heavens; All virtues, the sun and the moon, the shower and the dew, every spirit, fire and cold, ice and snow, lightning and

cloud; Earth, mountains and hills, and all that comes from the earth; Sea and rivers, fountains, sea creatures and all that move in the waters; Birds of heaven, animals and beasts, sons of men, Israel: Priests, servants of the Lord, spirits and souls of the just, holy and humble of heart. Ananias, Azarias and Misael, sing a hymn to the Lord, and exalt him above all for ever. Amen. *P* Bless the Lord. Glory and Honour to the Father. *P* Bless the Lord.

The two prayers appointed to follow the canticle normally alternate on the Sundays after Epiphany.

Benedicite is very widely used as a morning canticle. It is used on Sundays at Milan and was used every Sunday in the old Roman rite. It is also a morning canticle in Byzantine Orthodox, Chaldean and Maronite offices. It is never as condensed as in this old Spanish version.

THE FESTAL CANTICLES

1 *Confirmatum est cor meum* ('My heart exults the Lord'), 1 Sam. 2.1–10 (Apostles, a martyr, a martyr bishop, also Ascension).
2 *Qui sponte* ('When the people willingly offered' – song of Deborah), Judg. 5.2–31 (Martyrs and Confessors).
3 *Confitebor tibi* ('I will give thanks to thee, O Lord'), Sirach 51.1–38 (Confessors).
4 *Dominus de Sina* ('The Lord came from Sinai') Deuteronomy 33.2–29 (Martyrs).
5 **De nocte vigilat* ('My soul yearns for thee in the night'), Isaiah 26.2–20 (Circumcision and Purification).
6 **Cantemus* ('Let us sing to the Lord'), Exodus 15.1–19 (Invention of Holy Cross, 3 May, and Martyrs).
7 *Clamavi ad Dominum* ('I called to the Lord') Jonah 2.3–10 (two feasts of martyrs).
8 **Domine audivi* ('Lord, I have heard the report of thee'), Habakkuk 3.2–19 (St Rufina, 16 July and St Andrew).
9 *Magnificat*, Luke 1.46–55 (Christmas with OT canticle and Annunciation, 18 December).
10 **Vocavit Jacob* ('Then Jacob called his sons'), Genesis 49.2–27 (Christmas Day).
11 **Attende coelum* ('Give ear, O heavens'), Deuteronomy 32.1–43 (St Stephen).

12 *Surge inluminare* ('Arise, shine'), Isaiah 60.1–5 (Epiphany).
13 *Gaudens gaudebo ('I will greatly rejoice in the Lord'), Isaiah 61.10—62.7 (Common of one Virgin).
14 *Datio Dei* ('The gift of the Lord endures'), Sirach 11.17; 26.1–3; 16.23–4 (St Adrian and 17 June).
15 *Domine mi rex* ('My Lord, our King' – Song of Esther), Esther 14.3–19 (St Eulalia, 10 December).
16 *Benedictus*, Luke 1.68–79 (Epiphany with OT canticle, and Nativity of St John the Baptist).
17 *Nunc Dimittis*, Luke 2.29–32 (Purification with OT canticle).
18 **Ego dixi in dimidio dierum meorum* ('I said, in the noontide of my days I must depart'), Isaiah 38.10–20 (only in later feast of St Mary Magdalene inserted by Ortiz).

* = canticle also used on Sundays.

Festal Canticles Created for the 1502 Breviary

1 *Sacrificium salutare* ('He who returns a kindness offers fine flour'), Sirach 35.2–9 (Corpus Christi).
2 *Accesserunt* ('The same day Saducees came to him'), Matthew 22.23–32 (Office of the Dead).

The festal canticles are a later development, but in *Br*. we may discern a desire to keep the canticles from the *historical* books of the Old Testament in a pre-eminent place, so as to be in line with Sunday use. As can be seen, several days use Sunday canticles and this may well reflect original festal practice. A good example would be *Cantemus*, appointed for the Invention of the Holy Cross, probably because that feast would fall in Eastertide. This same paschal canticle was used for the lowest grade of martyrs, reflecting a time when the martyrs were seen as having imitated Christ our Passover in their lives and deaths. The antiphon for several martyrs is: 'Gloriosus Dominus in Sanctis, gloriosus et mirabilis' (col. 1010) which appears to be based on verse 11, 'Who is like thee, O Lord, among the gods, Who is like thee honoured among the Holy Ones, marvellous in his wonders, doing great things?' The old version that speaks of God honoured among the holy ones or saints was in the Vulgate rendered, 'Who is like thee, majestic in holiness' (Quis similis tibi, magnificus in sanctitate). In other words the festal/common use is dependent on the *Vetus Latina* text. In time other more appropriate canticles were selected for the more important feasts.

The song of Hannah, *Confirmatum est*, is used on many feasts, after Christmas, in August and September and also on Ascension Day. The use on this last day was again controlled by the *Vetus Latina* text:

> Dominus ascendit in coelos, et tonat: ipse judicat extrema terrae. Potens est, et dat virtutem regibus, et exaltat cornu Christi sui (col. 656, antiphon).
> The Lord ascends to the heavens and thunders: he judges the ends of the earth. He is powerful and gives strength to kings and exalts the horn of his anointed.

By contrast the Vulgate reads:

> Dominum formidabunt adversarii eius: et super ipsos in coelis tonabit ...
> The adversaries of the Lord shall be broken to pieces, against them he will thunder in the heavens.

The prayer also quotes these verses in the *Vetus Latina* version (col. 656).

De nocte vigilat is used for the Circumcision and the Purification and the antiphon used on those days stresses the theme of light, hence the selection of that canticle. The reasons for some selections now seem quite obscure or far-fetched; e.g., *Attende* is appointed for St Stephen, probably because of the words, 'Nomen Domini invocavi' ('I have called upon the name of the Lord'). On two feasts, St Vincent the deacon and St Clement, Jonah 2.3–10 *Clamavi ad Dominum* is appointed. In both cases it is likely that the theme is God's protection for seafarers – we may recall the legend that Clement was tied to an anchor and thrown overboard.

A feature that very much contradicts the standard expectations of daily offices in the West is that the New Testament canticles are used very little. *Benedictus* only twice, on Epiphany with an Old Testament canticle and on 24 June on its own. *Magnificat* is used at Christmas with an Old Testament canticle and on the Annunciation (18 December) on its own. It is also used in the Lady Office of Saturday (col. 214). The older tradition would appear to have known only Old Testament canticles, and when we find that the antiphon for the *Nunc Dimittis* on the Purification is in fact from Habakkuk 3: 'Ego in Domino gloriabor: gaudebo in Deo Jesu meo' (col. 1091) – 'I will rejoice in the Lord, I will joy in the God of my salvation', it seems likely that originally there was just the one canticle on this day, Habakkuk 3.

THE WEEKDAY CANTICLES

There are no fewer than 41 canticles appointed for use on weekdays, six for Advent,[15] six for the weekdays after Epiphany;[16] the 14 for the first half of Lent include some of those used on other days,[17] and the eight for the second half of Lent tend to be duplicated on feasts.[18] The various other fast days use canticles drawn from elsewhere, with one exception.[19] This extraordinarily large number of canticles is a Spanish peculiarity, and there is not the space here to go into them in detail.[20] Many show an advanced stage of festivalization, for instance, the use of Job in Advent, to stress the theme of God as incomprehensible; the 2 Samuel canticle, 'I took you from the pasture ... that you should be prince over my people Israel' is also used in Advent, and Zechariah 9 is often quoted in Advent antiphons. Martin Patino believed these Advent canticles to be in use in pre-Visigothic times.[21]

The ordinary weekdays are fragmentary but we can gain some idea of what may have been normal from the arrangements of the first three weeks of Lent. Only a few canticles on the weekdays of Lent have any obvious reference to that season. Pinell tried to establish an original series of weekday canticles as follows:

Genesis 12.1–3 etc.
Genesis 27.27–9; 28.3–4
Genesis 32.9–12
Numbers 23.7–10, 18–24
Deuteronomy 9.26–9
Tobit 13.13–23
Lamentations 5.1–22

They form a cycle that describes a growing human realization of the need for God's strength and pardon. Having set out on the Sunday, one must return there.

The prayers are more obviously penitential in Lent but, as with all the canticle prayers, there are problems of authenticity. Pinell believes them to be original,[22] and Janini does not.[23] Some found in *Br.* are not in *T2*. A good example of the prayers for the first half of Lent is that for the third Monday (col. 387) which accompanies the Isaian canticle of the vine:[24]

> O Lord, whose vineyard, Israel, brought forth only a harvest of thorns, increase your church with abundance of virtue; so that the hedge of which we were bereft, may be replaced by your

surrounding precepts; that the watchtower of the king and wine-vat of the altar so threatened by these thorns in which we have had a part, may receive the benefit of the rains that break out and douse their flames; that what is brought forth may not be a crop of thorns but the heavenly fruits with which you nourish us, and which you accept from us.

Pinell thinks this prayer ancient.

The second half of Lent concentrates on the betrayal and passion themes. Of the eight canticles, only two are used at any other time and they are well suited to the ethos of these weeks. Most used in this period is *Seduxisti* from Jeremiah 20.7–12, emphasizing dereliction, but also hope. Jeremiah 17.14–18 (*Sana me*) prays for delivery from enemies. The others are similar and most days there is a canticle collect, seemingly composed for this season; many of these are in *T2*. The following is the prayer to accompany *Seduxisti* on the Tuesday of the fifth week (col. 518 and *T2*, 178):

> Lord our God, let us not be held in derision by our enemies, nor wearied by the weakening attacks of the adversary: but you, our defence, deliver us from the gainsaying of the mischievous.

The fasts before Pentecost and in November use weekday canticles with the exception of *Memento Domine* from Lamentations 5.1–22.

CONCLUSION

Martin Patino concluded that the original basic stratum of canticles in *Br.* was independent, thematically and numerically, of the season; and that the usage of *Br.* was more ancient than that of the Tradition A manuscripts.

Both traditions had a daily canticle, followed on weekdays by the *Matutinarium* and on Sundays and feasts by the *Benedictiones*, this basic shape being in place by about the sixth century, which is before the two traditions diverged more radically. These two traditions are closer to each other than either is to any other, except that Milan and Ireland also place together the two ancient Paschal Vigil canticles from Exodus and Daniel.

The Tradition B use of the canticles is extremely important for understanding the old Spanish office; even though some of the prayers may not be ancient, the canticle use would appear to be so. Grisbrooke may stand for the authors who have maintained that *Benedicite* and Psalms

148–50 were found everywhere in the morning offices and (in nearly all of them the service concludes with a New Testament canticle or canticles'.[25] Actually the Chaldean and Maronite rites have no such arrangement, Milan has a New Testament canticle at the *beginning* of the office, and in Byzantine Orthodox use the New Testament canticle *precedes* Psalms 148–50. Further, ancient Spanish custom appears to have employed New Testament canticles only sparingly, and only included them from a relatively late date. The ancient structure of canticle followed by the praise psalms and prayer again appears to reflect the form of a miniature Paschal Vigil, and, like that vigil, it only employed Old Testament texts, the eucharistic readings 'fulfilling', as it were, that which the prophecies of the canticles and the other material had looked forward to in the course of the progression from night to morning.

It is very interesting also that the old Spanish tradition identified a very large number of Old Testament canticle texts, but never appears to have been attracted to the New Testament texts that have become popular in recent versions of daily prayer. Even the christological hymn of Philippians 2.5ff., that found its way into the Holy Week service of the Roman rite as *Christus factus est*, does not appear in these Spanish sources. Once again, it is clear that, in common with the wider tradition, in Spain, canticles were largely drawn from the Old Testament.

NOTES

1 *PL* 85, cols 452, 454 and 460.
2 Baumstark, *Comparative Liturgy* (London: Mowbray, 1958), pp. 35–6 and *Nocturna Laus* (Munster: Aschendorff, 1967), p. 175.
3 J. M. Martin Patino, 'El Breviarium Mozarabe de Ortiz, su Valor Documental para la Historia del Oficio Catedralicio Hispanico', Miscellanea 40 Comillas (1963), pp. 207–97.
4 ibid.; and J. Mearns, *The Canticles of the Christian Church Eastern and Western in Early and Medieval Times* (Cambridge University Press 1914), pp. 9ff. Codex Alexandrinus, Brit. Mus. Royal ID. v–viii – ff546b–569.
5 MS Turin. Bib. Naz. Bv11 30 (8th century). Martin Patino, op. cit., p. 229.
6 MS Berlin Deutsche Staatsbibliothek Hamilton 552 (9th century), Martin Patino, op. cit., p. 229.
7 Ms Vat. coptic 5 (10th century), Martin Patino, op. cit., p. 230; Mearns, op. cit., pp. 57–8.
8 Ms Vat. regin. lat. 11 (8th century); Mearns thinks from Narbonnese Gaul c. 705, op. cit., pp. 60–1.
9 Vespasian Psalter, 7th century.
10 Verecundus, Bishop of Civitas Juronensis, near Tunis, died 552. See Martin Patino, op. cit., p. 230 and Mearns, op. cit., pp. 57–8.
11 Martin Patino, op. cit., pp. 235 and 270–1.
12 J. Pinell, 'Los Canticos del Oficio en el Antiguo Rito Hispanico', *HS* 27 (1974), pp. 5–54, at pp. 47–50.
13 *T1* groups 22 canticles suitable for everyday use, including *Cantemus*, *PL* 86, cols 874–86.
14 J. Pinell, 'Las Oraciones "de Cantico" del Antiguo Rito Hispanico', *Didaskalia* VIII (Lisbon, 1978), pp. 197–329, at pp. 214 and 226.

15 Job 36.26–32; 37.3–12/2 Samuel 7.8–14 and 16/Zechariah 9.9–16/2 Maccabees 1.24–9/Isaiah 26. 1–8 and also *Gaudens gaudebo*, see above.
16 Genesis 12.1–3; 13.14–15; 22.17–18; 15.7; 17.1–4 and 6/Genesis 27.27–9; 28.3–4/Genesis 32.9–12/ Deuteronomy 9.26–9/Deuteronomy 32.36–9 and *Magnificat*.
17 Others are Lamentations 3.39–44/Esther 13.9–11 and 15–17/Genesis 49.1–27/Job 3.1–26/Numbers 23.7–10 and 18–24/Lamentations 5.1–22/1 Chronicles 29.10–18/Isaiah 5.1–7.
18 Non-duplicates are Jeremiah 17.14–18/Job 6.3–13/Jeremiah 20.7–12/Job 16.8–20/Job 19.7–27 and Jeremiah 15.15–21.
19 Day 3 of the fast before Epiphany, Tobit 13.11–18.
20 They are listed in an appendix to this chapter.
21 Martin Patino, 'El Breviarium', pp. 266–89.
22 Pinell, 'Las Oraciones', *passim*.
23 J. Janini (ed.), *Liber Misticus de Cuaresma* (Toledo: Istituto de Estudios Visigotico-Mozarabes, 1979), p. xlii.
24 Not in *T2*.
25 In *The Study of Liturgy*, ed. C. Jones, G. Wainwright and E. Yarnold (London: SPCK, 1978), p. 365. He has since revised his position: see 1992 revised edition, ed. C. Jones, G. Wainwright, E. Yarnold and P. Bradshaw, pp. 403–20.

APPENDIX: CANTICLES USED ON WEEKDAYS

Advent

1 *Ecce Deus magnus*, Job 36.26–32/37.3–12 (Monday of weeks 1, 3, 5 and 6).
2 *Ego tuli te*, 2 Samuel 7.8–14 and 16 (Wednesday of weeks 1, 3 and 4; Tuesday of weeks 4 and 5, Christmas Eve).
3 *Exulta satis*, Zechariah 9.9–16 (Friday of weeks 1 and 3, Wednesday of week 5).
4 *Dominus Deus omnium creator*, 2 Maccabees 1.24–9 (Monday of weeks 2 and 4, Thursday of weeks 4 and 5; (see also Lent 1).
5 **Gaudens gaudebo*, Isaiah 61.10–11; 62.1–7 Wednesday of week 2, Friday of weeks 4 and 5).
6 *Ecce civitas*, Isaiah 26.1–8 (Friday of week 2 and Saturday of week 5; also see Lent 1).

* = used also on a Sunday.

Weekdays after Epiphany Octave

1 *Egredere de terra tua* – Genesis 12.1–3/13.14–15/22.17–18/15.7/17.1–4, 6 – Monday (see also Lent 1).
2 *Ecce odor*, Genesis 27.27–9/28.3–4 (Tuesday; see also Fasts and Lent 1).
3 *Deus patris nostri*, Genesis 32.9–12 (Wednesday; see also Fasts).
4 *Domine, Domine, rex deorum*, Deuteronomy 9.26–9 (Thursday; see also Fasts and Lent 1).

5 *Vidit enim eos*, Deut. 32.36–9 (i.e. part of *Attende*) (Friday, from the common service for a sick person).
6 *Magnificat*, Luke 1.46–55 (Saturday).

The First Half of Lent

1 *Egredere*, Genesis 12 etc. (Monday of first week; see also weekdays).
2 *Quid murmuravit*, Lamentations 3.39–44 (Tuesday of first and Thursday of third week).
3 *Domine Deus rex omnipotens*, Esther 13.9–11, 15–17 (Wednesday of first and Saturday of third week).
4 *Ecce odor*, Genesis 27.27–9; 28.3–4 (Thursday of first week; see also weekdays and Fasts).
5 *Dominus Deus omnium*, 2 Maccabees 1.24–9 (Friday of first and third weeks; see also Advent).
6 *Domine, Domine, rex deorum*, Deuteronomy 9.26–9 (Saturday of first week; see also weekdays and Fasts).
7 *Attende coelum, Deuteronomy 32.1–43 (originally only vv. 36–9) (Monday of second week; see also fast before Epiphany).
8 *Vocavit Jacob filios suos*, Genesis 49.1–27 (Tuesday of second week; see also Christmas).
9 *Pereat dies*, Job 3.1–26 (Wednesday of second week).
10 *De Aram adduxit me*, Numbers 23.7–10; 18–24 (Thursday of second week; see also fast before Epiphany).
11 *Memento Domine*, Lamentations 5.1–22 (Friday of second week and Wednesday of third week; see also Fasts).
12 *Benedictus es Domine, Deus Israel*, 1 Chronicles 29.10–18 (Saturday of second week).
13 *Cantabo nunc*, Isaiah 5.1–7 (Monday of third week).
14 *Ecce civitas*, Isaiah 26.1–8 (Tuesday of third week; see also Advent).

The Second Half of Lent

1 *Sana me, Domine*, Jeremiah 17.14–18 (Mondays of fourth and fifth, Wednesday of fourth and Saturday of fifth weeks).
2 *Verba mea*, Job 6.3–13 (Tuesday of fourth week).
3 *Seduxisti me*, Jeremiah 20.7–12 (Thursday of fourth, Saturday of fourth, Tuesday of fifth week and Monday, Wednesday and Thursday of Holy Week).
4 *Nunc ecce*, Job 16.8–20 (Friday of fourth week).

5 *Ecce clamo vim patiens*, Job 19.7–27 (Wednesday of fifth week).
6 *Clamavi ad Dominum*, Jonah 2.3–10 (Thursday of fifth week; see also Feasts).
7 *Tu scis Domine*, Jeremiah 15.15–21 (Friday of fifth week).
8 **Ego dixi in dimidio*, Isaiah 38.10–19 (Tuesday of Holy Week; see also Feasts).

The Fast before Epiphany

Day 1 *Attende coelum*, Deuteronomy 32.1–43 (also Lent 1).
Day 2 *De Aram adduxit me*, Numbers 23.7–10; 18–24 (see also Lent 1).
Day 3 *Luce clara*, Tobit 13.11–18.

The Other Fasts

1 *Domine Domine rex deorum*, Deuteronomy 9.26–9 (Wednesday and Saturday before Pentecost, first days before Cyprian and Martin, second day before Cyprian; see also weekdays and Lent 1).
2 *Deus patris nostri*, Genesis 32.9–12 (Thursday before Pentecost and second before Martin; see also weekdays).
3 *Ecce odor*, Genesis 27.27–9; 28.3–4 (Friday before Pentecost; see also weekdays and Lent 1).
4 *Memento Domine*, Lamentations 5.1–22 (third days before Cyprian and Martin; see also Lent 1).

12

THE MORNING PSALM OR MATUTINARIUM, AND THE SONO

After the canticle or canticles, there normally follows the unit entitled *Matutinarium* or, on Sunday, Sono. As a result of misreading its purpose this unit is often treated as an antiphon to the Daniel 3 canticle *Benedictus es* in *Br*.[1] The unit is normally composed of an antiphon and psalm verse and both are usually drawn from the same psalm. Sometimes *Gloria* is stipulated as well. On Sundays and feasts the *Sono* may well be taken from other texts, at least as far as the antiphon goes. That the two probably have the same origin will emerge as we proceed. As we shall also see, not only are the *Matutinaria* and *Soni* usually taken from the psalms, they are normally taken from psalms that make reference to themes of light or morning. On many days in *Br.* the concluding prayer or *Completuria* of Matins, although separated from the psalm by Psalms 148–50, a reading(s), hymn and *supplicatio*, is the psalm collect of the *Matutinarium* psalm.

In almost all ancient liturgies are found such morning psalms and one of the most commonly found is Psalm 62, first mentioned in the Apostolic Constitutions. The large amount of evidence for the use of Psalm 62 in early morning offices is detailed by Bradshaw and Taft.[2] Baumstark also pointed out its near universality and remarked on the singularity of the East Syrian tradition in not having it and of Spain, in not using it daily.[3] As these authors point out, other psalms of a similar thrust were commonly added to Psalm 62 and, whereas in the East the tradition appears to have aimed at using all of them daily; in the West, they were spread over a period of time, usually a week, as can be shown by the following table:

	Old Roman	Benedictine	Milan (Psalmus directus)
Sunday	92/99 and 62/66	66, 117 and 92/99/62	92

THE MORNING PSALM OR MATUTINARIUM

Monday	5 and 62/66	5 and 35	53
Tuesday	42 and 62/66	42 and 56	66
Wednesday	64 and 62/66	63 and 64	69
Thursday	89 and 62/66	87 and 89	112
Friday	142 and 62/66	75 and 91	142
Saturday	91 and 62/66	142	89

There is no sign of there having been any morning psalms of this kind in the Celtic rite and the Milanese *psalmi directi* seem to be additions to the actual morning office, even though the psalms chosen are typically used as morning psalms elsewhere, at least in the cases of Psalms 92, 66, 142 and 89.

The old Spanish tradition not only had a large number of matutinary psalms, but they were employed less systematically and, eventually, the *Sono* was reduced to a single verse, with the result that Sundays and feasts lost any full morning psalm. Pinell listed the following psalms used in Spain:

5, 18, **35**, 42, 58, 62, **66**, **75**, **87**, 89, 91, 100, 107, 118 (w 145–52), 129 and 142.

Those underlined are found in old Roman use, those in bold in both old Roman and Benedictine uses. Psalm 64, used in *AL* and in a Sunday *Sono* for the Fifth Sunday after Epiphany in *Br.* (col. 230), should probably be added to the list.

The psalms quoted are accompanied by the antiphons alluding to the theme of light and, as mentioned above, the whole psalm must originally have been intended.[4] The *Completuria* was originally the psalm collect of the *Matutinarium*, summing up the morning service as expressed in that psalm. The repertoire of *Matutinarium* antiphons is quite small and there are more *Completuria*/psalm collects than antiphons.

The most complete set of *Matutinaria* in *Br.* are once again those of Lent:

Week 1	Pss. 5, 35, 66, 5, 66 and 42
Week 2	Pss. 62, 75, 66, 100, 77 and 89
Week 3	Pss. 42, 62, 18, 89, 107 and 100
Week 4	Pss. 87, 62, 5, 100, 62 and 62
Week 5	Pss. 87, 142, 62, 100, 5 and 142
Week 6 (to Thursday)	Pss. 62, 5, 62 and 58

Except that the *Completuriae* in the second half of Lent are concerned with the passion theme, there is no real difference between the two halves of the season. The use of Psalm 77 on the second Friday is unusual (col. 367). Of the sixteen psalms listed previously, 13 are used in this Lenten arrangement above, and of the remaining three listed by Pinell, Psalms 91 and 118 (vv. 145–52) are not found in *Br.* at all but are in *AL*.[5] Psalm 129 occurs only in a Sunday *Sono* in *Br.*

There appears to be then, a smaller selection of *Matutinaria* in *Br.* and, possibly, in Tradition B as a whole: namely, Psalms 5, 18, 35, 42, 58, 62, 66, 75, 87, 89, 100, 107 and 142, with 64 and 129 on Sundays and some others seemingly chosen for their seasonal references. This list provides only four psalms that are not normally found as morning psalms in other Western rites: 18, 58, 100 and 107.

AL's arrangement is more systematic:

Lent 1	Pss. 5, 18, 35, 42, 58 and 62
Lent 2	Pss. 64, 66, 75, 87, 89 and 91
Lent 3	Pss. 100, 107, 117, 118 (vv.145–52), 129 and 142
Lent 4 and 5	Pss. 5, 35, 58, 62, 64 and 75
Holy Week	Pss. 5, 18(?) and 58[6]

The whole repertoire is gone through in psalm order in the first three weeks in Lent, which looks like a later systematization. The shorter cycle for the period *de Traditione* appears to have been arrived at by choosing psalms which, besides their morning themes, possess verses that reflect the passion themes. As an example of such passion themes, the antiphon for Psalm 58 quotes from the second verse of the psalm:

> O rescue me from those who do evil and save me from bloodthirsty men.

There is nothing like this in *Br.*, which used ordinary *Matutinaria* even in this season.

In the fragmentary weekday cycle of *Br.*, Psalm 5 is used on Monday and Tuesday, 18 on Wednesday and 35 on Thursday, and the *Completuriae* are their psalm collects. This seems a more systematic use, but is there also any sign of a thematic approach similar to that suggested for the *Missa*?

On the first Wednesday and third Monday of Lent we find:

> Ps. 66: O God be gracious unto us and bless us and cause your face to shine upon us.
> Ps. 42: O send out your light and your truth; they have guided me in the right way.

THE MORNING PSALM OR MATUTINARIUM

Both are clearly matutinal but the first is as adequate to the theme of the Temptation in the Wilderness as any other and the second goes well with the confident prayer for rescue heard in the *Missa* for this day. This is hardly conclusive, and without a more detailed examination, one can only suggest the hypothesis that the *Matutinaria* were drawn from a general repertoire as they best suited the theme of the day. Later some were gathered into ordered series as in *AL*.

This presumed general repertoire would also supply the texts for the fast days outside Lent, where the *Completuriae* are proper to the season and there seems to be festal interest in, e.g., the use of Psalm 111 and a verse from elsewhere. Once again there is a growing tendency to turn the *Matutinaria* into festal units.

There are six *Matutinaria* for the weekdays of Advent, Psalms 35, 42, 66, 75, 89 and 117, the last being the one not found in the general repertoire, and used on the second Wednesday and fourth and fifth Fridays. (Pinell mentioned that this one is cited in MS Brit. Mus. 30.845 with the sign 'Mt' to indicate *Matutinarium*).[7] The *Completuriae* are seasonal. Some psalms are used more often than others. Of those omitted from the *Missae* in *AL*, four were *Matutinaria* (Psalms 42, 62, 66 and 107). All but 107 appear frequently in Western morning offices. In *Br.* Psalm 42 is given for nine days and supplies the text of the *Sono* on at least two Sundays; Psalm 62 is also given on nine days and, as a *Sono*, for two Sundays. Psalm 66 is given on six days and two Sunday *Soni*, and Psalm 107 on the Friday of the third week of Lent.

Other frequently used psalms are 5 (seven weekdays and three Sundays), 35 (eight weekdays) and 89 (nine weekdays). The rest are used much less and the most frequently used psalms for the *Matutinarium* and *Sono* are then:

5, 35, 42, 62, 66 and 89.

All these are in the Benedictine office, and only 35 is not in the old Roman office. All but 35 are used in Sunday *Soni*, where are also found Psalms 75 and 142 (on two Sundays and two weekdays each). Psalm 75 is found in the Benedictine and 142 in Benedictine and old Roman offices. It seems then possible that the oldest stratum of morning psalms in Spain was a very similar repertoire to that of Rome:

5, 42, 62, 64, 66, 89 and 142.

Further, the cycle of morning *Soni* may well witness to the original set of morning psalms. Psalm 62 may well have been one of the first, but the others must have been added at a very early stage. Martin Patino thought the cycle of psalms in the Sunday *Soni* after Epiphany in *Br.* to be primitive.[8] The eight Sundays in turn employ Psalms 5, 42, 62 (twice), 64, 66, 75 and 142 (cols 186–242). The Second and Third Sundays after Pentecost may well be the start of a repeat series; the texts are the same for those given for the First and Second Sundays after Epiphany (cols 701 and 704). The Sunday before the November fast refers one to the texts for the Sixth Sunday (col. 707).

The structure of the *Sono* is simple, as can be shown by that for the first Sunday after Epiphany:

> Verba mea auribus percipe Domine, Alleluia.
> Give ear to my words O Lord, Alleluia.

The antiphon is from verse 1 of Psalm 5 and the verse is:

> Intellige clamorem meum, rex meus et Deus meus. Quoniam ad te orabo. Alleluia. (Listen to the sound of my cries, my King and my God, it is you whom I invoke. Alleluia.)

Originally Psalm 5 may have been sung with the response 'Alleluia'. On the next Sunday we find the antiphon taken from verse 3 of Psalm 42: 'O send forth your light' and the psalm verse is verse 1. Whereas the first Sunday's *Sono* has no immediate relevance to the morning (as far as the verses quoted go), on the second Sunday the relevant verse is employed as the antiphon or response.

The present form of the *Soni* often entails the omission of the psalm verses that actually refer to light or morning, but it is also possible that this cycle of Sunday texts was designed to reflect the theme of resurrection common to all morning offices and not chosen simply because they happened to mention the word 'morning': 'It is you who bless the just man, Lord' (Psalm 5); 'Why are you cast down, my soul? – hope in God' (Psalm 42); 'For your mercy is better than life' (Psalm 62); 'You keep your promise with marvels' (Psalm 62); 'The earth has given its fruit' (Psalm 66); 'The earth feared and was still, when God arose to Judgement' (Psalm 75) and 'Turn not your face away from me, lest I be like those in the grave' (Psalm 142).

Pinell thought that the Sunday *Soni* were copied from the weekday *Matutinaria* and noted that they were sometimes the same texts. He saw the *Benedictiones* as the normal replacement for the *Matutinarium* on Sundays, parallel to the Milanese custom of using canticles but no Matutinary psalm on a Sunday.[9] It seems more likely to this author that there was a fusing of two Spanish traditions, one having two canticles on Sundays, and the other a canticle and a morning psalm. Matins in *AL* has similar texts, but in the Sunday appendix only *Soni* based on Psalms 62 and 107 are given, and the version of the former is unlike any used in *Br*.[10] The relatively small number of morning psalms with their resurrectional overtones, and the signs of a simple mode of execution, urge the conclusion that the Sunday *Soni* are in fact relics of a tradition having a morning psalm on Sundays as well as weekdays.

On four of the Sundays of Lent the *Soni* of *Br*. have a very strong morning theme:

Lent 2	From the morning watch	Psalm 129	(col. 326)
Lent 3	In the morning shall I stand	Psalm 5	(col. 382)
Lent 4	Wherefore hast thou cast me off?	Psalm 42	(col. 442)
Lent 5	O send out thy light, ... O God, my God	Psalm 42/62	(col. 503)

On the first two of these Sundays the *Completuriae* are psalm collects for Psalm 5 (see cols 328 and 384).

Leaving aside the very festal *Soni*, the following morning psalms are often found on Sundays: 5, 42, 62, 64, 66, 75, 129 and 142, of which the most commonly used are 5, 42 62 and 66. In Pinell's list of *Matutinarium* antiphons[11] there are six versions from Psalm 5 (all in *Br*.), three from Psalm 42 (also all in *Br*.), six from Psalm 62 (one not in *Br*.) and five from Psalm 66 (one not in *Br*.). Only one antiphon is from Psalm 35 (cited five times in *Br*.) and two from Psalm 89 (the second is found five times in *Br*.). It appears then that the basic psalm repertoire is 5, 35, 42, 62, 66 and 89, the lesser used psalms being 18, 58, 64, 75, 77, 87, 91, 100, 107, 117, 118 (vv. 145–52), 129, 142 and 147.

Pinell's grouping of the *Matutinaria* shows how a presumed earlier version may be corrected and sometimes amplified in later use. As an example, this *Matutinaria* from Psalm 5:

> Mane exaudies vocem meam, Domine; mane astabo tibi et adorabo te. (In the morning you will hear me Lord, I will stand before you and worship you.)

This is given for Tuesday after Epiphany octave (col. 197) and the first Monday of Lent (col. 265), citing the first verse of the psalm after this antiphon. A corrected version follows the Psalter and supplies 'videbo' for 'adorabo' on the fifth Friday of Lent (col. 548). Another version conflates the second half of v. 4 above with the first half of v. 5:

> Mane astabo tibi et videbo te quoniam tu es deus nolens iniquitatem. (In the morning I will stand before you and still see you; for you are a God who hates iniquity.)

This version is used on the Third Sunday of Lent (col. 382) and a corrected version on the fourth Wednesday of Lent (col. 468) – again the first verse of the psalm is given.

Pinell numbers amongst the most ancient of *Matutinarium* antiphons, this from Psalm 35:

> In tuo, deus, lumine videbimus lumen. (In your light God, we shall see light.)

In *Br.* this is appointed for five days, and in all cases the versicle that follows is taken from the verse of the psalm that immediately follows that from which the antiphon is drawn. Pinell emphasized the antiquity of these elements in the old Spanish office. The early antiphons were later corrected and amplified and, later again, texts of the psalms having no actual reference to light or to the morning begin to be used for the antiphon, as we see in the period *de Traditione* in *AL*. The psalm prayers presupposed the antiphon until replaced by prayers of a more festal type with no reference to the time of day. These appeared from at least the seventh century. With the use of the Daniel 3 Canticle on Sundays the *Sono* became downgraded and the *Completuria* was no longer its psalm collect but a morning prayer similar to those of Rome, Milan or Byzantium, on the days which were not festal or particularly seasonal.

Br. helps us to reconstruct the origins of the Spanish office because it possesses a number of psalm collects used as *Completuriae* at Matins. The following are English versions of two such collects, for Psalms 5 and 35 respectively:

> O our king and our God, remove from our hearts the errors and ignorance of the night, so that, renewed in the new man, in the morning you hear our voices and make us to stand before you at the break of day in good works; as we look upon you, grant us to share in the earnest of your Resurrection.

This was used on the first Monday of Lent (col. 267) and adapted, on the Monday after the Epiphany octave to read 'share in the earnest of your Epiphany' (col. 193).

> O Lord, in you is the source of light, in whose light we see light, nourish us in the knowledge of your glory; that as we thirst for a

share in life-giving gifts, the refreshment of our souls, we may be restored to the higher light of understanding.

This appears for the first Tuesday of Lent (col. 281), with the canonical psalms in Advent (col. 88), as a *Lucernarium* collect for Epiphany (col. 175), Sixth Sunday after Epiphany octave (col. 232) and the First Sunday after Pentecost (col. 695). Both prayers are also good examples of the resurrection theme in an ordinary weekday morning prayer.

Pinell tried to show a parallel between the *Lucernarium* and *Matutinarium* as both refer to light, the former to lighting the lamps and the latter to the morning light. The *Matutinarium*, however, retained a much simpler form.[12] The later festal *Soni* are complex and those of Vespers are often closely linked with the *Lucernarium*.

CONCLUSIONS

We note the frequency of Psalm 62 as a morning psalm and also the frequency with which Psalm 66 is used – both were used daily in the old Roman office. The continued recurrence of these psalms may point to a usage established at a very early date. We also note the fact that many of the psalms for the Sunday *Soni* are found in the old Roman morning office: 5, 35, 42, 64, 75 and 142, as well as 62 and 66.

The motive of choice of the Sunday psalms could be as much to do with the resurrection as with the new light of morning. We may well have another echo of distant origin in the Easter Vigil. If the repertoire of psalm collects is not earlier than the mid-sixth century, was there a primitive morning service consisting of a psalm of the morning, some intercessions and, perhaps, an extempore prayer that recalled the psalm? The very simple structure of the *Matutinaria* inclines one to the belief that they cannot be much later than the first half of the sixth century.

In the early stages, Lenten usage may have been to pick from the general repertoire *Matutinaria* that were best suited to the theme of the day's celebration or at least, not totally irrelevant to it. This selection led to the identity of new matutinary psalms for special occasions, e.g. Psalm 147 on Palm Sunday and Psalm 3 at Easter, and this development may well have started by the sixth century. As the original theme was obscured with increasing festivalization, the *Completuriae* lost their connection with the morning psalm and, from at least the seventh century, are more often festal or seasonal.

The final development is the festal *Sono*. The morning psalm, already reduced to a single verse except perhaps on weekdays, is now another festal unit composed of various scriptural texts.

NOTES

1 *T1* does not support this misreading.
2 P. F. Bradshaw, *Daily Prayer in the Early Church* (London: Alcuin/SPCK, 1981); R. Taft, *The Liturgy of the Hours in East and West* (Collegeville: Liturgical Press, 1986).
3 A. Baumstark, *Nocturna Laus* (Munster: Aschendorff, 1967), p. 170.
4 J. Pinell, 'El *Matutinarium* en la Liturgia Hispana', *HS* 9 (1956), pp. 61–85, at p. 62.
5 *Antifonario Visigotico Mozarabe de la Catedral de Leon (AL)* ed. L. Brou and J. Vives (Madrid: *Monumenta Hispaniae Sacra, ser. lit.* 5, 1959), col. 123v.
6 See J. Pinell 'Las *Missae*, Grupos de Cantos y Oraciones en el Oficio de la Antigua Liturgia Hispana', *ArchL* 8 (1954), pp. 145–85, at p. 160.
7 Pinell, 'El *Matutinarium*', p. 72.
8 J. M. Martin Patino, 'El Breviarium Mozarabe de Ortiz, su Valor Documental para la Historia del Oficio Catedralico Hispanico', *Miscellanea 40 Comillas* (1963), pp. 207–97, at p. 220.
9 Pinell, 'El *Matutinarium*', pp. 81–3; and 'Los Canticos del Oficio en el Antiguo Rito Hispanico', *HS* 27 (1974), pp. 5–54, at p. 15.
10 *AL*, cols 296 and 296v.
11 Pinell, 'El *Matutinarium*', pp. 67–73.
12 Pinell, ibid., pp. 80–5.

13

THE LAUDATE PSALMS

Psalms 148, 149 and 150 together are one of the most universal and primitive features of Matins. The old Spanish rite is no exception and so far as *Br.* is concerned, the three are cited to be used on all Sundays and feasts. They are always grouped together under one antiphon and there is only one *Gloria* at the end of all three. On certain weekdays however, only one of the psalms, Psalm 150, is appointed to be used, something not found outside Spain.

The weekday arrangements are as follows:

Advent weekdays: Psalm 150, except that on Monday of the Second Week and Thursday of the Fourth and Fifth Week 'Psalm 148' (which signifies all three) is appointed, although the antiphon is taken from Psalm 150 (col. 73). Also, on the second Friday and the fifth Saturday 'Psalm 148' is cited and the antiphon is from Psalm 148 itself (col. 78).

January fast: first and third days cite 'Psalm 148' but with antiphons from Psalm 150 (cols 151 and 171). Psalm 150 is cited on second day (cols 151ff.).

Weekdays after the Epiphany octave: Monday to Thursday, Psalm 150 (col. 192–205). Friday, the Office of the Sick (very unusual), Psalm 116 and Saturday, being largely derived from the festal material for 18 December, cites all three (cols 209 and 214).

Weekdays of Lent: Normally Psalm 150, but for all Wednesdays and Fridays (and a few other days), and on Monday, Tuesday and Thursday of Holy Week 'Psalm 148' is appointed (cols 265–597).[1] There is a clear pattern of all three psalms being used on Wednesday and Friday throughout Lent on all but one day (strangely the Wednesday) in Holy Week. Since we have already found that these days were the ones on which the Eucharist was celebrated in Lent, it is likely that we here have the earlier pattern, the use of Psalm 150 on other weekdays being perhaps a later simplification.

The fast before Pentecost: Psalm 150, except on the Saturday, all three (col. 662ff.).

The fast before St Cyprian: Psalm 150 every day (col. 709ff.).

The fast before St Martin: Psalm 150, except on the last day, all three (col. 724ff.).

The offices of the Sanctoral and the common of Saints in *Br.* appear to know only the singing of all three psalms, an interesting exception being the common for the Departed which cites Psalm 150 alone (col. 988).

Turning to the Sundays we find only a very small repertoire of antiphons of the Laudate psalms, e.g.,

> Laudate Dominum de caelis. Alleluia, Alleluia. Laudate eum in excelsis. Alleluia, Alleluia. (col. 55) (Praise the Lord from the heavens, Alleluia, Alleluia. Praise him in the highest. Alleluia, Alleluia.)

This is appointed for all the Sundays of Advent (with some variation in number of Alleluias), for the Sundays after Epiphany octave, Friday and Saturday of Easter week and the Sundays of Eastertide including that after Ascension; the Sundays after Pentecost, before the November Fast, and for the Advent of John.

This basic form reappears with slight variations, sometimes being lengthened into the next verse, on most feasts and in the common offices. The antiphon is simply the first verse of the set and may well be a relic of an unchanging simple form of these psalms, sung right through with only Alleluia as a refrain.

AL has a set of three antiphons on the *Laudate* psalms which may well have been sung together, since only the last has *Gloria*. The first quotes the first two verses of Psalm 148, the second the first verse of Psalm 149 and the third appears to repeat the first verse of Psalm 150 twice.[2] The only time that anything similar is found in *Br.* is on the feast of St John the Evangelist which has both the basic form as given above, and the following:

> Alleluia. Confessio ejus super coelum, et terram. Alleluia. Exaltabit cornu populo suo. Alleluia. *V* Hymnus est omnibus sanctis ejus. Alleluia. (col. 131) (Alleluia. His praise is above

the earth and heaven. Alleluia. And he shall exalt the horn of his people. Alleluia. *V* The praise of all the saints is his. Alleluia.)

Taken from the last two verses of Psalm 148, it is also appointed for two other feast days and for the common of Confessors.

On the Third, Fourth and Fifth Sundays of Lent and Palm Sunday the antiphons for the *Laudate* psalms are of similar form to the last example, and all quote verses of Psalm 148. That for Palm Sunday has verse 12 of the psalm as the antiphon but the verse is from another source or is an adaptation (col. 567). For Good Friday, Psalm 139, 'Rescue me Lord, from evil men', is given as the '*lauda*' (col. 607).

Returning to the weekdays, a generally common pattern emerges in the use of Psalm 150 on many weekdays. The first verse introduces the psalm:

Laudate Dominum in sanctis ejus. Alleluia. Alleluia. Laudate eum in firmamento virtutis ejus. Alleluia. *Psalmus CL*. *P* Laudate Dominum. *V* Gloria, et honor Patri, et Filio. *P* Laudate eum in firmamento. (col. 61). (Praise the Lord in his saints. Alleluia. Alleluia. Praise him in the firmament of his power. Alleluia. *Psalm 150*. *P* Praise the Lord. *V* Glory and honour to the Father and the Son. *P* Praise him in.)

On the Wednesdays and Fridays of Lent all three psalms are to be sung and the antiphons all quote Psalm 148. When Psalm 150 alone is used, the antiphon from verse 1 above is found 11 times (without Alleluia). Once again, it seems that Psalm 150 was originally sung with an alleluiatic refrain. In the old Roman use, the antiphon for these psalms on Sundays was simply 'Alleluia' three times, verses of Psalm 148 supplying the antiphons for Monday to Wednesday and of Psalm 150 for Thursday to Saturday.

The ordinary antiphon in the Benedictine office of Sunday was also 'Alleluia' and there was a similar set of antiphons for the weekdays. In Milan it was customary to sing Psalms 148–50 with Psalm 116 added, as often found in some Eastern sources (e.g. East and West Syrian[3]). The Egyptian 'psalmodia of the night' has Psalms 148–50 with 'Alleluia' after each verse. This may be a relic of a cathedral office of the morning.[4]

It has been suggested that these psalms came into the cathedral office from the monastic office as the conclusion of the all-night psalmody.[5] Hanssens did not agree[6] and more recently Taft showed how Cassian appeared to treat these psalms as a separate office, and he also emphasized that they came at the end of the morning, not the night office. If the ancient morning office comprised more than Psalm 62 alone, then that 'more' was Psalms 148–50.[7] The strength of Taft's case is now recognized by Bradshaw who, in reviewing Taft's book, suggested that these psalms may have been the first element of the morning office to acquire a fixed, formal place, other elements, even Psalm 62, coming later.[8]

It is no longer possible to state, as Baumstark did, that these psalms entered Christian worship from the synagogue.[9] They do, however, seem to be at the core of nearly all early Christian morning services that are known, including those of Spain. Here the old Spanish office appears to have undergone very little alteration, at least in Br. and sources of the same tradition. It may well be the central element of the old Spanish Matins, originally perhaps sung with the simple response 'Alleluia'. Lent called for responses without 'Alleluia' and from these developed the antiphons sung at the beginning and end of the three psalms. Later may have come the practice of using Psalm 150 alone on weekdays but its antiphons do display a simple, presumably primitive, structure.

At the earliest stages, prayers would no doubt have followed these psalms. The elements that now follow them are later insertions. The psalm of praise would have been the climax of the morning office, the praise of God who restores life after the darkness of the night that signifies death. That this unit remained so little unchanged may show that some memory of its centrality was kept. This centrality may have been emphasized by a ceremonial use of incense such as appears to have been the case in Milan.[10]

NOTES

1 The exceptions of second Monday and fourth Thursday may be copyists' errors.
2 *Antifonario Visigotico Mozarabe de la Catedral de Leon* (*AL*), ed. L. Brou and J. Vives (Madrid: *Monumenta Hispaniae Sacra*, ser. lit. 5, 1959, f. 296v.
3 See, e.g., R. Taft, *The Liturgy of the Hours in East and West* (Collegeville: Liturgical Press, 1986), pp. 232, 241.
4 ibid., p. 256.
5 See, e.g., P. F. Bradshaw, *Daily Prayer in the Early Church* (London: Alcuin/SPCK, 1981), pp. 109–10.
6 J. M. Hanssens, *Nature at Genese de l'office des Matines* (Rome: *Analecta Gregoriana* LVII, 1952), pp. 105–6.
7 Taft, op. cit., pp. 192–209.
8 In *Worship* 60.6 (1986), pp. 544–6.
9 A. Baumstark, *Comparative Liturgy* (London: Mowbray, 1958), p. 38; and see J. W. McKinnon, 'On the Question of Psalmody in the Ancient Synagogue', *Early Music History*, 6 (1986), pp. 159–91.
10 See *Beroldus, sive Ecclesiae Ambrosianae Mediolanense Kalendarium et Ordines*, ed. M. Magistretti (Milan, 1894; reprinted Farnborough: Gregg, 1968), p. 44.

14
READINGS IN THE OLD SPANISH OFFICE

There is an automatic assumption, especially in the English-speaking world and perhaps due to Anglican influence, that the Divine Office has readings from Scripture. An examination of the earliest evidence shows no sign at all of readings at the cathedral offices. Taft, following Zerfass and Mateos, points to their almost total absence from the East Syrian Liturgy, which is one of the most primitive to survive. There are some indications that Egypt had readings at the morning office in the fourth century, and in Cappadocia they appear to have had readings at Vespers and at the Vigil.[1] Traces of the primitive pattern can still be found in many Eastern rites. In the West readings were originally found only in monastic vigil and not at the cathedral Matins and Vespers. This is certainly how Taft interprets the evidence from Caesarius, for example.[2] The monastic night Vigils, together with the eucharistic liturgy, were the proper place for reading the Scriptures, not the morning and evening services of the people as a whole.

A very interesting piece of evidence about Roman practice is a letter written by Theodemar, Abbot of Montecassino, 777–97, who believed that readings were introduced to the Roman office at some time in the late sixth or early seventh century. Bradshaw notes that there was still no short reading at Prime or Compline as late as the ninth century.[3]

Monks introduced systematic reading into their vigils in order to fulfil their need for meditational material, and these spilled over into the cathedral offices in two forms in the West: a brief reading from memory, the 'Little Chapter', and a systematic reading in course. The latter was confined to the night office of originally monastic provenance, as we see in the Nocturns with their nine Sunday and Feast-day readings of the old Roman office and the similar arrangements of St Benedict. Lessons in the Milanese night office appear not to be indigenous to that rite.[4] Magistretti believed such readings to have come in the fifth or sixth century, but Righetti thinks it more likely that they result from the Carolingian reforms.[5] In the Milanese night office, these readings do give the impression of having been 'tacked on' after the psalmody, even on Sundays and feasts which in Roman use had the readings dispersed among the psalmody.

All other services in the old Roman and Benedictine rites acquired a 'Little Chapter', a mere verse or two of Scripture that could be committed to memory as required by Benedict.[6] This custom of the 'Little Chapter' was resisted by Milan, at least as far as Lauds and Vespers were concerned, though the minor hours did acquire one under the title of *Epistolella*. Even in the modernized Milanese office Sunday Vespers has no reading. The Celtic rite did have a Gospel reading after the *Laudate* psalms but Curran thinks this may well have been moved from its original place in the Vigil to the end of Lauds.[7]

Old Spanish Vespers never acquired reading of Scripture, but Matins did. The most complete arrangement is found in Lent, for which there is provided in *Br.* a series of lengthy readings in course from the 'Law and the former Prophets'. These lengthy Lenten readings follow the *Laudate* psalms and precede the hymn, a position for a lengthy reading in course not found elsewhere and thus, on comparative evidence alone, they look suspiciously like much later insertions. The course reading is also spread over the cathedral minor hours of Terce and None and the Masses of Sunday, Wednesday and Friday. The early sources quoted by Pinell do not give any hint of readings; e.g. the Bobadilla ordo: 'in matutinis dicantur psalmi matutinarii tres, deinde responsum et laudes, sequente ymno et dominica oratione' – 'In Matins are said three morning psalms, then the responsory and the *laudes*, followed by a hymn and the Lord's Prayer.'[8] Similarly, Fructuosus in the seventh century made no mention of readings at this point, but Isidore did expect there to be reading in the Monastic office.[9]

The system of readings commences on the Monday of the first week of Lent with Genesis 2.1—3.24 and, with some omissions, Genesis is read up to and including Matins of the Wednesday of the second week. At Terce on that day, Exodus is started and, with more omissions, is read up to and including Terce of the Saturday of the second week, finishing at Exodus 18.27. On the Third Sunday, at Matins and Mass, are read two sections of Numbers: 13.1—14.24 and 22.2—23.10 and the next day one reading from Deuteronomy 34.1–12 at Matins. In the following week there are readings from Joshua and Judges and, at Matins on the Fourth Sunday, the whole of Ruth is read. The Mass commences the reading of 1 Samuel and 2 Samuel which is finished at Matins of the Friday of the fifth week. From Terce that day to Maundy Thursday Matins inclusive, there are readings from 1 and 2 Kings, though with a reading of Lamentations on the Tuesday of Holy Week at Terce, and finally Isaiah 50 at Terce on Maundy Thursday. Also excepted from this scheme are the Matins and Mass readings of Palm Sunday: 1 Samuel 16.1–13a (not read in the fourth week) and Deuteronomy 11.18–32 respectively.

There appears to be a discernible theme in this series of readings. The series commences with the creation and first sin of humankind, passes on to Cain and Abel (omitting the flood which is featured in the Easter Vigil – *PL* 85, cols 448–9) and tells of the Tower of Babel. Abram goes into Egypt and parts from Lot; God makes a covenant with him and changes his name. Abraham intercedes for Sodom but its sin leads to destruction; Isaac is born and Hagar dismissed. Isaac meets and marries Rebecca; Jacob seizes the initiative from Esau; Jacob goes away and meets Rachel; they deceive Laban and return to be reconciled with Esau. The Joseph cycle details his slavery, experiences in prison, rise to power, dealings with his brothers and their eventual reconciliation. Israel goes down to Egypt with all his people. The Exodus accounts are of the birth of Moses, the burning bush, the message to Pharaoh and the plagues, the flight as far as the edge of the Red Sea. The crossing of the Red Sea is left to the Easter Vigil (*PL* 85, cols 451–2). Also from Exodus are the account of the people's complaint at Massah and Meribah, with the defeat of Amalek and Jethro's advice to appoint elders. From Numbers comes the negative reaction to the report of those sent to spy out the land, and the story of Balaam; from Deuteronomy the death of Moses. Joshua tells first of Rahab, the fall of Jericho, the sin of Achan and the victory over the Amorites. It finishes with the defeat of the five kings and the covenant and death of Joshua. From the Judges comes the story of Gideon and his refusal to be a king, also the life of Samson, the murder of the Levite's concubine and the civil war that follows. Then comes the whole story of Ruth.

From the Mass of the Fourth Sunday of Lent, the theme of oscillation between obedience and disobedience to God's will continues. The story of Samuel's birth and calling, the capture of the Ark and Israel's demand for a king, lead to the history of Saul's reign and eventual failure to obey God. The selection and anointing of David is omitted here and used at Matins on Palm Sunday. The series continues with David's career before becoming king. David reigns but commits adultery with the wife of Uriah the Hittite and their child dies. The killing of Amon by Absalom and his later revolt and death lead to the struggle to succeed David, Solomon's ascent and his apostasy. The cycle concludes with a few of the Elijah stories and his succession by Elisha.[10]

We find here a constant concern to illustrate the truth that men and women do sin and are sinful. Some of the most heinous crimes that people can commit are unswervingly related in considerable detail and at some length. There is another side; there are plenty of examples of repentance and sorrow and, in general, one could say that while humanity's total depravity is taken very seriously indeed, so is the fact of God's forgiveness of sinners and his continued faithfulness to his faithless people.

Bishop suggested that these readings, complemented at Terce and None by readings from the sapiential books, formed a series of the catechumenal lectures followed (at the hours) by three Antiphons, except on Wednesdays and Fridays when the Eucharist followed. He also mentioned a Milanese parallel of catechism at the third and ninth hours on the Mondays to Fridays of Lent. All of this would be found in the cathedral rather than the parish churches of a particular town.[11] The Milanese parallel is the more revealing when we recall that Ambrose spoke of the 'daily moral discourse when the history of the patriarchs or the precepts of the Proverbs were read'.[12] In twelfth-century Milan the Heptateuch was to be read from Septuagesima to the middle of Lent and included the book of Ruth. This arrangement spread the reading over six weeks, whereas in Spain these particular books were covered in three, as we have seen. In Spain, Lent originally lasted three weeks and Bishop's theory was that this series of readings from the Heptateuch was read then, but was later pushed back to what became the first three weeks and the continuing series of readings from the books of Samuel and the Kings were then added for the second half of Lent. Bishop also showed that Tradition A books like *OV*, while having a slightly different arrangement of the cathedral 'minor hours' and also different days on which Mass was celebrated, were yet using a similar system.

The sapiential readings comment on the historical; some examples will show this: on Tuesday of the first week Genesis tells of Abram in Egypt and is preceded by Proverbs 5.15—6.3a, which includes an exhortation to rejoice in the wife of one's youth – in Egypt Abram pretended that Sarai was his sister. At Sext, Isaiah 5.8–16 is read and has the words 'My people go into exile for want of knowledge' and at None, the account of God's covenant with Abram is preceded by Sirach 2.1–4 urging hearers to cleave to the Lord and not depart from him.

Other sources show interesting parallels. The Bible of Alcala has marginal notes that indicate the beginnings of readings and in some cases the ends too. Genesis and Exodus are divided between Matins, Terce and Sext (on two occasions None) of the first two weeks of Lent. Of 29 readings, 17 start in the same place as those in *Br.* and seven are appointed for the same service of the same day. Two of the 17 are to finish at the same point.[13] This is representative of Tradition A which, as Martin Pintado has shown, arranges similar material somewhat differently and does not use the Wisdom literature in the same way.[14] The Tradition A systems are parallel methods of ordering the same material to provide an overview of God's dealings with his often erring people, and thus forming a comprehensive catechetical instruction for those to be baptized. This may not have differed greatly from what obtained in Milan. Martin Pintado believes the arrangement of *Br.*, of Tradition B, to be the more ancient: it avoids centonizing readings, associates the sapiential readings with the historical ones and keeps the custom of two Old Testament readings even on the days when there is a Mass. Martin Pintado said that the readings found in *Br.* at Matins and Mass on the Second, Third, Fourth and Fifth Sundays of Lent and Palm Sunday are the same as those in *T5* of the tenth century.[15] This, again one of the very few Tradition B manuscripts, also gives the Mass readings for the Wednesdays and Fridays of Lent, the same ones to be found in *Br.* So far, then, Ortiz must have remained close to the sources and may well have used this very manuscript.

In the introduction to his edition of *T2*, Janini points out that this manuscript lacks much in the way of references to readings in the first three weeks of Lent but, in the last three weeks, there are references to the beginning of readings from the historical books.[16] In fact such references are found for 20 days, usually at Matins and None, and they are all indicated as starting at the same place as those given in *Br.*[17] In the first three weeks there is reference to a daily, unchanging reading of a passage from Proverbs (3.5–7) at Matins, which is not found in the Lenten services in *Br.* but is appointed for the four days of the fragmentary weekday cycle.

Janini concluded that for the first three weeks Ortiz used MS Toledo 35.8, the *Liber Commicus* of Toledo, as a guide for building up a series of readings to cover the gaps left by *T5*. In doing so he juggled readings about, sometimes lengthening or shortening them. The prophetic readings were just added in, not being found in 35.8, and in the last three weeks Ortiz took the incipits of *T2* and finished the readings wherever the mood took him, filled in the spaces and provided new prophetic readings. He also mixed up Vulgate and other versions of the Scripture. Martin Pintado suggested that *T2* followed ordinary weekday use in the last three weeks of Lent and that monastic influence had reduced the reading of the first three weeks to the short sapiential one.

It is at least possible that Ortiz had before him another source which fitted in with the readings of *T5* and was different from 35.8. This other source is only an hypothesis, but so is the theory that has Ortiz simply inventing things that do not fit in with the few manuscripts that still exist today. It would have been simpler for him to introduce the more complete system of 35.8 *in toto* and forget about *T5*. Whatever may be true about the sources that existed in about 1500, it is still possible that this system of readings originated as a set of catechetical instructions for those to be baptized at Easter. As such, they would probably date from the fourth or fifth centuries, when baptism of adults was still the norm; their content includes the then common themes of such catechism, such as choosing the way of life over the way of death.[18] The daily reading of Proverbs 3.5–7 which Ortiz probably did omit, perhaps to transfer it to weekdays that lacked any reading, provided an appropriate general preface addressed to those who would seek true wisdom:

> Trust in the Lord with all your heart, and do not rely on your own insight. In all your ways acknowledge him, and he will make straight your paths. Be not wise in your own eyes; fear the Lord and turn away from evil.

Originally the catechetical instructions were no part of the daily evening and morning services. Once infant baptism became the norm, the process may have been that one reading was transferred to Matins and the others, with Antiphons, were formed into cathedral minor hours, the extra reading at Sext from the prophets perhaps being added then.[19]

It may have been partly from a desire to imitate Roman and Benedictine practice that readings were inserted into the morning service, but those uses know only a 'Little Chapter' at this point. The use of Proverbs 3.5–7 on weekdays in *Br.* is the nearest parallel to a Little Chapter in the old Spanish Matins (there is a similar reading for Terce on those days, cols 192 and 193). Most of the Matins readings in *Br.*, though not so long as the Lenten ones, are much longer than those that compose the Little Chapter in other traditions. The use of the sapiential literature remains a general chracteristic of these short Spanish readings, and the whole series could be described as general moralizing,[20] although those for Advent Sundays are mostly prophetic[21] and do largely harmonize with the eucharistic readings of those Sundays. Feast-day readings are obviously chosen to suit the day, and the other fasts show a predilection for sapiential readings that emphasize the observance of particular seasons. This whole system of readings is in stark contrast with those of the old Roman and Benedictine systems of *lectio continua* and the Little Chapter. The only continuous reading, the Lenten one, is completely different in style and purpose from that of the monastic meditative reading of Scripture in course.

We may conclude:

1 Readings are not original components of the old Spanish cathedral Matins, either as a continuous series or as a Little Chapter. Alongside this however, there may have been a series of catechetical instructions in cathedrals during Lent, based on the Law and the Former Prophets, with commentary from the sapiential books.
2 A cathedral vigil on certain days may have involved readings from the Old Testament, the Epistles and the Gospels; and this may have existed by the seventh century.
3 By the sixth or seventh century, infant baptism was more common, and there were no catechumens to instruct. A desire to increase the edificatory element of the cathedral offices may have led to the readings being transferred there in Lent.
4 Later again, a series of sapiential readings of a generally edifying character was established on Sundays – while too long to be 'Little Chapters', these never became a continuous system either.
5 Finally, appropriate readings are identified for saints' days and other festivals. That these occur in a position more akin to that of the Little Chapter may show that any awareness of the *Missa* unit as constitutive of the old Spanish vigil was now lost, so the readings were not included at that point.

NOTES

1 R. Taft, *The Liturgy of the Hours in East and West* (Collegeville: Liturgical Press, 1986), pp. 34–41.
2 ibid., pp. 103 and 152–3.

3 P. F. Bradshaw, *Daily Prayer in the Early Church* (London: Alcuin/SPCK, 1981), p. 137.
4 W. C. Bishop, ed. C. L. Feltoe, *The Mozarabic and Ambrosian Rites* (London: Alcuin/Mowbray, 1924), p. 121.
5 M. Righetti, *Storia Liturgica* (Milan: Ancora, 1946), p. 688.
6 *Rule of St Benedict* 12.
7 M. Curran, *The Antiphonary of Bangor* (Dublin: Irish Academic Press, 1984), pp. 186–7.
8 Quoted in J. Pinell, 'El Oficio Hispanico-Visigotico', *HS* 10 (1957), pp. 385–427, at p. 420.
9 See *PL* 83, cols 876–7 – Chapter 6 of *Regula Monachorum*.
10 Genesis 2.1—3.24/4.1–26/5.1–29/11.1—12.8/12.10—13.18/15.1—17.21/18.1–33/19.1–29/20.1—21.33/24.1–67/25.19—26.5a/27.1—28.4/29.1–28/31.17—32.1a/32.3–30/37.2b–36/39.1—40.22/41.1–45a/41.46—43.14a/43.15b—45.16/45.16—46.7/46.28—47.12/47.15b–26/47.27—48.22/49.18b—50.6. Exodus 1—2.10/2.11—3.15/3.15—6.1/6.29—8.31a/9.1–33/9.34—10.19/10.21—12.41/13.17—14.24/22.2—23.10. Deuteronomy 34.1–12. Joshua 1.1—3.5/5.13—6.27/6.27—7.26a/8.1–30/9.3–27/10.1–27/24.1–31a. Judges 1.1–26/6.1–24a/6.33—7.25/8.4–32/13.2–25a/14.1—15.19/16.1–31/19.1—20.26/20.28b—21.25. Ruth. 1 Samuel 1.1–20/1.20—2.1a, 11–26/2.27—3.19a/4.1b–18/7.1–17/8.1–22a/9.1–25a/9.26—10.25a/10.26—11.15/12.1–24/14.47b—15.21/17.1–37/17.37–54/17.55—18.30/19.1—20.8a/20.8–42/21.1—23.18/23.19—24.22/25.2–39/26.1–24/28.3–25/29.1—30.25/31.1. 2 Samuel 2.4/2.8–32a/3.1–28/3.28—5.8/11.1–27/12.1–25/13.24—14.33/15.1—16.15/16.16—17.23/18.1—19.8/19.11—21.22. 1 Kings 1.1–48/1.49—2.12/2.12—3.3a/3.5–28/11.4–24/12.33b—13.31/17.2–24/18.1–40/18.41—19.21. 2 Kings 2.1–22/6.24—7.20.
11 Bishop, op. cit., pp. 87–9.
12 E. J. Yarnold, *The Awe-Inspiring Rites of Initiation* (Slough: St Paul's, 1971), p. 11 – *Catechism* 1, 5, 6.
13 D. de Bruyne OSB, 'Un système de Lectures de la Liturgie Mozarabe', *Revue Benedictine* XXXIV (1922), pp. 147–55.
14 V. Martin Pintado, 'Las Lecturas Cuaresmales de Antiguo Testamento en la Liturgia Hispanica. Estudio de Liturgia Comparada', *Salmanticensis* XXII.2 (1975), pp. 217–69, esp. 218–9.
15 ibid., pp. 219–20.
16 J. Janini (ed.), *Liber Misticus de Cuaresma* (Toledo: Istituto de Estudios Visigotico-Mozarabes, 1979), pp. xxxviiiff.
17 Janini, ibid., pp. 267–8 (appendix).
18 See, e.g., R. Grant, 'Development of the Christian Catechumenate' in *Made Not Born* (Notre Dame, IN: University Press, 1976), pp. 32–49.
19 Though we should note the existence of a parallel prophetic reading at the Sixth Hour of the modern Byzantine Orthodox rite on Lenten weekdays.
20 For the Sundays after Epiphany and Pentecost: Proverbs 25.1–13/Ecclesiasticus 2.2b—3.12/9.1b–7/Wisdom 6.21—7.7/Sirach 1.1–9a/6.37—7.11/32.19—33.1/34.14—35.6/2.7–17/Wisdom 1–7a/Sirach 7.35—8.8/9.10–16.
21 Sirach 24.22–32/Isaiah 22.15–23/Ezekiel 34.22—35.31/Isaiah 42.10–16a/Micah 4.1–10/Isaiah 7.10—8.10.

15

THE MORNING HYMN

By contrast to Vespers, only 12 hymns are appointed in *Br.* to follow the reading and precede the final prayers at Matins. Also in contrast to Vespers most of them are not Spanish in origin.

For ordinary Sundays after Epiphany and Pentecost *Splendor paternae gloriae* (col. 149), attributed to St Ambrose, is appointed. It was also the ordinary morning hymn in Milanese Lauds. The hymn is found in Benedictine Lauds on Monday, and was eventually inserted at the same place in the Roman Breviary. It is without doubt a very suitable hymn for the morning:

O Splendor of God's glory bright,
O thou that bringest light from light,
O Light of light, light's living spring,
O Day, all days illumining.[1]

The following hymns are appointed for weekdays:

Mon.	*Fulgentis auctor aetheris*	'Author of the shining heaven'	(col. 192)
Tues.	*Deus aeterni luminis*	'God of everlasting light'	(col. 197)
Wed.	*Deus Pater ingenite*	'God the Father unbegotten'	(col. 201)
Thurs.	*In matutinis surgimus*	'At morning we rise'	(col. 205)
Fri.	*Aeterne lucis conditor*	'Eternal creator of the light'	(col. 310)
Sat.	*Deus creator omnium*	'Creator of the earth and sky'	(col. 318)

(The last two are only given for Lent in Br.) All six are well-known morning hymns.

At least one document gives *Te Deum* as the Sunday morning hymn at this point in Matins.[2] *AL* makes reference to several seasonal and festal hymns at Matins but not to any hymn for Sundays after Epiphany or Pentecost. *T5* of Tradition B gives the hymns of the Lenten Sundays as they are in *Br*.

Outside of seasons and particular feasts with their own proper hymns, there may have been a custom in Tradition A regions of using the *Te Deum* as the morning hymn but it appears nowhere in *Br*. for Matins.[3] Tradition B areas may have been slower to introduce any hymn at this point, at least until the influence of seasonal and festal customs became stronger.

Other hymns appointed for morning only include another of non-Spanish origin, the well-known *Hostis Herodes impie* (col. 184) of Sedulius ('Why, impious Herod, shouldest thou fear') for Epiphany. It is not a particularly matutinal hymn and in Benedictine use it comes at Vespers.

Caterva matrum personet ('A crowd of mothers of the people') (col. 135) for Matins of the Holy Innocents is purely festal. The same may also be said of the hymns in the Sanctoral of *Br*. that are appointed for Matin, with a few rather tenuous exceptions. The Advent hymns *Cunctorum rex omnipotens* ('Almighty King of all creation') (col. 57) (which should be seen as including the shorter version *Cunctorum rerum* (col. 61)) and *Ecce Salvator omnium* ('Behold the saviour of all') (col. 73) are of Spanish origin. Both are seasonal and the former has a reference to the people in the darkness awaiting the coming of Christ, thus suiting it for morning use. *Noctis tempus jam praeterit* ('Now the time of night is past') (col. 446) is used in the morning of both Sundays and weekdays in the period *de Traditione*. This hymn makes reference to cockcrow in its first verse in speaking of Peter's betrayal, but the main theme is the passion and betrayal of Jesus Christ. To these hymns we may add Ambrose's *Hic est dies verus Dei* ('Here truly is the day of God') for Easter (col. 618) as it is appointed for the Matins of the Sundays of Eastertide up to the Ascension, but it is not a specifically morning hymn.

The hymns at Vespers and at Matins were probably first added to reflect festal and seasonal themes rather than the hour of the day. Possibly the ordinary Sundays and weekdays (where not encroached upon by the rapidly increasing number of saints' days) did not have hymns at first or only had a very small selection. As has already been said concerning the hymn at Vespers, the hymns are interpolated and they comment on already established forms. As a result, they add little to our knowledge of the primitive core of these offices, and this is especially so in the case of Matins.

Several hymns, not necessarily very late ones, are appointed for both evening and morning celebrations. These are all either festal or seasonal and include such hymns as *Vox clara ecce intonat* ('Hark, a herald voice is calling')[4] and *Verbum supernum prodiens* ('High Word of God who once didst come').[5] Both of these would be more suited to Advent mornings. We find several hymns of purely seasonal theme for Advent-Christmas-Epiphany, some of the Lent Sundays and Palm Sunday, Ascension and Pentecost.

One of the more interesting of these hymns is that for what *Br.* calls the First Sunday of Lent: *Alleluia piis edite laudibus* (col. 259). The use of *Alleluia* in Lent would strike most Western Christians as strange, but in Spain the actual fast did not commence until the Monday of the first week of Lent.[6] The hymn with its frequently repeated refrain of *Alleluia* is almost a solemn farewell to this word of praise for the duration of Lent. Perez de Urbel dates the hymn to the seventh century.[7] The first two verses are given as an example:

Alleluia piis edite laudibus
Cives aetherei, psallite unanimiter
Alleluia perenne. (Sing Alleluia forth in duteous praise,
Ye citizens of heaven; O sweetly raise,
An endless Alleluia.)

Hinc vos perpetui luminis accolae
Ad summum resonate hymniferis choris
Alleluia perenne. (Ye powers who stand before the eternal light
In hymning choirs re-echo to the height,
An endless Alleluia.[8])

The hymn for the other days of Lent, *Benignitatis fons Deus* (col. 152), is appointed for Matins and Vespers on all these days. It is of Spanish origin and is found in many of the sources, and as we might expect, is heavily penitential. Verses 1, 4 and 5 will serve for examples:

Source of all kindness, O God,
Whose goodness has no end
Beyond all wicked evil
Always the holy always the good.

A suppliant voice is raised to you,
O creator, spare! it says,

> Again us spare, it cries beseeching,
> Pardon us that, which we have done.
>
> Let us your anger not have to drink.
> Nor punishment grind us down:
> Come quickly to shine on the contrite,
> And grant us joy.

The hymns for the saints' days are, as we might expect, suitable for celebrating these heroes of faith. The praises of the saints are often sung at considerable length, e.g. in Prudentius' hymn for the feast of Sts Fructuosus, Augurius and Eulogius on 21 January, *Felix Tarraco, Fructuoso vestiris* (cols 1062–5). This Fructuosus was bishop of Tarragona and martyred in 259, and Prudentius leaves no stone unturned in the telling of the story of the holy bishop and his two deacons resulting in a hymn, in *Br.*, of no fewer than 41 verses.

Prudentius had many less skilled imitators who seem to have done little more than take the *Acta Sanctorum* and translate them wholesale into Latin doggerel. Another lengthy example from a later date is the hymn for Matins on the feast of Sts Julian and Basilissa on 9 January (col. 1034), which has 35 verses. In fact the great length of some of these hymns, including those of Prudentius, inclines one to conclude that they were not originally intended for directly liturgical use.[9]

Isidore and Fructuosus said nothing of readings in the office and metrical hymns seem to have been inserted immediately after the morning praises, and before the concluding prayers. This would be a simple extension of the theme of morning praise, but would isolate the *Completuria* (when it was a psalm collect) from the Matutinary psalm. There were readings of some sort or other by the time of our manuscript sources, i.e. the ninth or tenth centuries. It is most likely then, that with hymns being inserted in the office from the seventh century, the readings may well have begun to be inserted in or around the eighth century, and inserted at this point in Matins (i.e., between the praise psalms and the hymn) in a possible imitation of Benedictine usage. Their introduction, however, still further disrupted the unitary theme of the morning celebration, while moving the meaning of Matins in another direction that was more to do with particular seasons and the feasts of saints.

NOTES

1 *English Hymnal* (OUP 1933), No. 52.

2 M. Férotin (ed.), *Liber Mozarabicus Sacramentorum* (Paris: *Monumenta Ecclesiastica Liturgica*, 1912), 708–9 (MS of 10th. cent.).
3 It is appointed for Sunday Prime, *PL* 86, col. 944.
4 *English Hymnal*, No. 5.
5 *English Hymnal*, No. 2.
6 See J. Janini, 'Cuaresma Visigoda y Carnes Tollendas', *Anthologica Annua* 9 (Rome: Santa Maria di Monserrato, 1961), pp. 11–83.
7 J. Perez de Urbel, 'Origen de los Himnos Mozarabes', *Bulletin Hispanique* 28 (Bordeaux, 1926), pp. 113–39, at p. 136.
8 *Hymns Ancient and Modern*, NS, 188.
9 Perhaps they were similar to those lengthy 'chanted sermons', the *Kontakia* of ancient Constantinople.

16

THE CONCLUDING PRAYER OF MATINS – THE COMPLETURIA

The *Supplicatio* that introduces the *Completuria* at Matins is no different from those that introduce the *Completuriae* at Vespers, so there is no need to say anything more about it. Similarly the Lord's Prayer and *Petitio* have already been dealt with, as has the dismissal formula. The Blessing was, as we have seen, originally confined to Vespers and in Tradition B the blessings at Matins are entirely dependent on those at Vespers, which have been examined earlier.

The examination of the Vespers *Completuriae* established the background and purpose of the concluding prayers at the evening and morning offices. The following will examine the morning *Completuriae*, those that do have a definite connection with the time of day and which are, thus, counterparts of the evening prayers. The very large number of purely seasonal and festal *Completuriae* will not be examined; many are used at Vespers and at Matins interchangeably.

It has already been pointed out that in Tradition B, the *Completuria* at weekday Matins is often the psalm prayer of the *Matutinarium*. In this prayer were developed the concepts that had been outlined in the antiphon given with the psalm. There are however, rather more examples of the prayers than there are of the antiphons. Two examples of these prayers were given above in the chapter on the Matutinarium (see pages 118–19) and both show clearly the ideas of emerging from the night as if awaking from the dead and being restored to new life at the break of day. The morning office is always in some way connected with the resurrection.

Weekday *Completuriae* are mostly psalm collects, while those of the fasts are proper to each of the four fasting periods, and are not psalm collects (see cols 152, 663, 709 and 248). The weekdays of the second part of Lent have *Completuriae* proper to the season, many of which are common to both Traditions A and B.[1] These prayers are not very matinal in their language and style.

The *Completuriae* on Sundays are not normally psalm collects although they are clearly matinal. Interestingly however, the Second and Third Sundays of Lent do use psalm collects at this point: *Expectatio* (col. 328) is a prayer on Psalm 5, as is *Clamoris nostri* (col. 384). This latter is actually the psalm collect of the *Sono* of this Sunday.

> Standing here in the shining presence of eternal light we offer our morning vow to you, who receive the cries of our prayers: that daily the lustre of the eternal may shine upon us, and vanquish the foul darkness of the night and the encroaching mist of error; may we be kept in the shining rays of his true Son.

This is probably a survivor of an older use in which psalm prayers served to conclude Sunday as well as weekday offices. The ordinary Sundays have *Completuriae* that are basically morning prayers.

The following is for the sixth Sunday after the octave of the Epiphany (col. 235):

> Now the east brightens, now the day hastens, now darkness flees, dawn blushes with most pure light: the heavens are brightened by the sun whose rays enlighten the world; all hasten, all hurry, to rejoice in the Lord's favour, he who is ever known as creator and defender.

Another example is the following, from the Eighth Sunday after the Epiphany octave (col. 243):

> In the morning hours, invoking the presence of the true morning star, whose heavenly splendour is sprinkled upon our breasts and gives joy to our hearts: so with souls illumined and enlightened in faith, may we adore for ever our leader and prince of light.

Once again the theme of resurrection light in the morning appears to be the dominant idea. It can be said that the morning office is the time of rejoicing in the gift of a new day, as a rising to new life brought about by the power of God who raised Jesus Christ from the dead.

NOTES

1 See, e.g., J. Janini (ed.), *Liber Misticus de Cuaresma* (Toledo: Istituto de Estudios Visigotico-Mozarabes, 1979), p. 125 (#788).

17

MATINS – SOME CONCLUDING REMARKS

At the beginning of the seventh century, old Spanish Matins appears to have comprised the canonical psalms, the *Missae Psalmorum*, a *Missa Canticorum*, a fifth *Missa* of the morning psalms (including the *Laudes* (Psalms 148–50)), a hymn (probably) and prayer. The general shape is similar to what is found in the later manuscripts and in *Br*. There is a difficulty however, in that our information for this period is largely from monastic sources. The ternary groupings of the canonical psalms, and the Psalter in course appear to be clearly of the monastic night office.

The morning office proper, Psalm 50, canticle/canticles, morning psalm, *Laudes*, (hymn) and prayer, are all of the cathedral office. The most primitive morning element appears to be Psalms 148–50. If, with Hanssens, Taft and Bradshaw, these psalms are seen as the kernel of the morning office, it may be possible to work backwards to see how the office grew.

The canticle and the *Matutinarium* are ancient. The former recalls the Easter Vigil, and such canticles as the Exodus *Cantemus* and the *Benedicite* are found everywhere in the ancient Christian world as Easter hymns. We have also seen that, by the sixth century certainly, a specifically morning psalm – often Psalm 62 – was an element of morning prayer (p. 112). It is difficult to gauge how primitive the use of this psalm is; it does not occur as consistently at Milan as in Spain. As Pinell suggests, there may be the convergence of two traditions, one using a canticle or canticles and another using a morning psalm. The Milanese *Psalmus Directus* comes *after* the *Laudes* and only includes one or two of the psalms regularly used in the mornings elsewhere. For these reasons, I would disagree with most of the authorities and suggest that the Milanese *psalmus directus* may not be ancient. The morning office at Milan still retained, up to its most recent changes, a primitive order of canticles on Sunday and Psalm 50 on weekdays, both arrangements being followed by Psalms 148–50. Something similar seems probable in Spain.

The use of Psalm 50 at the beginning of the morning office, a sort of penitential act at the end of the darkness of night, is also very ancient.[1] The very fact that Psalm 50 is often found beginning the whole office of Matins in *Br.* may well witness to the memory of that psalm and, perhaps, its accompanying prayer, as being the primitive invitatory which was also preserved by the monastic usage of the canonical psalms on Sundays.

Isidore, Fructuosus and the ordo of Bobadilla were legislating primarily for monastic communities and as we have seen (p. 76–7), groups of twelve psalms in sets of three were considered the desirable norm by the late fourth century to provide material for monastic prayer in the night, and similar forms appear to have been used in Spain (see p. 79). Spain resisted, more successfully than most places, the tendency to monasticize the cathedral office but the *Missa* of three psalms or Antiphons must have its origin in a cathedral version of the monastic vigil. The relics of older vigils on feasts would explain the greater number of *Missae* for feasts which some at least of the more devout laity and secular clergy would have attended. The monks recited the Psalter and, because of the repeated legislation obliging them to the cathedral office as well as their own, ended up having the 'mini-Vigil' of the cathedral office that developed in imitation of the monastic one, as a duplication of their own. (This could only be at a date later than Isidore, Fructuosus and Bobadilla, who seem to know only a cathedral morning prayer, following the monastic vigil and without any cathedral vigil.)

Hanssens pointed out that originally Matins was the office of dawn. In the Mediterranean basin, there is an interval of one and a half (or more) hours in winter and two (or more) hours in the summer between dawn and sunrise.[2] If the dawn of the new light of another day is seen as symbolic of the resurrection of Christ, then the period immediately before dawn is one of waiting in prayer, i.e., the Vigil, no matter how brief that vigil may be: perhaps just a canticle, a morning psalm with a theme of waiting such as 'O God you are my God, for you I long', preceded maybe by the confession of sinfulness and the need for God's forgiveness so well expressed in Psalm 50. Here are the basic elements of a primitive morning office to end the night. Only later, with the overwhelming influence of monasticism on the whole of church life, will the vigil that extended further back into the night with a long series of psalms and prayers, to become an integral part of the daily prayer that most people experienced.

The primitive office, having praised God through the power of the risen Jesus, was emboldened to pray for the Church and the world. It used the Lord's Prayer from an early stage, but let the people go with a blessing only later, when the lively awareness of the presence of the risen Christ had perhaps dimmed, and more assurance of divine blessing was desired.

Later additions between the praise psalms and the prayers soon included the morning hymn, though only generally in the old Spanish office after Toledo IV in 633. The hymn may well have first appeared as an element that celebrated any occurring feast, in an office that still largely concentrated on the time of day. In Milan, where this element was probably in use at a far earlier date, it came after the psalms of praise and before the prayer, and that is probably the position the Spanish office adopted it from. The readings may have been added later again, and the processional/devotional appendices perhaps came in imitation of Vespers only after their original processional nature had been lost to sight.

As was emphasized by both Baumstark and Hanssens,[3] the old Roman morning office, distinguished from the night office by being called *Lauds*, retained many features of the primitive morning prayer that we have also seen surviving at Milan and in Spain. In all these offices it appears to be clear that there are indeed the relics of an assembly to beg for God's forgiveness and wait upon his love, that love shown forth in the risen Christ (symbolized by the sunrise), who gives strength to his faithful people to pray in confidence to God, now that they have come safely through the dangers of the night to new life in him.

NOTES

1 See, e.g., J. M. Hanssens, *Nature et Genèse de l'Office des Matines* (Roma: *Analecta Gregoriana* LVII, 1952, p. 70.
2 ibid., pp. 9–10.
3 A. Baumstark, *Comparative Liturgy* (London: Mowbray, 1958), p. 38; and Hanssens, op. cit., pp. 13–18.

Part Three

Conclusion

The conclusion falls into three sections. In the first we shall sum up what has been learnt about early Western European cathedral offices from this old Spanish material, while in the second we will survey some recent attempts at revising daily prayer, and in the third, we will try to draw up principles for approaching the composition of services of daily prayer that are informed by this once widespread non-Roman tradition.

EARLY WESTERN EUROPEAN CATHEDRAL OFFICES

Monastic v. Cathedral

We should not drive too deep a distinction between monastic and cathedral offices. Outside of the rather rarified atmosphere of Egyptian monasticism a purely monastic office is difficult to find. The phenomenon of urban monasticism, or monasteries within easy reach of cities, can be seen exerting an important influence as early as the pilgrimage of Egeria. She described offices of a monastic type, but indicated that they were connected with churches frequented by the people as a whole; were led by clergy appointed to the task rather than monks who were then largely lay; and attracted the attendance of the more devout ordinary laity.[1] This was happening at a time when a church order such as the *Apostolic Constitutions* appears to be laying down a much more slimmed office than anything described by Egeria. It is of course likely that there were many different practices, but also some likelihood that a document such as a church order was trying to prescribe a *minimum* of common practice.[2] If, as Bradshaw has suggested, we should see the cathedral and monastic offices as two contrasting modes of prayer, one a strongly ecclesial 'eucharistic' offering of praise and prayer, and the other a meditation on the word of God as nourishing the spiritual life,[3] then we should also recognize that many devout laity wanted spiritual nourishment as well as an ecclesiological role, and monks needed to be aware of their place as members of the Church as well as individuals seeking 'prayer without ceasing'.

As Baumstark pointed out and others have since largely accepted, one of the most obvious features of the cathedral office was that it used selected psalms rather than the Psalter in course, which was a monastic practice. It was also the practice of monks in antiquity to recite the appointed section of the Psalter in course during the night, or before the cathedral offices of Vespers and Matins, the day hours utilizing fixed psalms. Originally the Spanish monks recited the Psalter in course overnight and so we see traces of a Psalter in course only at Matins in *Br.* and in the services of Lent in *Br.* and *AL*. The old Spanish Vespers and Matins use a range of vesperal and morning psalms but they are all chosen for the time of day, not as part of a *psalmodia currens*. However, we have seen evidence that, just as the monks in Spain were required to follow both cathedral and monastic ordos, so they had their own night-time psalmody which appears, at least in part, to have immediately preceded the cathedral Matins, and thus be in principle open to the wider community's participation. The attempt at a recitation of the Psalter in course in the sources we have examined shows its relative lateness by being spread over Matins, Terce, Sext and None (and also, to a very limited extent, Vespers) in *AL*. In *Br.* little or no order had been established, though the fragmentary weekday cycle may be evidence that such an attempt was made. There was simply no need for *another* Psalter in course if it existed elsewhere, such as at the monastic night offices.

The cathedral office was very much a people's office and easily remembered responses to the psalms can still be detected. The cathedral office was given richness and variety by presbyteral prayers, rather than antiphons that might require trained cantors, and many of these psalm prayers are found in *Br.* The cathedral office was also far more ceremonious and we can see traces of light ceremonies at Vespers and possibly incensations both at Vespers and, perhaps in parallel with Milan, during Psalms 148–50 at Matins. These features all emphasize the celebratory rather than meditational traits of the cathedral office as opposed to the monastic type.

The use of Old Testament canticles at the morning office, as reflecting the Vigil origin of the service, is also an ancient cathedral feature found, as we have seen, almost everywhere and used very extensively in the old Spanish rite. Although the Easter Vigil has readings, the cathedral office, precisely because it was celebratory rather than meditational or edifying, does not at first seem to have featured readings. The continued absence of readings from the old Spanish Vespers eloquently testifies to this fact. The system of readings at the other offices, especially in Lent, appears to have been imported into the office from a defunct catechumenal instruction.

It seems likely that the introduction of New Testament canticles into the office is largely from monastic influence, especially at Vespers. The old Spanish office uses such canticles as *Benedictus*, *Magnificat* and *Nunc Dimittis* only at Matins on certain appropriate feasts. It should be remembered that outside of the non-Spanish West, the *Magnificat* is never used at Vespers.[4]

Monastic offices tend to have basically similar structures; this is not necessarily true of cathedral offices and attempts to make them show similar structural forms are misguided. The old Spanish morning service of Psalm 50, an Old Testament canticle, a Matutinary psalm, Psalms 148–50 and prayer, is not exactly the same shape as the Vespers with its vesperal psalm, two other psalms and prayer. There is no reason why the two offices should have the same form, since their function is different.

Ancient Spain and its Nearest Neighbours

There are numerous parallels between the old Spanish offices and those that were found elsewhere in Europe. The most obvious parallels are with Milan. At Vespers, they share the *Lucernarium* and other chants with a probably similar function, the relics of selected psalms and psalm prayers, the processional appendices. In the morning, there are the paschal canticles *Cantemus* and *Benedicite* or Psalm 50 on weekdays, and the obvious centrality of Psalms 148–50. Even the nocturnal Vigil services that must have been followed in Milan, with their very different form from those of Rome, are parallel to those of the Spanish monks.[5] The Milanese offices also show differences of structure one from another, Vespers, for example, having the hymn at the beginning, and Matins after Psalms 148–50. Hymns at Milan are ancient and both rites appear to utilize hymns to emphasize the original elements of both services, the lamp lighting at Vespers and the praise psalms at Matins. The Gallican parallels are from accounts such as those of Gregory of Tours and Caesarius.[6] Here we find Psalm 50, *Benedicite* and the praise psalms at Matins and a *Lucernarium* and a final blessing at

Vespers. In Ireland too, we find canticles and praise psalms in the morning.[7]

The old Roman morning office, that part entitled *Lauds* in the later books, started with Psalm 50 on weekdays, had selected morning psalms, an Old Testament and Psalms 148–50. The 'Little Chapter', the hymn and the *Benedictus* were all later additions. Similarly, the survival of the versicle from Psalm 140 at Vespers and the evidence of other types of Vespers with three 'antiphons', may suggest that the old Roman cathedral Vespers was, in its most primitive form, not so unlike that which we have found in Spain. There seem to be sufficient Western parallels for the conclusion to be reached that the forms in the old Spanish books of both traditions were once quite common throughout the Christian West.

The Vigil Structure of Daily Prayer

The cathedral office is basically a vigil. Vespers and Matins are, in their normal everyday form, the beginning and end of a night dedicated to a prayerful watch. This obviously could not be an every-night event for most people, but the two separate services can symbolize a night that is to be overcome by the power of God, death to be defeated by life. In many places, anciently, there was a vigil that did occupy a great part of the night on the eves of Sundays and feasts. The connection of the bringing in of the lights, the *Lucernarium*, with an evening meal that may be noted in some sources, is illustrative of the community gathering to eat so as to have the strength to spend the night in vigil (see p. 6).

The prayers at Vespers in the old Spanish rite are frequently ones that ask protection for the night,[8] or that look forward to praising God joyfully in the morning.[9] The same themes of sorrow for sin and the confidence that God's people have in his power to overcome the darkness of sin and death, are found in the concluding prayers quoted above, pp. 41–2. At Matins, the vigil emphasis is continued in prayers that God may strengthen his people, as in those of the Sunday *Missae* quoted at pp. 89–92. These lead on to Matutinary psalms and prayers that see the people renewed in their resurrection faith, and conclude in prayers that pour out expressions of confident trust that, in the morning light, the risen Christ will be present to his people (see p. 139).

The internal evidence of the texts and structural units is complemented by the way that in *Br.* and in the MSS, the offices are largely arranged in the order, Vespers and Matins, and there is often no

'Second Vespers' or, if such a service exists, it exhibits the chracteristics of a weekday office, the First Vespers of Monday. To this we can add the unusual rubric at the beginning of Vespers for the third Monday of Lent in *Br.*: 'Ad Vesperum in tertia feria'; i.e. 'At Vespers on Tuesday' (col. 396). (The wording is not found in *T2*.)

The modern Russian use of Vespers and Matins on the eves of Sundays and feasts, called 'All-night Vigil',[10] also reflects a similar understanding of the vigilial nature of the cathedral office. This is even more clearly seen in the practices of some Old Ritualist Orthodox in Bukovina in the 1920s, as described by Cyrille Korolevsky.[11] Here an Akathist (or devotional service) and Little Vespers were celebrated in the afternoon of Saturday. The Vigil, consisting of Great Vespers (i.e. the full festal form), Matins and Prime, was celebrated from midnight to about 5 a.m., and the eucharistic Liturgy, preceded by the day hours, followed after a gap at 9 a.m. The Old Ritualists probably held tenaciously to what would have been common practice in Russia before the middle of the seventeenth century: practices brought to them by Greek missionaries in the tenth century, which would seem to have been not unknown to seventh-century Spaniards, even if the latter were different in many details.

Prayer to Sanctify the Night

The prayers and other structures of the cathedral office and the way that these were anciently used show that the priority was to sanctify the night rather than the day. Since the offices centre on the mystery of Christ's death and resurrection and may have their distant origin in Jewish evening and morning practices of recalling Passover at night and Covenant in the morning, it is then more logical to use the night as the symbol of the life-denying sin that is overcome by Christ, the risen Lord. Echoes of something similar may be found in Psalm 129's singing of waiting for the dawn, in order to celebrate the morning sacrifice, and in the ideas that surrounded the evening sacrifice of the Temple. Vigils were also not unknown to paganism but were often orgiastic, which may probably explain the tendency after the fourth century to insist on 'fasting' from sexual intercourse before celebrating or receiving the Eucharist. These tendencies were even more obvious in monastic traditions and so, not only do we find a night-to-morning dynamic in the old Spanish cathedral office, we also find an elaborate system of monastic vigils (see p. 78ff.).

Cathedrals and Parishes in Spain

What has already been said above shows that the offices of *Br.* do indeed reflect a tradition of cathedral office that must have been common in Western Europe. The basic structures are also found in the Tradition A MSS. Some differences, such as the addition of a versicle after the hymn in Tradition A, the common use of a Blessing to finish Matins, the eventual disappearance of most full psalms, may well be later developments in the old Spanish office. The tendency to add extra features, to duplicate, to include more festal material, to elaborate the musical execution of some pieces – all this would speak convincingly of later development from a primitive simplicity. In *Br.* and the few remaining Tradition B manuscripts, there is evidence that the Church of Sts Justa and Rufina in Toledo did hold tenaciously to a less elaborate, more parochial tradition, a tradition that had not worked out a really tidy, comprehensive system of psalm use, except where the old selected psalms were concerned; a tradition that hung on to half-remembered cycles of texts and old Latin versions of psalms and canticles. Like all old Spanish neums, those of *T2* are indecipherable, but if the sample page given as a frontispiece in Janini's edition is typical of that manuscript, then the music would appear to have been far simpler than that in *MP*, as illustrated by Plate II in Gilson's edition.[12] Janini did suggest a parochial use as being the origin of Tradition B.[13] If this were a simplification of the office of the great metropolitan churches, it seems likely that the original simplification took place at some date prior to most of the surviving Tradition A manuscripts and the elaborate musical and highly festal tradition that they represent.

It may finally be recalled that most of the material with which we have dealt, if not its final arrangements, appears to have been in existence by the end of the seventh century. Little real development took place during the period of Muslim domination and that which did, the addition of more hymns and the tendency of saints' days to obliterate the temporal cycles, was a development that can be seen elsewhere in medieval Europe.

ATTEMPTS AT REVISION

This part of the conclusion examines, in outline, whether and to what extent, modern understanding of the ancient cathedral offices of Vespers and Matins has informed the revisions of the daily offices at present in use in Roman Catholic, Church of England and

American Lutheran communities, and goes on to suggest ways in which that understanding should hopefully inform future developments. We shall also examine the very influential, but hitherto unofficial, English compilation *Celebrating Common Prayer*.

Revising a Revision – The Roman Catholic Liturgy of the Hours
For half of this century Roman Catholic clergy have used the Breviary of Pius X. This revised the old Roman office and spread the recitation of the Psalter over all the offices, not just over Vespers and Matins. The Second Vatican Council mandated redistribution of the Psalter through a longer period than a week and this has become a recitation of the whole Psalter (more or less) over five offices, in the course of a month. Some principle of selection has been achieved at Lauds and Vespers; the former has three 'psalms', the first a morning psalm, then an Old Testament canticle and third, a praise psalm – not necessarily 148, 149 and 150, but one that can broadly be described as laudatory. Many of the morning psalms used anciently in Spain have found their way into this office but Psalms 148, 149 and 150 are spread over the Sundays of the month and their daily role in the ancient office is largely lost to sight. Vespers proved more difficult, but psalms of a broadly vesperal nature have been supplemented by those that have some reference to God's protection of his people. The order of Compline utilizes appropriate psalms but Psalm 142, used on Tuesdays, also appears as the *morning* psalm on the fourth Thursday.[14] The remainder of the Psalter is spread over the Office of Readings (that replaces Matins) and a single minor hour. The selection has meant that the morning and evening offices may stand on their own, but the continued insistence on the normative ideal of recitation of the Psalter in course means that private recitation remains common practice and can still be perceived as burdensome.

Although Vatican II spoke of sanctification of the day *and* the night, this was forgotten very quickly, and it is clear, in the General Instruction prefaced to the revised office, that Lauds and Vespers are to sanctify the day. This renders the continued use of a First Vespers somewhat anachronistic. A great advantage has been gained by the provision of prayers for the time of day, many from the various psalm prayer sources. Unfortunately, the use of proper collects of the day on all Sundays, on Feasts and Commemorations, on even the weekdays of Advent, Christmastide, Lent and Eastertide, means that these are not likely to be so important as vehicles that convey the meaning of the daily office.

Antiphons, that started out as simple responses, have become yet more complex with the result that even when the psalms are sung, they, rather incongruously, are often said. The hoped-for psalm collects to draw out the meaning of these psalms have only now begun to materialize.[15] The use of ceremonial elements such as incense is unreflectingly tied to the New Testament canticles *Benedictus* and *Magnificat*. These latter are said to have been in 'popular use for centuries in the Roman Church' – which rather begs the question as to how one defines the word 'popular'. To further complicate matters, other New Testament canticles have been inserted at Vespers, to make up for the lack of vesperal psalms no doubt, showing once again the continued ignorance of the Vigil structure of ancient offices, in which New Testament material was confined to the mornings, as the realization of that which had been anticipated in the night.

The great variety of different texts makes it impossible for any but the more highly trained, to recognize the traditional features of daily prayer. The failure to perceive the differences between a celebratory people's office and an edifying private reading for clergy and religious is exhibited by the increased size of the 'Little Chapters' and their very much greater variety. Lengthy readings from the Bible and the Fathers at the Office of Readings seem more concerned with making sure that the clergy read something rather than celebrate anything. Certain units, such as Responsories, have been retained with little understanding of their origin as psalms after readings. There seems to be little likelihood that the long ones in the Office of Readings will be sung and their form is likely to simply baffle even intelligent lay people.

A good point is the provision of intercessions, something hardly provided for in the old office, except on the rare occasions that the *Preces Feriales* were used. The General Instruction speaks eloquently and movingly of a public office of cathedral type,[16] but all the book provides is a complex book of private prayer used by clergy and small groups of religious (among the few who use it in common) and, here and there, by a few of the laity. The problem is that it remains monastic in its desire to be a source book for meditation and edification, rather than a celebration of the Church gathered for prayer.

Overall there has been a desire to make all the offices structurally the same. This is particularly noticeable in the novel idea of placing the hymn at Lauds and Vespers at the beginning of those offices, just as if they were minor hours. The placing of the hymn after the Psalter in course made it, with the *Magnificat* or *Benedictus*, part of the climax of the office – something that once would always be sung, even when the psalms were recited in a monotone recitative.[17] Hansjakob Becker has also argued that the complex of Little Chapter (plus a Responsory in the Benedictine rite), Hymn, Versicle, and *Magnificat* indicate the relics of the central core of Vespers with its light ceremony and raising of evening incense.[18] Apparently this idea, which has commended itself to other forms of revision (see below), came from Canon A.-G. Martimort, who rigorously pressed it upon other members of the revision body, many of whom expressed misgivings.[19] The tendency to ignore the testimony of many scholars and go for a pragmatic solution to the difficulties of getting priests to pray the office is well detailed by Stanislaus Campbell's recent book on the revision process.[20]

Revising a Revision – From Common Prayer to Alternative Services

The provision of the Alternative Service Book is far simpler, but is itself a reform of Cranmer's reform of the monastic-type office that was found in the Sarum Breviary – itself simply a version of the old Roman office. *ASB*'s offices are almost interchangeable. Leaving aside the canticles of the Old Testament that may be used in the morning, there is nothing but an updated version of the collect of Prime that is explicitly matutinal.[21] The evening is better, with the introduction of the Eastern evening hymn, 'O gladsome light' and Psalm 133 (134) as alternative invitatories. The Sarum collect for Compline remains as the third collect.[22]

The Psalter in course and Readings remain the major features of this office, so that with few attempts to make the psalms suit the time of day (or at least, not be totally unsuitable to those times) the office remains monastic in origin and inspiration. The provision of the Book of Common Prayer for seasons and feasts was very limited and *ASB* provides some variety, but again, this seems to be at the expense of the original purpose of daily services at morning and evening, that is, to celebrate those times. The continued use of a *Capitella de Psalmis* form of intercession and the relegation of freer intercessions until after the actual office, shows a failure to grapple seriously with the question of intercessory prayer as a part of the office.

Both Roman and Anglican provisions provide a large amount of edificatory material that was once part of ancient monastic offices, rather than those of the secular churches. The readings of the Scriptures at the Eucharist may be said to be proclamatory, while those of the monastic office were to provide food for meditation in a world which had few books. Even in the sixteenth century, many could not read, which was, no doubt, a powerful influence upon a reformer such as Cranmer to provide edificatory services. It needs to be asked in these days whether large chunks of Scripture should really be part of the daily office, except where a daily Eucharist is not normal and then, as can be seen in many Orthodox countries, perhaps such readings should be a sort of brief ante-communion or 'dry mass', added to the office and acting, in such a context, as a reminder of the basically eucharistic nature of all Christian worship, even when the sacrament is not or cannot be celebrated. We shall, however, return to this question below.

It would appear that the Matins and Evensong of the Alternative Service Book have not proved popular. However, most cathedrals and other institutions with choral foundations have retained the offices of the Book of Common Prayer which are structurally little different, but which attract quite healthy congregations in some British cities. Even the said offices in the *BCP* form seem to have their enthusiasts – there does in fact seem to be a desire among some at least for a more substantial reading of the Psalter than is provided in *ASB*, which is spread over too long a period of time to encourage prayerful familiarity. The major reasons for the continued popularity of the *BCP* offices may be more to do with the language, and the music in which that language is frequently clothed, than with questions of theology and structure.

Probably because there may not be the same tradition of obliging the clergy to daily recitation of the office, the morning and evening offices of the Lutheran Book of Worship of some of the Lutheran churches in the USA and Canada are better at providing a cathedral style of office. No attempt has been made to use the entire Psalter but appropriate psalms are provided over a four-week period. One of a small number of praise psalms is always used at the Morning Office, Psalm 140 (141) is normally the first psalm at Vespers and an appropriate psalm prayer may always follow each psalm. In the evening office there is a concern to have a genuine *Lucernarium*. Major criticism must be the tendency to put both services into a structural straitjacket. The continued question of the New Testament canticles *Benedictus* and *Magnificat* and what, if any, place they should have in the daily offices is not really faced. The use of the New Testament canticle at Vespers seems to contradict the whole concept of the evening prayer as commencing a vigil that would use Old Testament material to look forward to the praise of the risen

Christ at dawn. Besides, the new Lutheran office has followed the modern trend and put the office hymn at the beginning, which is in line with Milanese usage but which in the Lutheran book, as well as in the present-day Milanese use (and since at least the ninth century), means that the office has two unrelated climaxes, both of which attract the use of ceremonial such as incense. As with the general instruction of the Roman Breviary, received wisdom identifies the use of incense with the fact that these canticles are from the Gospel, whereas we may recall that Amalarius knew of a tradition that associated incense at Vespers with Psalm 140 (p. 10) and the Milanese custom, still used in Beroldus' time, was to offer morning incense at Psalms 148–50 (see p. 124).

A Different Way Forward? Celebrating Common Prayer[24]

As with a number of other recent liturgical books, this has so many possible alternatives that it seems quite difficult to see what the shape of its liturgical services really is. The book is consistent with a modern Western outlook that prefers to conceive of the day running from morning to evening, and the rubrics only provide for First Vespers on feasts of great solemnity.[25] This will tend to leave Vigils hanging in the air, except that the vigil appears to be a replacement for First Vespers.[26] In order to be consistent with our treatment so far, we shall examine Vespers and Matins, or Evening and Morning Prayer, in that order – though, as with the Roman office, many remarks one can make will apply to both offices. Also, again for consistency, we shall continue to use the numbering of the psalms used by the Septuagint and Vulgate texts.

The evening service, Vespers for short, starts with a greeting, blessing of light and 'O gladsome light', to which may be added verses from Psalm 140 and a prayer.[27] This appears to owe a great deal to the revised Ambrosian rite, and actually could form the nucleus of a central core of Vespers if thought through more consistently. However, treated effectively as an optional, rather high-church opening, it misses its opportunities and looks too dispensable.[28] That this is a pity is well shown by the excellent prayers which talk of walking in the light of Christ, exactly as in many ancient orders, but in modern idiom.

The psalmody which follows is based on selecting psalms to suit a theme for each day of the week, or, in a major season, the same theme for each day of the week. This means that Sunday evening commemorates the resurrection, and its round of seven psalms may be used on each day of the week in Eastertide.[29] Some Sunday evening psalms are traditional morning ones, e.g. 102 and 135 that are parts of Sunday Matins in modern Byzantine use. The psalms for Saturday are those for the 'Kingdom season' (the weeks before Advent). This means that the tendency for seasonal themes, whether they be good or bad, to take over from the daily rhythm is very dominant. It is not my brief at present to examine the weekday themes, but any such system has a certain artificiality about it,[30] and the seasonal material can sometimes end by 'flogging' an at least ailing horse! The psalm prayers for several psalms, especially for Psalms 112 and 113[31] on Sunday nights would suit the morning better, if our interpretation of traditional orders is correct.

CCP provides a possible way of reciting the whole Psalter, which raises the question as to what role such a recitation has, and if it does have a role, how that role should be worked out practically. Simply stretching the Psalter over longer and longer periods (which does nothing to aid familiarity with the psalms) does not seem to really grapple with the problem, one which should perhaps be addressed by those whose spirituality was traditionally grounded upon the Psalter, namely monks and nuns.

The use of the psalms in *CCP* does seem to have an edificatory role rather than a ritual one – it is reinforcing a message. The edificatory element is heightened by the use of readings, of which there can be two, at both morning and evening. Since the canticles can be used between or before the readings, it is not clear what their role is intended to be.[32] This book provides no fewer than 67 canticles, and the 35 from the Old Testament (including Deutero-canonical books, e.g. the Prayer of Manasses[33]) do integrate six or seven of the ancient ones with paschal overtones. The New Testament ones include similar texts to those in the Roman Breviary, poetic texts from the epistles and Revelation that do not have a detectable history as Christian hymns. Fourteen of the 'canticles' include ecclesiastical compositions like the *Te Deum* and the *Gloria in excelsis*, and the compositions of individuals.

The principle of selection shows great ingenuity, but gives the impression of ransacking Scripture and elsewhere for something to cover every eventuality, rather than starting from the basic symbols of night and day, death and life, creation and re-creation, sorrow, joy and hope – such things may be found, but scattered over the week or year, or just throughout the book.

The purpose of the Responsory at Vespers on Sunday appears to be to reintroduce the theme of light: 'The Lord is my light and my

CONCLUSION

salvation'.[34] Its purpose at other times is not clear at all. Similarly, the *Magnificat* is given a light theme on Sunday, and a totally different one on other days.[35] We have already pointed out that there is no clear reason for this canticle to occupy the position it does in Western evening services. Once again, the prayers are often good, as the collects frequently look forward beyond sleep to the new day, though that is mainly seen as the eternal day which traditional orders most emphasized in the mornings.

The morning offices are similar in structure, with an attempt to provide an alternative to the Light ceremony that sets the weekday theme, even to the point of making optional the phrase most redolent of earlier understandings: 'Now, through the deep waters of death you have brought your people to new birth by raising your Son to life in triumph'.[36] The Sunday Matins feels itself on safer ground and sings of the resurrection, expecting the same psalm to be sung each Sunday, even if it is only Psalm 116, the shortest, rather than one of 148–50, which only turn up on weekdays in Eastertide.[37] On weekdays, the tendency to cling to seasonal and weekday themes takes over after the opening, and then the idea of waking comes back with the Responsory and the *Benedictus*, which latter does lend itself to morning use far more readily than the *Magnificat* to evenings.

Like the new Roman Breviary, this office attempts to take a 'cathedral office' principle of selectivity, but also falls into the trap of an over-complexity that puts many people off. However, a major criticism is to do with shape: the Roman office and *CCP* both start with something that establishes time of day (albeit the hymn has to carry this virtually alone in the Roman form); there is then a rather obvious sag, with the Roman offices trying to maintain the evening or morning themes without attempting to order them, and *CCP* tending to lose itself in arbitrarily chosen seasonal-type themes. The readings beg the question as to whether offices are for edification or prayer, and many are asking whether reading passages from Scripture is becoming overdone, in view of the greater centrality of the role of eucharistic lectionaries. Reading the Bible is a good thing; the question is how best to do it. The two styles try to recover the time of day at the *Magnificat* and *Benedictus*, but in the case of the former, by imposing interpretive material upon it. The prayers are often good, but sometimes half-hearted attempts to inject an otherwise missing eschatological thrust.

The dynamic of the early Church offices was to move from awaiting the light, celebrating it and praying in it for protection, this initiating a night of prayer (even if one was going to bed). In the early morning, rising as if from death and sin, and growing in an ever-increasing crescendo of praise, one finally came to expression of faith and hope in the greater light, the risen Jesus symbolized first by the evening lamp, and now by the morning sun. The new offices have not really accepted that interpretation, and consequently remain individual and unconnected, their internal cohesion often difficult to follow; and the principles of selectivity have often led to greater confusion and a lack of clarity of purpose. We have tried to argue that the original purpose of daily, public prayer, as witnessed to in ancient Spain, was to move the Christian from darkness to light (though in such a way that in the evenings one was not left entirely in darkness, while the process of entering into the new day in the morning was gradual rather than immediate); the newer offices have some, even many, of these elements in their forms, but ordered in such a way that for all the similarity of structure between the two 'hinge' hours of prayer, there is no cohesion of purpose.

The General Instruction of the Roman Liturgy of the Hours stresses the long-standing traditional use of the Church of Rome, without any sign of awareness that the people's office in Rome was, in early times, of a structure very different from that of the monastic communities who took over the daily worship in the great basilicas from the secular clergy. The almost total absence of public celebration of the Liturgy of the Hours in ordinary Roman Catholic parishes shows that for all its good points, this liturgy of the hours is simply not a daily service that priests and people can *celebrate* together. The desire of Anglican reformers to retain the Cranmerian forms, that were focused on teaching a population with little knowledge of Scripture, ignores the possibility that that form may no longer be an effective way of doing just that and, moreover, edification does not seem to be the primary reason for celebrating the daily office.

Some Independent Experiments

Attempts have been made to provide a genuine celebration of the evening and morning prayer. A number of scholars connected with the University of Notre Dame brought out *Morning Praise and Evensong* in 1973.[38] This provides a simplified Lauds and Vespers based on the modern Roman form for each day of the week. The vesperal celebration begins with a light ritual, with hymn and prayer of thanksgiving and then, Psalm 140 (141). The rest of the structure is not so successful but, with only one incensation (the book suggests a second at the Gospel canticle) and good use of the simple sung responses or metrical psalms provided, the present writer knows of very positive responses to this evening service from ordinary Roman catholics who were expecting a Marian devotion and Benediction. The morning office is more similar to that of the Roman Breviary but probably more accessible to people.

The Lutheran Book of Worship, already mentioned, was used recently at a church in London, who normally have the Vespers from this book on a Sunday night. They use the option of having a light brought in and with a very high standard of singing, both congregational and choral, provide a very satisfying evening service. One major difficulty here, is that in this pastoral context, Vespers has been the normal Sunday worship of a different congregation from that which assembles in the morning.

At the Anglican Church of St James', Haydock, Lancashire, Fr George Guiver CR, at the request of the then vicar, the Revd Dr Paul Nener, compiled a simple parish office. The morning office had the form: psalm with collect, canticle with collect, reading, hymn and intercessions and prayer. The form of Evensong was the same but with a canticle from the New Testament. On Saturday night, the Evensong commenced with a *Lucernarium* and the hymn 'O gladsome light' and there was more ceremonial. The hymns at least were sung and the result was a congregation with whom to share the daily office, especially on a Saturday night.

A final experiment known to this author was in the work done in his parish at Towcester, Northamptonshire, by the Revd Dr T. J. G. S. Cooper, then head of the RC diocese of Northampton's adult education programme. Dr Cooper took over an evening service with Benediction when he arrived in the parish and transformed it into Vespers, with a *Lucernarium* in the winter. Other offices for both morning and evening, making use of simple chants and responses, psalm prayers etc., were used on the great feasts and sometimes attracted a sizeable proportion of the congregation. Dr Cooper's experiments were shown in full to the Panel of Monastic Musicians in January 1988 at Douai Abbey. Taking note of some criticism, he produced a highly simplified version which was used to close a day course on Liturgy given by the present writer. The service opened with the bringing in of the light, the hymn 'O gladsome light' and the thanksgiving for light. The incense psalm, 140, with a prayer then followed, and two other psalms with prayers continued the theme of prayer for protection and intercessions; the Lord's prayer and a solemn blessing concluded the service. (NB there was no *Magnificat*.) The whole service lasted half an hour and was well sung by all present after a short practice. The developments in Dr Cooper's experimental services arose from his further consideration of the basic elements and function of the daily office.

SOME POSSIBLE PRINCIPLES FOR DAILY PRAYER

There needs to be more thought given to the function of the daily offices and then the form may follow as a natural expression of that function. If the early Church had thought it simply a good and pious idea to pray in the morning and in the evening, it is likely that we would have even more bewilderingly different forms of daily prayer than we in fact do. The truth of the matter is that there are broad structural similarities, and even recurrent scriptural texts, that indicate the essentially vigilial function of the daily services of Vespers and Matins almost everywhere.

It is possible to see that, throughout the Christian East, Egeria's daily vigil of psalmody leading to the morning office at dawn/sunrise finds constant parallels. Even in the ancient West the same was true. We have already seen this in the detailed treatment of the old Spanish office, and in Milan, prior to recent reforms, similar forms could also be found. Matins began with the hymn *Aeterne rerum*, that talks of stirring from sleep,[39] a responsory, the first part of the Daniel 3 canticle, *Benedictus es*, and then ten or so psalms in course (Monday to Friday); these were followed by three readings with responsories. On Saturdays, Psalm 118 was used, with the Exodus 15 canticle, the 'Song of the Sea', instead of the current psalmody. On Sundays, there was again no Psalter in course, but three canticles, and the *Te Deum* after the last reading. The *Te Deum* was a late addition (1440), and the Roman habit of inserting 'Deus in adjutorium' at the beginning of the morning part of the office only dates from 1625.[40] Once again we find a night-time continuous psalmody, at least from Monday to Friday, but the arrangement of the Psalter into what were called *decuriae*, that spread it over a two-week period, may not have existed before the Carolingian era.[41] The readings were adapted from the old Roman office,[42] but the responsories were probably from Milanese sources. The weekday responsories invoke God's protection and often refer to night, 'Meditatus sum nocte cum corde meo' ('I think upon you in the night time with my whole heart') or morning, 'In matutinis meditabor in te'[43] ('In the morning will I meditate on you'). It is possible that, before the system of the

CONCLUSION

decuriae, there may have been simply three selected psalms and prayers as in the weekday pre-matinal vigil in Milan.

The structures of the Ambrosian rite in the morning are informative, and we really need to grasp the overall shape of that office, pre-matinal and matinal. The Sunday canticles of the pre-matinal vigil: Isaiah 26.9ff, 1 Samuel 2 and Habakkuk 3, preceded by *Benedictus es* from Daniel 3, were followed by a procession with the *Antiphona ad Crucem*, then the Exodus 15 'Song of the Sea' and the *Benedicite*; Psalms 148–50 and 116 now followed, and a selected psalm; then the *Laus Angelorum Magna*, a form of the *Gloria in excelsis* similar to the Byzantine Great Doxology.[44] This means that, taking into account the seasonal use of Deuteronomy 32, Milan used no fewer than seven of the canticles of the Greek canon, only the canticle of Jonah being missing of the Old Testament ones (it also seems to have been a tradition that did not originally admit the New Testament canticles, *Benedictus* and *Magnificat*). On weekdays there may have been three psalms at the pre-matinal vigil, then Psalm 50 preceded the praise psalms – canticles may have been confined to Sundays, because of their ancient connections with the Paschal Vigil. Saturdays retained an interestingly more festal aspect, with a pre-matinal vigil of the Exodus 15 canticle and Psalm 118; then the resurrectional Psalm 117, instead of Psalm 50, preceded the praise psalms.

The structures of these offices would appear to show, in the first place, a vesper service which may have prefatory psalmody, but which basically comprises an evening act of worship involving lights and/or incense, and then moves into prayer; and then, a morning service that takes up the vigil where it was left off at Vespers; psalmody and/or readings of a basically monastic kind are carried out while it is still dark, and then the service moves towards the light, employing canticles and psalms with a clear resurrection reference, reaching its climax at the full light of the new day, and looking forward to the eternal day; all of this exactly parallels what we have seen in the old Spanish tradition. It should be noted that I am not defending this interpretation by pointing to the universal use of certain psalms. Psalm 140 is very widely found, but is used differently in different places; Psalm 62 is widely used in the morning, but not at all in the Chaldean Matins, and although it turns up elsewhere in the West, e.g. Rome, it has no place in the Milanese office. Psalm 50 is found a great deal in the mornings, and Psalms 148–50 are pretty much universal, but, in the final analysis, what I am pointing to is the underlying *criterion* of selection, and not what was actually selected.

In his article '"Thanksgiving for Light", Towards a Theology of Vespers', Robert Taft emphasized the evening light as standing for the lamp of the Heavenly City, where there is no darkness or night, but only the day, and Christ himself is the lamp.[45] This is fine as far as it goes, but it is in fact impossible to interpret Vespers entirely apart from Matins. There is an incompleteness at Vespers; many orders have a lengthy, meditative psalmody to begin, then a more dramatic climax is reached at the showing of light, or some other ceremony connected with light and/or incense; after which, with intercessory material, the service can quite rapidly finish. On some occasions there might be readings, processions etc. that extend the service further into the night, but normally there is a relatively quick ending. In the morning, preferably before it is light, there may be a lengthy monastic psalmody, which starts in quite a low-key fashion, but again, more ritual and drama come later. Deliberate reminders of the Easter Vigil, such as the Exodus 'Song of the Sea' and the *Benedicite*, lead into the first light, and the outburst of praise, (Psalms 148–50 etc.) that greeted the sunrise makes clear that the lamp of the night before is only an indicator of the full glory of the light of Christ. The end of the Matins looks forward to the eternal day, and the light that will never be put out. Hence the purpose of daily prayer in the evening and the morning is to move from darkness and death, to light and life.

In the modern age it is likely that all-night vigils could only be attractive as very occasional occurrences. On the other hand, it would still be possible and even desirable for preparation for the Sunday Eucharist to include Vespers on Saturday night, with its emphasis on the forgiveness of sins giving a more communitarian dimension than was present in the old individual, devotional confession on a Saturday night. In the morning, suitable songs of praise might be an effective 'warm up' to the Liturgy of the Eucharist in which, for instance, the young, who may be going elsewhere for their own liturgy of the word, could joyfully and actively participate.

The tendency among Roman Catholics, and some Anglo-Catholics in the past, was to see their participation in an evening service with Benediction of the Blessed Sacrament as a sort of extended thanksgiving for Communion in the morning. Perhaps the slow recovery of the Eucharist precisely as 'Thanksgiving' may have contributed to the flagging popularity of evening services conceived in such a way. More needed may be the 'run-up' to Eucharist/Thanksgiving, rather than the 'run-down' from individual and over-personalized communion.

The vigilial nature of the office could continue in the week and, in places that have a daily Eucharist in the morning, the pattern would be similar to Sunday only simpler. If an evening Eucharist were the norm, such an office could still be usefully vigilial and, by emphasizing morning as a time to celebrate the resurrection, might help to avoid dull legalism, the sort of thing characterized by the students of the Venerable English College in Rome in the 1970s naming a rather unintelligent kitten 'morning prayer' because he was half asleep and not all there!

A very wide variety of texts, antiphons and the like militates against ordinary parish celebration. Simple responses are preferable to complex antiphons; they are easy to memorize and sing. To bring out the meaning of the psalm, it might be better to use psalm prayers. Mention of singing may remind us that, among the few places where any sort of popular office has been established or never lost in England and Wales, are the cathedrals and other establishments of choral foundation. Although not popular in the sense of being services where all present join in vocally, they often do attract quite sizeable congregations. In those places where a more congregational syle has been established, e.g. Westminster Roman Catholic Cathedral on Saturday night and Sunday morning, a very large increase in those attending can be seen. The daily service is basically a sung form of prayer. Psalms are songs and should be treated as such. Variety can be assured by change of tune and judicious use of hymns and prayers.

What do we do about readings? A course of Bible study is very useful and may be the basis of some shared study and reflection; it may not necessarily be the purpose of the Liturgy of the Hours to provide the place for such study. However, ancient precedent may give us a workable idea for both psalms and readings. Ancient forms such as those we have discussed from Spain tended to keep the Psalter in course, together with any series of readings, as an introduction to the vesperal or matinal act of prayer. This opening service was very often the monastic office, and therefore not a 'mere preliminary', but something that the monastics and the more devout, or leisured, of the laity could easily also attend. Those without such leisure could time their arrival in church for the lamp-lighting and prayer at Vespers, and for the sunrise praise and prayer at Matins. Instead of the modern tendency to heap up the ceremonial and sung celebration of the hour at the beginning of the office, it would be possible to envisage a relatively low-key and flexible period of reading and psalmody, the *Lucernarium* at evening, and the morning praise then being both a climax and, for those with less time, a free-standing service. Such a flexible period of reading and psalmody could vary in length according to the community using it. A rigorously monastic style could entail recitation of the psalms (excluding those used in the 'people's service') over the period of a fortnight or a month; and also include meditative reading of sizeable sections of Scripture if desired. A less rigorous form, perhaps suited to a busy clergy team, might have a series of selected psalms and/or scriptural passages for about 20 minutes to half an hour. In both cases the 'popular' service following might only last about 15 to 20 minutes, fully sung and with some ceremonial. A parish team might have the 'monastic' form only once daily, either morning or evening, especially where there was a daily Eucharist, which latter might follow or be followed by the 'popular' service.

Another point to bear in mind with such a system would be that any day hours or forms of Compline should really be entirely free-standing and in no sense seen as a necessary part of the whole round of prayer, but a clearly additional devotion, employing, for example, a small number of selected psalms, and short chapter-type readings.

In all cases, older forms of office should be a warning as to how quickly the concern with the time of day can be swamped by seasonal and festal material. It is right that the major seasons and feasts be recognized but the Eucharist should perhaps be the privileged place for much of this material, and especially its Liturgy of the Word. The use of a Sunday collect, rather than an evening or morning one, reduces the liturgy of time to reiteration of the same themes as at the eucharistic celebration.

There may be a place for processional appendices or other devotions at the end of the daily services – that would be a good way of including seasonal or festal themes. In some places, e.g. Liverpool Roman Catholic Cathedral, a station was made at the Lady Chapel at the end of Vespers on Sunday in which the antiphon of Our Lady appointed to follow Compline was often sung.

If the function of the evening office is to celebrate the evening, the time of the Passover meal, of the Last Supper, and to recognize in the lamp the presence of the Lord Jesus among his people, then the early Christians did not so much talk about it, as do it, in greeting the light and thanking God, in singing of that light and of their need for the presence of Christ in their midst. From that developed the form of the

CONCLUSION

Lucernarium, the primitive vesperal service. If the function of the morning office was to recognize the need for God's forgiveness and then praise the risen Lord for that forgiveness – the Lord not now represented by mere artificial light but by the glory of the sunrise – then doing this meant assembling at the end of the night of vigil, with its remembering of God's good deeds to his sinful people, to acknowledge sin, but also to praise God for his forgiveness and his promise of new life represented by the new day's light. These differing functions could imply different shapes, as we have tried to show was indeed the case in the past. The high point of Vespers comes with light and incense and tails off relatively quickly in intercession for and blessing upon all of God's people as they enter upon the night. The high point of Matins comes after confession of sin and longing for forgiveness, and after the shout of praise, confident prayer leads on to a day dedicated to and blessed by God. The attempts to force the ancient offices into a preconceived structural straitjacket do not work, and even less do rather dogmatic attempts to impose such a shape on today's churches.

The purpose of this work has been to try and identify, from the Spanish sources seen in their context, what some of the basic features of daily office really are and what their function as offices might have been. This has been done in order to contribute to the groundwork that must be done so that modern Western European Christians may one day, hopefully, have the opportunity to celebrate again the new life of the risen Christ in daily communal, or even family prayer.

NOTES

1. See J. Wilkinson, *Egeria's Travels* (London, 1971), pp. 123–5.
2. For the nature of the Church Orders see Paul Bradshaw, *The Search for the Origins of Christian Worship* (London: SPCK, 1992), pp. 80–110.
3. ibid., p. 189.
4. The author was once asked by a surprised Georgian Orthodox after her first experience of Anglican Evensong: 'Why do they sing the Magnificat in the evening?' – for all Orthodox it is indelibly associated with the morning!
5. M. Magistretti (ed.), *Manuale Ambrosianum* (Milan, 1905), pp. 53–6 for example of vigil Vespers of Christmas, and Epiphany (pp. 87–9). Also W. C. Bishop, ed. C. L. Feltoe, *The Mozarabic and Ambrosian Rites* (London: Alcuin/Mowbray, 1924), pp. 114–15.
6. See, e.g., R. Taft, *The Liturgy of the Hours in East and West* (Collegeville: Liturgical Press, 1986), pp. 146–56.
7. Further references may be found in my 'Daily Prayer: Its Origin in Its Function', *Studia Patristica* (1997), pp. 364–88.
8. E.g. *Vespertinum* after Epiphany (col. 215): 'O God; who send your mercy by day and declare your love by night; protect us we beseech you and bring us to salvation by day and at night, defend us at rest.'
9. E.g. *Vespertinum* (col. 228): 'Save us Lord, who cry to you and let the tears we have shed at evening be turned to joy for us by the morning of rejoicing, by the help of your speedy assistance.'
10. *Vsenoshchnoe Bdenie*.

11 In *Stoudion* IV (1927), pp. 123–37: 'Chez les Staroveres de Bucovine'.
12 J. Janini (ed.), *Liber Misticus de Cuaresma* (Toledo: Istituto de Estudios Visigotico-Mozarabes, 1979), frontispiece of fol. 32 of MS. J. P. Gilson (ed.), *The Mozarabic Psalter* (London: Henry Bradshaw Society, 1905), plate II, illustrating fol. 188b.
13 Janini, op. cit., pp. xxx–xxxi.
14 One of the Six Psalms of Byzantine Matins, it is also found in both orders of Compline in that tradition. It is really a psalm for use at night: e.g., 'He has forced me to live in darkness, like those long dead'.
15 See selection in Brian Magee (tr.), *Psalm Prayers* (Dublin: Veritas, 1990).
16 For example, 'General Instruction on the Liturgy of the Hours' (Rome, 1970), in *The Divine Office*, Vol. I (London: Collins, 1974), pp. xix–xcii, at pp. xxxiiff., paras 20ff.
17 See J. Jungmann, 'Essays in the Structure of the Canonical Hours. 1. Psalmody as the Introduction to the Hours' in *Pastoral Liturgy* (London: Challoner, 1962), pp. 157–62.
18 'Zur Struktur der "Vespertina Sinaxis" in der Regula Benedicti', *Archiv für Liturgiewissenschaft* 29 (1987), pp. 177–88.
19 Well described in Stanislaus Campbell, *From Breviary to Liturgy of the Hours* (Collegeville: Liturgical Press, 1995), esp. pp. 179–181. Also personal recollections of Very Revd Archimandrite Boniface (Luyckx), related to author in August 1992.
20 Campbell, op. cit.
21 *ASB*, p. 60, #23.
22 *ASB*, pp. 62–3 (#32) and 70 (#45).
23 *Lutheran Book of Worship* (Minneapolis: Augsburg and Philadelphia: Board of Publication, Lutheran Church in America, 1978).
24 London: Mowbray, 1992.
25 See *Celebrating Common Prayer*, p. 3, n1.
26 See pp. 184ff.
27 ibid., pp. 26–7.
28 The alternative opening includes the classical *night* Psalm 133, see ibid., p. 28.
29 ibid., p. 29.
30 Systems of particular devotions on days of the week are well known in the Roman rite where they do not really influence the Liturgy, except perhaps on Saturday; Milan had a system of votive masses for each day of the week (*Messale Ambrosiano, dalla Pasqua all'Avvento* (Milan: 1942, 95*–133*) which still appears to be in use; and the Byzantine weekday offices reflect daily themes to a certain extent, notably on Wednesday and Friday. That all these systems are arbitrary is well demonstrated by the fact that Milan prays for the Holy Spirit on Thursday, CCP on Monday; and in honour of the angels on Tuesday, Byzantium on Monday!
31 *CCP*, pp. 634–5.
32 See, e.g., ibid., p. 29.
33 ibid., p. 212.
34 ibid., p. 31.
35 ibid., and *passim*.
36 ibid., p. 13.
37 ibid., p. 15.
38 W. Storey, F. Quinn and D. Wright, *Morning Praise and Evensong* (Notre Dame: Fides, 1973).
39 *Breviarium Ambrosianum, Hiemalis* I, 1*: 'Surgamus ergo strenue:/Gallus jacentes excitat,/Et somnolentos increpat:/Gallus negantes arguit.'
40 P. Borella, *Il Rito Ambrosiano* (Brescia: Marcelliana, 1964), p. 240.
41 See W. C. Bishop, ed. C. L. Feltoe, *The Mozarabic and Ambrosian Rites* (London: Alcuin/Mowbray, 1924), pp. 114–15, 122.
42 P. Borella, 'Il Breviario Ambrosiano' in M. Righetti (ed.), *Storia Liturgica*, Vol. III (Milan: Ancora, 1946), pp. 615–16.
43 Magistretti (ed.), *Manuale*, pp. 401–2.
44 The readings at Nocturns were obviously of Roman provenance, and the *Benedictus*, which started the morning office, was almost certainly a borrowing from elsewhere, as we can see by its replacement in Advent and certain other times by Deuteronomy 32; *Brev. Ambr. Hiemalis* I, 8*–11*.
45 In *Beyond East and West* (Washington, DC: Pastoral Press, 1984), pp. 127–49, 138.

BIBLIOGRAPHY

ORIGINAL SOURCES

Amalarii Episcopi Opera Liturgica Omnia, ed. J. M. Hanssens SJ (Roma, Vatican: *Studi e Testi* 138–40, 1948–50).
Antifonario Visigotico Mozarabe de la Catedral de Leon, ed. L. Brou and J. Vives (Madrid: Monumenta Hispaniae Sacra, ser. lit. 5, 1959). (*AL*)
Antiphonale Monasticum (Tournai: Desclee, 1934).
Beroldus, sive Ecclesiae Ambrosianae Mediolanense Kalendarium et Ordines, ed. M. Magistretti (Milan, 1894, reprinted Farnborough: Gregg, 1968).
Breviarium Ambrosianum (4 vols) (Milan, 1944).
Breviarium Gothicum, ed. F. A. Lorenzana (Paris: J. P. Migne, *Patrologia Latina* 86, 1862). (*Br.*)
Breviarium Monasticum ... pro omnibus sub regula S. Patris Benedicti militantibus (2 vols) (Bruges: Desclee de Brouwer, 1930).
Breviarium Romanum ex decreto SS. Concilii Tridentini restitutum ... (4 vols) (Tournai: Desclee, 1894).
Breviarium Secundam Regulam Beati Isidori, ed. A. Ortiz (Toledo, 1502).
Directorium Mozarabicum ad Divinum Officium debite persolvendum et Missam Gotho-Hispanicam recte peragendum intra Sacellum et Duas Toletii Paroecias pro vertente anno MCMXXXV (Toledo, 1934).
Diurna Laus (Milan: Centro Ambrosiano, 1990).
William Durandus, *Rationale Divinorum Officiorum* (Venice, 1599).
Liber Commicus seu Lectionarium Missae, ed. G. Morin OSB (Maredsous: *Anecdota Maredsolana I*, 1893).
'Las Horas Vigiliares del Oficio Monacal Hispanico', ed. J. Pinell OSB (Monserrat: *Liturgica 3 – Scripta et Documenta 17* (1966), pp. 197–340). (*T3*)
Horologion (Vatican: Polyglot Press, 1937).
Liber Misticus de Cuaresma, ed. J. Janini (Toledo: Istituto de Estudios Visigotico-Mozarabes, 1979). *T2*.
Liber Misticus de Cuaresma y Pascua, ed. J. Janini (Toledo: Istituto de Estudios ..., 1980). *T5*.
Liber Mozarabicus sacramentorum, ed. M. Férotin (Paris: *Monumenta Ecclesiastica Liturgica*, 1912).
Liber Orationum Psalmographus, ed. J. Pinell OSB (Barcelona-Madrid: Monumenta Hispaniae Sacra IX, 1972). (*LOP*)
Les Ordines Romani du Haut Moyen Age, II Les Textes, ed. M. Andrieu (Louvain: Spicilegium Sacrum Lovaniense, 1948).
Le Liber Ordinum en usage dans l'Eglise Wisigothique et Mozarabe de Espagne du V a X siècle, ed. M. Férotin (Paris: *Monumenta Ecclesiastica Liturgica*, 1904).
Liber Vesperalis juxta ritum Sanctae Ecclesiae Mediolanensis (Rome: Desclee, 1939).
Liturgia Horarum (Vatican: Polyglot Press, 1975).
Manuale Ambrosianum (2 vols) ed. M. Magistretti (Milan, 1905).
Missale Mixtum, ed. F. A. Lorenzana (Paris: J. P. Migne, *Patrologia Latina* 85, 1862). (*MM*)
The Mozarabic Psalter, ed. J. P. Gilson (London: Henry Bradshaw Society, 1905). (*MP*)

Oracional Visigotico, ed. J. Vives and G. Claveras (Barcelona: *Monumenta Hispaniae Sacra I*, 1946). (*OV*)
Passionario Hispanico (2 vols) ed. J. Fabrega Grau (Madrid-Barcelona: *Monumenta Hispaniae Sacra* 6, 1953 and 1955).

STUDIES OF THE OLD SPANISH LITURGICAL TRADITION

Abbreviations: ArchL = *Archivos Leoneses*
 ALW = *Archiv für Liturgiewissenschaft*
 EL = *Ephemerides Liturgicae*
 HS = *Hispania Sacra*
 JTS = *Journal of Theological Studies*
 SE = *Sacris Erudiri*
 SL = *Studia Liturgica*
 SP = *Studia Patristica*

Akeley, T. G., *Christian Initiation in Spain* (London: Darton, Longman and Todd, 1965).
Bernal, J. 'Primeros Vestigios de Lucernario en Espana', *Liturgica III – Scripta et Documenta* 17 (Monserrat, 1966), pp. 21–50.
Bishop, W. C., ed. C. L. Feltoe, *The Mozarabic and Ambrosian Rites* (London: Alcuin/Mowbray, 1924).
Blume, C., *Hymnodia Gotica* (Leipzig: *Analecta Hymnica*, 1897).
Brockett, C. W., *Antiphons, Responsories and Other Chants of the Mozarabic Rites* (Princeton Studies in Music, 1969).
Brou, L., 'Liturgie "Mozarabe" ou Liturgie "Hispanique"?' *EL* 63 (1949), pp. 46–70.
——, 'Le Psautier Wisigothique et les Editions Critiques des Psautiers Latins' , *HS* 8 (1954), pp. 337–60.
——, 'Ou en est la question des Psalter Collects?' *SP* II (1957), pp. 17–20.
——, 'Etudes sur le Missal and le Breviaire "Mozarabes" imprimés', *HS* 11 (1958), pp. 349–98.
——, 'Deux mauvaises lectures' in *Miscellanea Mgr. H. Angles I* (Barcelona, 1958–61).
Callewaert, C., 'Le Carême Primitif dans la Liturgie Mozarabe', *SE* (Steenbrugge, 1940), pp. 507–16.
de Bruyne, D., 'Un système de Lectures de la Liturgie Mozarabe', *Revue Benedictine* 34 (1922), pp. 147–55.
de Mora Ontalva, J. M., 'Nuevo Boletin de Liturgia Hispanica Antigua', *HS* 28 (1975), pp. 209–37.
Gamber, K. (ed.), *Codices Latini Antiquiores* [2 vols] (Fribourg: *Spicilegii Friburgensis Subsidia*, 1968).
Janeras, V., 'Combinacion de los Oficios temporal y festivo en la Liturgia Hispana', *AL* 8 (1954), pp. 186–225.
Janini, J., 'Cuaresma Visigoda y Carnes Tollendas' in *Anthologica Annua* 9 (Rome: Santa Maria di Monserrato, 1961), pp. 11–83.
——, 'Las Collectas Psalmicas del *Liber Ordinum*', *HS* 28 (1975), pp. 103–24
——, 'El Oficio de Pentecostes del Oracional Visigotico y el Breviario de Cisneros', *Analecta Sacra Tarraconensia* 57-8 (1984–5), pp. 101–10.
—— and Gonzalvez, R., *Manuscritos Liturgicos de la Catedral de Toledo* (Toledo: Diputacion Provincial, 1977).
Jungmann, J., 'The Pre-Monastic Morning Hour in the Gallo-Spanish Region in the 6th Century' and 'Matins in the Mozarabic Liturgy' in *Pastoral Liturgy* (London: Challoner, 1962), pp. 122–57 and 138–51.
King, Archdale A., *The Liturgies of the Primatial Sees* (London: Longmans, 1957).
Lorenzana, F. A. and Fabian y Fuero F., *Missa Gotica seu Mozarabica et Officium itidem, Gothicum, diligenter ac dilucide explanata* (Puebla de los Angeles, 1770).
Martin Patino, J. M., 'El Breviarium Mozarabe de Ortiz, su Valor Documental para la Historia del Oficio Catedralico Hispanico', *Miscellanea 40 Comillas* (1963), pp. 207–97.
Martin Pintado, V., 'Las Lecturas Cuaresmales de Antiguo Testamento en la Antigua Liturgia Hispanica. Estudio de Liturgia Comparada', *Salmanticensis* XXII, *fasc*. 2 (1975), pp. 217–69.
Perez de Urbel, J., 'Origen de los Himnos Mozarabes', *Bulletin Hispanique* 28 (Bordeaux, 1926), pp. 5–21, 113–39, 209–45 and 305–20.
Pinell, Jordi, 'Las *Missae*, Grupos de Cantos y Oraciones en el Oficio de la Antigua Liturgia Hispana', *ArchL* 8 (1954), pp. 145–85.

——, 'El Liber Horarum y el Misticus entre los Libros de la Antigua Liturgia Hispana', *HS* 8 (1955), pp. 85–107.
——, 'El *Matutinarium* en la Liturgia Hispana', *HS* 9 (1956), pp. 61–85.
——, 'Vestigis del Lucernari a Occident' in *Liturgia I – Scripta et Documenta* 7 (1957), pp. 91–149.
—— 'El Oficio Hispanico-Visigotico', *HS* 10 (1957), pp. 385–427.
——, 'Una Exhortacion Diaconal a la Plegaria en el Antiguo Rito Hispanico, La *Supplicatio*', *Analecta Sacra Tarraconensia* 36 (1963), pp. 3–23.
——, *De Liturgiis Occidentalibus, cum Speciali Tractatione de Liturgia Hispanica* (pro manuscripto, Rome: Istituto di Sant'Anselmo, 1967).
——, 'Fragmentos de Codice de Antiguo Rito Hispanico', *HS* 27 (1972), pp. 185–208.
——, 'Los Canticos del Oficio en el Antiguo Rito Hispanico', *HS* 27 (1974), pp. 5–54.
——, 'Unité et Diversité dans la Liturgie Hispanique' in *Liturgie de l'Église Particulière et Liturgie de l'Église Universelle*, 22nd St Serge Conference in Paris (Rome: Edizioni Liturgiche, 1976), pp. 245–60.
——, 'Las Oraciones "de Cantico" del Antiguo Rito Hispanico', *Didaskalia* VIII (Lisbon, 1978), pp. 197–329.
——, *La Liturgia delle Ore* (Rome: Pontificio Istituto Liturgico, 3rd edition, 1983).
Porter, A. W. S., 'Early Spanish Monasticism', *Laudate* (Nashdom Abbey), X, 37–39 (1932), pp. 2–15, 66–79, 156–67; XI, 44, pp. 199–207; XII, 45 (1934), pp. 31–52.
——, 'Studies in the Mozarabic Office', *JTS* 35 (1934), pp. 266–86.
——, 'Cantica Mozarabici Offici', *EL* 49 (1935), pp. 126–45.
Rivera Recio, J. F. (ed.), *Estudios sobre la Liturgia Mozarabe* (Toledo: Diputacion Provincial, 1965).
Rojo, C. and Prado, G., *El Canto Mozarabe* (Barcelona, 1929).
Triacca, A., review of Pinell's *Liber Orationum Psalmographus* in *EL* 87 (1973), pp. 284–300.
Vives, J., 'El Oracional mozarabe de Silos', *Analecta Sacra Tarraconensia* 18 (1945), pp. 1–25.

A SELECTION OF GENERAL STUDIES OF THE DAILY OFFICE, AND STUDIES RELATING TO VARIOUS ASPECTS OF THE OFFICES

Baumstark, Anton, *Comparative Liturgy* (London: Mowbrays, 1958).
——, *Nocturna Laus* (Münster: Aschendorff, 1967).
Becker, Hansjakob, 'Zur Struktur der "Vespertina Sinaxis" in der Regula Benedicti', *Archiv für Liturgiewissenschaft* 29 (1987) pp. 177–88.
Borella, P., 'Il Breviario Ambrosiano' in Righetti, M., *Manuale di Storia Liturgica* (Milan: Ancora, 1946), pp. 603–41.
——, *Il Rito Ambrosiano* (Brescia: Marcelliana, 1964).
Bradshaw, Paul F., *Daily Prayer in the Early Church* (London: Alcuin/SPCK, 1981).
——, *The Search for the Origins of Christian Worship* (London: SPCK, 1992).
——, 'Cathedral vs. Monastery: The only Alternative for the Liturgy of the Hours?' in J. Neil Alexander (ed.), *Time and Community* (Washington, DC: Pastoral Press, 1991), pp. 122–36.
Campbell, Stanislaus, *From Breviary to Liturgy of the Hours* (Collegeville: Liturgical Press, 1995).
Cattaneo, Carlo, *Il Breviario Ambrosiano* (Milan, 1943).
Cuming, G. J (ed.), *Hippolytus: A Text for Students* (Bramcote: Grove Liturgical Study 8, 1984).
Curran, M., *The Antiphonary of Bangor* (Dublin: Irish Academic Press, 1984).
Cutts, David and Miller, Harold, *Whose Office?: Daily Prayer for the People of God* (Bramcote: Grove Liturgical Study 32, 1982).
de Clerck, Paul, *La prière universelle dans les liturgies latines anciennes* (Münster: Aschendorff, 1977).
de Vogue, A., *The Rule of St Benedict: A Doctrinal and Spiritual Commentary* (Kalamazoo: Cistercian Publications, 1983).
Dehne, Carl, 'Roman Catholic Popular Devotions', *Worship* 49 (1975), pp. 446–60.
Gamber, Klaus, *Sacrificium Vespertinum* (Regensburg: Pustet, *Studia Patristica et Liturgica* Fasc. 12, 1983).
Grant, R., 'Development of the Christian Catechumenate' in *Made Not Born* (Notre Dame, IN: University Press, 1976), pp. 32–49.
Grisbrooke, W. Jardine, 'Cathedral Office and Monastic Office' in *SL* 8 (1971–2), pp. 143–59.
——, 'The Laudate Psalms; A Footnote', *SL* 20 (1990), pp. 162–84.
——, 'The Formative Period – Cathedral and Monastic Offices' in Jones, C., Wainwright, G., Yarnold, E. and Bradshaw, P. (eds), *The Study of Liturgy* (revised edn, London: SPCK, 1992), pp. 403–20.

Guiver, George, *Company of Voices* (London: SPCK, 1988).
Hanssens, J. M., *Nature et Genèse de l'Office des Matines* (Rome: *Analecta Gregoriana* LVII, 1952).
Jungmann, J., 'Essays in the Structure of The Canonical Hours. I. Psalmody as the Introduction to the Hours' in *Pastoral Liturgy* (London: Challoner, 1962), pp. 157–62.
King, A. Archdale, *The Liturgy of the Roman Church* (London: Longmans, 1957).
Mateos, J. 'The Morning and Evening Office', *Worship* 42 (1968), pp. 31–47.
McKinnon, J. W., 'On the Question of Psalmody in the Ancient Synagogue', *Early Music History* 6 (1986), pp. 151–91.
Mearns, J., *The Canticles of the Christian Church Eastern and Western in Early and Medieval Times* (Cambridge: Cambridge University Press, 1914).
Mohrmann, C., 'À propos des collectes du Psautier', *Vigiliae Christianae* 6 (1952), pp. 1–19.
Pinell, J., *Las Oraciones del Salterio 'Per Annum' en el nuevo Libro de las Horas* (Rome: Edizioni Liturgiche, 1974).
Pudichery, S., *Ramsa* (Dharmaram College, 1972).
Raya and De Vinck (eds), *Byzantine Daily Worship* (Allendale, NJ: Alleluia Press, 1969).
Righetti, Mario (ed.), *Storia Liturgica*, Vol. II (Milan: Ancora, 1946).
Storey, William, 'The Liturgy of the Hours: Cathedral versus Monastery', *Worship* 50 (1976), pp. 50–70.
——, Quinn, F. and Wright, D., *Morning Praise and Evensong* (Notre Dame: Fides, 1973).
Taft, Robert, *Beyond East and West – Problems in Liturgical Understanding* (Washington, DC: Pastoral Press, 1984).
——, *The Liturgy of the Hours in East and West* (Collegeville: Liturgical Press, 1986).
Uspensky, N., *Evening Worship in the Orthodox Church* (Crestwood, NY: St Vladimir's Seminary Press, 1985).
van Dijk, S. J. P., 'The Medieval Easter Vespers of the Roman Clergy', *SE* XIX (1969–70), pp. 261–363.
Vellian, Jacob, *East Syrian Evening Services* (Kottayam: Indian Institute for Eastern Churches, 1971).
Vogel, Cyrille, *Medieval Liturgy: An Introduction to the Sources* (Washington, DC: Pastoral Press, 1986).
Wilmart, A. and Brou, L., *The Psalter Collects* (London: Henry Bradshaw Society, 1949).
Winkler, Gabrielle, 'Über die Kathedralvesper in Verschiedenen Riten des Ostens und Westens', *Archiv für Liturgiewissenschaft* 16 (1974), pp. 33–102.

INDEX OF NAMES

Amalarius, Bishop of Metz 10, 153
Ambrose, Bishop of Milan 29, 63

Baumstark, Anton xiii, 96, 112, 124, 142, 144
Bishop, W. C. xi, xii, 4, 5, 73–5, 78
Bradshaw, Paul F. vii, xv, 69, 112, 124, 125, 140
Brou, Dom L. xiii, 75

Caesarius, Bishop of Arles 69, 145
Campbell, Stanislaus xiv
Cisneros *see* Ximenez de Cisneros

de Vogüé, Dom Adalbert 77

Egeria 6, 76, 143

Férotin, Dom M. xi
Fructuosus, Bishop of Braga 61–2, 136, 141

Gregory VII, Pope viii
Grisbrooke, W. Jardine xiv, 107, 108n
Guiver, George xvi
Gregory of Tours 69, 145

Hanssens, J. M. xii, 141, 142

Isidore, Bishop of Seville 3, 8, 14, 22, 26–7, 34, 54, 62, 66, 73, 78, 126, 136, 141

Janini, José xv, 98, 106, 129
Jungmann, Josef xiii

Leander, Bishop of Seville 67, 80
Lorenzana, Francisco Antonio, Archbishop of Toledo x, xvii, 30, 33, 89, 98

Magistretti, Marco 54
Martin Patino, J.M. xiii, 48, 97, 106, 107, 116
Martin Pintado, V. xiv, 129, 130
Mateos, Juan xiv, 125

Ortiz, Alfonso ix, xiv, xv, 17, 21, 30, 33, 45, 46, 59, 83, 98, 129, 130

Porter, A. W. S. xi, xii, 4, 5, 73–5, 78

Taft, Robert F. xvi, 69, 76, 122–5, 140, 160

Uspensky, N. D. 5

Winkler, Gabriele xiv, xvi, 10, 55

Ximenez de Cisneros, Francisco, Archbishop of Toledo ix

INDEX OF SUBJECTS

Ambrosian rite *see* Milan
Antiphona 14, 17–22, 54
Antiphonary of Léon xi, xiii, 9, 11, 12, 17, 21, 24, 25, 36, 43, 51, 52, 65, 66, 68, 73–5, 76, 79, 93, 113, 114, 116, 122, 144
Aurora (office of) 44, 44n

Bangor Antiphoner 55, 126, 146
Barcelona, Council of (540) 61, 62, 71, 72, 95
Benedictine Office 29, 34, 63, 69, 77, 113, 115, 123, 126, 130, 131, 134, 151
Benedictio 44–6
Bobadilla, Ordo of 3, 14, 54, 61, 62, 126, 141
Braga, Council of (563) 30
Breviary, Lorenzana edition of 1776 x
Breviary, Ortiz edition of 1502 ix, xiii
Breviary, Roman xiv, 1, 36n, 59, 64, 69, 77, 96, 103, 108, 112, 113, 115, 118, 119, 123, 125, 126, 130, 131, 145, 146, 149–51, 153, 155, 156, 159

Canonical Psalms 61, 65, 66, 71, 119, 140, 141
Celtic rite *see* Bangor Antiphoner
Completuria 40–3, 56, 62, 82, 83, 136, 138, 139

De Traditione (2nd part of Lent) 18, 18n, 19, 23, 32, 41, 42, 51, 71, 72, 83, 88, 89, 93, 107, 110, 111, 114

Gerona, Council of (517) 43, 61

Laudes 14, 21, 22–6, 27n, 46, 54
Liber Commicus xi

Liber Misticus ix, xii
Liber Orationum Psalmographus xiv, 66, 68, 83
Liber Ordinum 43, 52
Liturgy of the Hours *see* Breviary, Roman
Lucernarium 3, 5, 6, 7–13, 14, 17, 22, 29, 40, 54–6, 119, 146, 152, 157, 162

Matutinarium 14, 80, 81, 107, 112–20, 138, 140
Milan, Rite of 9, 10, 17, 27, 29, 34, 39, 40, 48, 54, 56, 63, 64, 69, 77, 79, 96, 101, 103, 107, 112, 113, 115, 116, 118, 123–6, 128, 133, 140–2, 144, 145, 153, 158, 159
Missa Psalmorum 61, 62, 73, 75–7, 81, 85, 88, 90–5, 114, 115, 131, 140, 141, 146

None ix, x, xvi, xxii, 81–3, 126, 128, 129, 144

Orationale *see* Verona

Passionary xii, 92
Psallendum 4853, 62

Sext ix, x, xvi, xxii, 81–3, 128–30, 144
Sono (or Sonum) 3, 14–17, 56, 112, 113

Terce ix, x, xvi, xxii, 80–3, 86, 126–30, 144
Toledo viii, xiii, xv, 83, 148
Toledo, Fourth Council of (633) 3, 30, 34, 40, 43, 61, 142

Verona Orational x, xii, 63, 65, 73, 83, 128
Vespertinum *see* Lucernarium